Ethics, American Foreign Policy, and the Third World

Ethics, American Foreign Policy, and the Third World

David Louis Cingranelli
State University of New York at Binghamton

St. Martin's Press
New York

Senior editor: Don Reisman
Managing editor: Patricia Mansfield-Phelan
Project editor: Cheryl Friedman
Production supervisor: Katherine Battiste
Art director: Sheree L. Goodman
Cover design: Jeannette Jacobs Design
Cover art: Diego Rivera, *Distributing Arms,* ca. November 19, 1928. Mexico City, Secretaría de Educación Pública, Court of Fiestas. Photograph: Founders Society, Detroit Institute of Art.

For information, write:
St. Martin's Press, Inc.
175 Fifth Avenue
New York, NY 10010

ISBN: 0-312-05669-9 (paperback)
      0-312-06519-1 (hardcover)

Library of Congress Cataloging-in-Publication Data

Cingranelli, David L.
    Ethics, American foreign policy, and the third world / David Louis Cingranelli.
        p.   cm.
    Includes bibliographical references.
    ISBN 0-312-05669-9 (pbk.), 0-312-06519-1 (hardcover)
    1. United States—Foreign relations—Moral and ethical aspects.   2. United States—Foreign relations—Developing countries.   3. Developing countries—Foreign relations—United States.   4. United States—Foreign relations—1945-1989.   5. United States—Foreign relations—1989-   I. Title.
E183.7.C56   1992
327.730172′4—dc20   92-50013
                                                                                CIP

Published and distributed outside North America by:

THE MACMILLAN PRESS LTD.
Houndmills, Basingstoke, Hampshire RG21 2XS and London
Companies and representatives throughout the world.

ISBN 0-333-58893-2

A catalogue record for this book is available from the British Library.

To my parents, Louis and Josephine Cingranelli,
whose love and encouragement over the years
have been a constant source of inspiration for me.

Acknowledgments

I would like to thank Scott L. Bills, Stephen F. Austin State University; Robert Elias, University of San Francisco; David P. Forsythe, University of Nebraska at Lincoln; James M. Lutz, Indiana University at Fort Wayne; Richard A. Melanson, Brown University; Kathleen Pritchard, Marquette University; Brian Ripley, University of Pittsburgh; and Andrew J. Rotter, Colgate University, for the assistance they rendered in the preparation of this book. In addition, the staff at St. Martin's Press has my thanks, especially my editor, Don Reisman, and my project editor, Cheryl Friedman. An abundance of detailed suggestions were provided by Brian Ripley and Scott L. Bills.

Preface

When Jimmy Carter was elected president of the United States in 1976, he announced that human rights would be "the soul of our foreign policy." The ensuing debate over the proper role of human rights considerations sparked my interest in the relationship between moral values and foreign policy. I wondered whether such a bold statement of purpose would have any effect on U.S. behavior toward other nations, especially developing ones where human rights were fragile and U.S. influence great. Even if the new policy rhetoric brought changes in this behavior, I wondered whether the changes would produce effects different from those spawned by past policies.

In 1981 I began working on a series of projects with students and colleagues on various aspects of human rights, including one project on the relationship between the human rights practices of developing countries in Latin America and U.S. foreign policy toward those countries. A paper based on that research, co-authored with Thomas E. Pasquarello, was published in 1985.[1] It demonstrated that America's leaders had considered the human rights practices of governments in Latin America when making some, but not all, kinds of foreign aid decisions. That research convinced me to write this book. My earlier work had focused solely on Latin America and examined only foreign aid allocations, neglecting other instruments of foreign policy such as trade, military intervention, and the exercise of influence over the lending policies of international financial institutions. It presented a picture of the allocation of foreign aid in 1981 and 1982, but gave little evidence of how either aid allocations or human rights conditions were changing as a result of the newly stated policy goal. Finally, its focus on human rights and foreign aid precluded attention to the other foreign policy goals of the United States and how they might have affected foreign aid policies.

---

[1]David L. Cingranelli and Thomas E. Pasquarello, "Human Rights Practices and the Distribution of American Foreign Aid to Latin American Countries," *American Journal of Political Science* 25, No. 3 (August 1985): 539–563.

I decided to address a broader set of questions by examining U.S. policies toward a more representative group of developing countries and by incorporating more information about the historical development of U.S. foreign policy toward the Third World. As the project progressed, I gradually came to the conclusion that the moral and ethical dimensions of foreign policy–making were crucial and that foreign policy behavior flowed naturally from some basic ethical and moral choices.

Philosophers have offered several standards by which particular acts can be judged as moral or immoral. These standards, derived from rational arguments concerning what kinds of things are "good" and why, are usually reducible to maxims. At one end of the moral continuum are ethical egoists, who argue that asking "what is good?" is the same as asking "what is in my long-term self-interest?" The basic premise of this school of thought is that there is nothing inherently immoral about the pursuit of individual or national self-interest. The most important question in the context of foreign policy, however, is how much responsibility the leader of one nation should have to protect the welfare of the peoples of other nations. Should the United States, for example, in its attempt to advance its own economic and military interests, be concerned about any negative impacts on developing countries?

Implicitly or explicitly, utilitarianism is the moral standard U.S. policymakers most commonly use to justify all public policies, including foreign policy. Even within the field of political philosophy, utilitarianism operates as a standard against which all other political philosophies must be judged.[2] The utilitarian maxim is "Act so as to bring about the greatest good possible, not just for you, but for all actors." In other words, choose the act with the best total consequences. According to this standard, policymakers act immorally if they do not think through the full range of consequences a policy will have on others, if they expect the total consequences of the action chosen to be worse than if some other course of action is pursued, or if they know that the announced policy will not really be implemented or has a very small chance of being successful even if implemented. Utilitarians emphasize the idea that acts are not morally good in and of themselves. Rather, the moral good or evil of an act depends entirely on its consequences for others to whom the person acting should be held responsible. In the context of international relations, utilitarians recognize that the same act — for example, breaking a treaty — may have good or bad consequences in different situations.[3] Therefore,

[2]Will Kymlicka, *Contemporary Political Philosophy* (New York: Oxford University Press, 1990), p. 9.

[3]See William K. Frankena, *Ethics* (Englewood Cliffs, N.J.: Prentice-Hall, 1973), for an extended discussion of utilitarianism.

whether it would be right or wrong to break a particular treaty would depend on the particular circumstances. For this reason, those who prefer absolute rules sometimes refer to utilitarianism derisively as "situational ethics."

Another approach to deciding what is right and what is wrong is to choose a process for deciding on the best moral principles and then to abide by the results of that process. One reason why democracy is so valuable is that it provides a process for choosing among alternatives even when the advocates of different positions are unwilling to compromise. Many people accept a truly democratic process as fair and legitimate and are, therefore, willing to abide by the results whether or not they like them. For this reason, some have argued that democracy or, to use the more general term, self-determination is the most fundamental value in the sphere of politics. When a nation resolves to abide by decisions reached in the United Nations, it essentially places faith in a process that is felt to transcend any particular moral principles. But no process is ever entirely neutral. The most important decisions in the United Nations, for example, are decided by the United Nations Security Council, where any one of the five permanent members (China, France, the Russian Federation, the United Kingdom, and the United States) may cast a binding negative vote. Most matters of less importance are decided by the General Assembly, where the one-nation/one-vote rule gives small and large countries equal weight.

In an attempt to construct a process that would be impartial, some philosophers have proposed that the best principles would be the ones approved by a hypothetical "ideal observer." Briefly, an ideal observer would be one who (1) is impartial or unbiased, (2) has full knowledge of the pertinent facts of the situation, and (3) can empathize fully with every person involved in the situation. According to this view, knowing that the ideal observer approves X is the same as knowing that X is right.[4]

John Rawls has developed a theory of justice using a variation of the "ideal observer" criterion. Recognizing that it was difficult for anyone judging among several alternative ethical and moral principles to be unbiased, he suggested that the observer could don a "veil of ignorance" to achieve impartiality.[5] The veil of ignorance would enable a person to choose principles for making decisions about the distribution of scarce valued things in ignorance of the place in society the person would have. Under such circumstances, he contends, everyone would agree on two principles for dividing scarce valued things among competing interests.

[4]John Hospers, *An Introduction to Philosophical Analysis* (Englewood Cliffs, N.J.: Prentice-Hall, 1967), p. 570.

[5]John Rawls, *A Theory of Justice* (Cambridge, Mass.: Belknap Press, 1971), p. 12.

Rawls's first principle of justice is that "each person is to have an equal right to the most extensive total system of basic liberties compatible with a similar system of liberty for all."[6] His second principle is that any social inequalities are to be "to the greatest expected benefit of the least advantaged" and subject to "conditions of fair opportunity."

Charles Beitz has extended Rawls's principles, stressing their redistributive implications, to develop less familiar, more radical principles for international social justice. Regarding the distribution of resources among nations, he predicts that, operating under the veil of ignorance and not knowing the resource endowments of their own societies, "the parties would agree on a resource redistribution principle that would give each society a fair chance to develop just political institutions and an economy capable of satisfying its members' basic needs."[7] Rawls and Beitz, as well as others who have attempted to find a compromise position between the values of liberty and equality, have staked out what may be called the "liberal equality" position.

Still another moral position is that of the neo-Marxists, who favor absolute equality, even at the expense of liberty. They appeal to a more radical theory of justice in which the existence of private property is considered intrinsically unjust. The unequal distribution of property, political power, and well-being among individuals and among nations of the world is, therefore, doubly unjust. As a first and modest step in the right direction, neo-Marxists believe U.S. foreign policy should be designed to support a radical redistribution of wealth and power from the more advantaged nations to the less advantaged.

The major purpose of this book is to locate U.S.–Third World relations within this rich debate over standards for moral conduct and to provide a historical perspective. As I see it, the main controversy can be reduced to different conceptions of (1) what "good" should be maximized and (2) to whom national leaders should be held morally responsible. Part I describes four moral positions that represent the four logical combinations of answers to these two questions. Each moral position incorporates a view of the nature of humankind and a related empirical theory from which a set of propositions are derived explaining the nature of international relations. From that theoretical explanation, we can infer the set of goals that actually motivate U.S. foreign policy toward the Third World, as well as the moral and ethical values that should guide it.

Standard treatments of American foreign policy and international

[6]Ibid., p. 302.

[7]Charles R. Beitz, *Political Theory and International Relations* (Princeton, N.J.: Princeton University Press, 1979), p. 141.

relations often ignore or give only brief attention to moral principles, North-South relations, and historical developments prior to World War II. Therefore, the discussion of the moral dimensions of U.S. foreign policy toward the Third World in Part I is followed, in Parts II and III, by a historical overview of significant developments in U.S.-Third World relations. This overview, which begins with the early years of the American republic, is necessary because moral choices take on meaning only in the context of real-life situations that force decisions to be made. Only an understanding of the particular situations that led to interventions or to major new policy initiatives allows us to consider the kinds of values that often conflict and the kinds of tradeoffs that must be made among them. A historical overview also enables us to see in concrete terms the kinds of real policies that flow from the application of alternative sets of moral principles. It also helps make sense of the extensive anti-Americanism we often find among Third World peoples today. Part IV focuses on present and future policies, which are of immediate interest. However, an awareness of the past public statements of U.S. leaders, and of policy actions and their consequences, is essential if we are to understand present developments and to predict the future.

Consideration of the values and objectives that motivate U.S. foreign policy toward the Third World is especially important at this juncture in history. The plight of the Third World, and the response of the United States to it, expose the kinds of tradeoffs U.S. leaders have been willing to make between values generally associated with the pursuit of national self-interest and those associated with altruism and humanitarianism. American value tradeoffs are particularly significant and far-reaching because, since World War II, the United States has been the acknowledged leader of the industrialized democracies and the leading contributor to most important international lending organizations including the World Bank and the International Monetary Fund. U.S. foreign policy toward developing countries, therefore, has had—and will continue to have—a profound effect on the character of North-South relations and on the welfare of people living in less developed countries.

America's relations with Third World countries are also becoming increasingly important to the welfare of U.S. citizens. More than ever before, the United States is vulnerable to threats emanating from Third World regimes or from people living in Third World countries. The Atlantic and Pacific oceans once provided the United States some security from external threats, but they will not protect us from environmental degradation perpetrated by other nations, from the export of dangerous drugs to our shores, from the effects of externally supported terrorism, or from militant Third World leaders. Few Third World states have nuclear weapons, but many that are unfriendly to the United States have developed frightening chemical and biological weapons. American leaders must decide how the United States should respond to these potential threats.

Finally, in the name of anti-communism, since World War II the United States has conducted morally reprehensible foreign policies toward some Third World countries. It has developed close relationships with repressive, but anti-communist, dictators in the Third World, including three generations of Somozas in Nicaragua, Ferdinand Marcos in the Philippines, and Mohammed Reza Pahlavi, the former shah of Iran. American leaders have also attempted to undermine some pro-communist regimes in the Third World, in some cases even financing the assassination of Third World leaders. Many ostensibly successful U.S. policies have had terrible consequences for the poor and powerless in Third World societies. Chile, in the aftermath of the assassination of Salvador Allende, is a case in point.

Of course, it is difficult to write about the future of any aspect of international relations when the world is changing so quickly. With the historic transformations taking place in the former Soviet Union and in Eastern Europe, U.S. leaders will have the opportunity to reassess past policies and modify them in response to a new, less threatening climate in East-West relations. Failure to do so will call into question the rationale of anti-communism that was used to justify nearly a half century of U.S. intervention in Third World politics. Chapter 11 discusses three possible scenarios for U.S. foreign policy toward the Third World in the twenty-first century. The United States' response in 1991 to Iraq's invasion of Kuwait and to subsequent provocative acts by Saddam Hussein's regime gives us some concrete evidence about the direction U.S. foreign policy toward the Third World will likely take in the aftermath of the Cold War.

In the small contemporary body of literature dealing specifically with ethics and U.S. foreign policy toward the Third World, both neo-Marxists and neoconservatives have been disproportionately represented. Both sides have focused on the moral and practical failures of U.S. foreign policy toward the Third World. However, they have ignored progressive elements in that policy or have treated them with derision. In this book I have tried to stake out a more balanced approach.

DAVID LOUIS CINGRANELLI

Contents

Ethics, American Foreign Policy, and the Third World

PART I

Morality and Foreign Policy: Contending Views

CHAPTER 1

A Typology of Moral Positions

A moral foreign policy may be defined as one in which the motives, intentions, dispositions, or traits of national character manifested in that policy are virtuous, right, and consistent with the responsibilities of leaders to their peoples and with one nation's responsibilities to others. The purpose of this work is to consider three related questions about morality and U.S. foreign policy. First, should U.S. policy toward the Third World be guided by moral principles or by expediency and national self-interest? Second, if morality is important, which moral values should dominate? Finally, to what extent has U.S. foreign policy toward the Third World been moral as it actually has been conducted?

These are not academic questions. Important moral issues are at the center of many, if not most, of the United States' important foreign policy decisions that touch on the Third World. The U.S. government must decide whether it should remove all sanctions against South Africa even before a black majority government assumes power, assist friendly Third World governments when they are threatened by internal revolutions or by outside forces, eliminate barriers to trade with less developed countries, support the economic stabilization loan requirements of the multilateral development banks, make the promotion of human rights a major foreign policy goal, change the level of foreign aid to less developed countries, increase the ratio of economic to military aid, or decrease the extent to which foreign aid is tied to purchases in the United States. It must also decide whether to use coercive means (even military intervention), economic sanctions, or covert action to stop some Third World states from sponsoring terrorism, from developing chemical, biological, or nuclear weapons, from serving as the bases of operation for drug traffickers, or from seriously abusing the human rights of their citizens.

Study of the words and actions of the United States' leaders over the past two hundred years, along with the exhortations of scholars addressing these subjects, reveals the existence of four main types of answers to these questions. These answers are presented in the form of a typology in this

3

chapter. A foreign policy action can be evaluated in moral terms only if we can assume that the national leaders involved in this action have free choice. Some structuralist interpretations of international relations are not fully compatible with this assumption inasmuch as they emphasize that the international system is an anarchy without an authoritative lawmaker and enforcer. In an anarchy, all interactions are competitive. Because the survival of the weak is not assured, maintaining and accumulating power to produce national security becomes the all-consuming objective of the rational leader. In short, any choice to do otherwise is severely limited, if not illusory.[1]

Although this perspective possesses some undeniable truth, it implies that the leaders of nations have less freedom of choice than they do in reality. American policymakers do indeed face some constraints that affect choices on foreign policies toward the Third World, but these checks serve to keep choices within predictable bounds rather than determine them in any strict structuralist sense. One source of these limits comes from the external international environment. Because of the anarchic character of the international system, U.S. leaders have always been particularly attentive to the preferences of leaders of powerful military regimes and to significant changes in the relative power capabilities of those regimes. With changes in those preferences or power capabilities, the latitude for choice available to U.S. leaders and the expected payoffs associated with particular foreign policies also change. The recent radical transformations in what was formerly the Soviet Union, for example, will likely have a systematic effect on all subsequent U.S. foreign policy decisions, including those decisions that affect the Third World.

Domestic societal forces may also limit the decision-making latitude of leaders.[2] Domestic forces are likely to be particularly influential when the foreign policy involves states with much less power capability and, therefore, much less ability to retaliate. Under these circumstances, U.S. presidents are more likely to be swayed by domestic electoral concerns and the domestic political culture than by the preferences of the leaders of the target nations. While in office, U.S. presidents are expected to maintain the support of the majority of American citizens. That backing will probably elude them unless their foreign policy choices accord with the dominant moral philosophy of the American public. As it pertains to foreign policy, a moral philosophy answers questions about what foreign policy goals are right and wrong and what means of affecting the behaviors of other governments and their peoples are acceptable. Although the citizens of a state can never achieve unanimity on these questions, they can develop a dominant or majority position. In any nation, this dominant moral philosophy must be consistent with other central values in the political culture. It also evolves over time based on how the public perceives the consequences of the national government's previous responses to action-forcing events in the international arena.

Action-forcing events represent a challenge to officially stated government policy, to widely shared conceptions of the national interest, or to the nation's dominant moral philosophy. National opinion leaders tend to require the government to respond to these occurrences, so even the decision to take no action will be viewed as an important policy decision. For the United States, examples include Iraq's invasion of Kuwait in August 1990, the killing of U.S. missionaries in El Salvador in 1989, the kidnapping of U.S. diplomats in Iran in 1979, attempts by foreign governments such as Saudi Arabia, Mexico, and Chile to nationalize the assets of U.S.-based multinational corporations, and the establishment of a Soviet missile base in Cuba in 1962. Whereas all "crises" are also action-forcing events, they demand a fast response to a rapidly changing situation; not all action-forcing events make such a demand.

Within the boundaries enforced by external and societal constraints, U.S. leaders may pursue a wide range of actions in response to such events. Following the work of others, including the political scientists, Alexander George and James David Barber, and the historians, John Lewis Gaddis and Robert Caro, we can assume that leaders come to office with something George called an "operational code"—a set of assumptions and a political philosophy about the world that tend to govern when the leader responds to action-forcing events afterward.[3] These convictions are formed long before leaders reach high office and, as Henry Kissinger has written, they "are the intellectual capital they will consume as long as they continue in office."[4] Their operational codes will form the foundation and shape the character of their administrations' foreign policies toward the Third World. These codes will determine their views of U.S. interests in the world, potential threats to them, appropriate means, feasible responses, the sources of political instability in the Third World, and the relative importance of North-South relations. Their foreign policy actions during their terms of office will reflect those views.

THE TYPOLOGY

As part of their operational codes, leaders must take positions on two fundamental questions — *what values should they advance, and to whom should they be held responsible?* Answers to these questions represent the moral premises of the leader's foreign policy. Based on the logical combination of the answers to these two questions, we can categorize each ruler or administration as Nationalist, Exceptionalist, Progressive, or Radical Progressive (see Figure 1.1). Although there are only four cells in this typology, the position each administration takes on these two questions should be regarded as being located on a continuum. That is, in the making of foreign policy, different leaders have given more or less emphasis to advancing the ideals held by their own citizens and have taken more or less responsibility for advancing the welfare of people who are citizens of other nations.

A citizen may reject the leader's choice of moral positions on basic philosophical grounds and, accordingly, evaluate as immoral most or even all of that leader's subsequent foreign policy actions. Or the citizen may accept the leader's choice of moral premises as valid. Then the morality of particular foreign policy actions should be evaluated on more technical grounds. That is, even if a particular leader's moral premises are accepted as valid, particular foreign policy actions should be judged as immoral if

Leaders Should Be Held Responsible to:

	Their Own Citizens	Community beyond International Borders
Leaders Should Promote:		
National Ideals	Nationalist	Exceptionalist
Universal Ideals	Progressive	Radical Progressive

FIGURE 1.1   A Typology of Positions on Morality and U.S. Foreign Policy

the leader (1) did not try to think through the full range of policy consequences for others; (2) expected the total consequences of the actions chosen to be worse than if some other available course of actions had been pursued; (3) knew that the stated policy really would not be implemented; or (4) recognized that the policy had little chance of being successful even if implemented.

In the United States, the political culture provides an important source of values that may guide foreign policy; these values include individualism, democracy, political equality, republicanism, capitalism, the rule of law, and civilian control of government. These ideals are endorsed in numerous documents developed during the nation's founding period, especially the Declaration of Independence, the records of the 1787 debates at the Philadelphia Constitutional Convention, the Constitution itself, and the records of the ratification debates. These documents provide a powerful statement about what the Founding Fathers wanted the new nation to stand for, or, in other words, what motives, intentions, dispositions, or traits of national character the founders considered to be virtuous. Many U.S. presidents have seized on some of those virtues as "goods" to be maximized in other nations through U.S. foreign policy. Such leaders would be characterized as either Nationalist or Exceptionalist.

But are these national values also universal or do some values transcend the moral practices of particular communities? The political philosophers, Terry Nardin and Alan Donagan, are among those who argue that a transcendent common morality exists and that it is knowable through the exercise of reason.[5] Clearly, the values differ from culture to culture. In some cultures, for instance, individualism may be less important than the good of the community, and elections may not be viewed as essential to self-determination. Capitalism may be seen as perpetuating an unjust class structure and as providing an obstacle to a more desirable emphasis on spiritualism. In such a culture, central economic planning may therefore be chosen as the best way to promote macroeconomic prosperity. All leaders who seek to conduct a moral foreign policy must decide whether their own nation's foreign policies should be based on advancing the ideals held by their own citizens or on realizing more universally accepted values as well.

The important universal values and principles that have application to U.S. foreign policy include (1) self-determination or autonomy, (2) nonintervention into the affairs of other states except under extraordinary circumstances, (3) the rejection of certain means no matter how worthy the ends, (4) social, political, and economic justice, (5) the existence of (and obligation to protect) universal human rights (as those rights are defined in international agreements), and (6) a commitment to multilateral as opposed to unilateral action — especially toward less developed countries. In real situations, these values and principles may conflict with each other and with other nonuniversal principles. Rulers who choose to place a relatively high degree of emphasis on promoting such universal values as opposed to others would be categorized as either Progressive or Radical Progressive.

Having chosen which universal values are to be maximized, leaders must next decide to whom they are willing to be held morally accountable. According to one school of thought, leaders should be morally answerable only to the citizens they represent. They should be agents of their people in the same way as lawyers are agents of their clients. In this capacity as agents, they should make decisions ensuring the survival, sovereignty, security, and economic prosperity of their states. All other goals must be consistent with, if not contribute to, this one. If the ends pursued by leaders neglect this role as agent too much, they are immoral.[6] Beyond ensuring the survival of their state, leaders should, according to this view, maximize the utilities or social happiness of their own citizens. The utilities of people living outside national boundaries should be assigned little or no importance in foreign policy decision making.

Four fundamental arguments have been raised against moral obligations extending beyond the United States' national borders. The first is that there are no universal values, so it is ethnocentric and arrogant of U.S. leaders to suggest what is best for other states. To do so constitutes an unwarranted and unwanted intrusion into their internal affairs. The second is that, however good and right such principles may be, achieving them is well beyond American power. Third, the statement of moral principles requires a consistency of application that the U.S. government is not prepared to maintain. Fourth, even if there are universal moral principles regulating human conduct, they do not apply to the affairs of governments, or, in the words of Edmund Burke: "Nothing universal can be rationally affirmed on any moral or political subject."

In contrast, many believe that the conduct of a moral foreign policy is important and that morality requires that a nation recognize its global responsibilities. Unless national leaders recognize duties to those living beyond their national borders, Stanley Hoffmann writes, "the world is doomed to remain a jungle, and the arrangements of international law will be no more than temporary artifices."[7] Some rulers have claimed to be advocating the interests of constituencies living beyond their own nation's boundaries. Mohandas Karamchand Gandhi, an advocate of nonviolence and internal reform of Indian society, led that country's quest for political independence, but his moral messages against colonialism and materialism were addressed to a world community. In advocating the League of Nations after World War I, President Woodrow Wilson claimed that he was concerned not only with promoting the well-being of the American people, but also with preserving world peace. In the 1991 War in the Persian Gulf, Saddam Hussein professed to be acting on behalf of all Arab people, not just the citizens of Iraq. Both Exceptionalists and Radical Progressives accept the notion of moral duties beyond national borders.

When the two dimensions are put together, the distinctiveness of each of the four perspectives becomes apparent. For Nationalists, the main societal interests that government should advance through foreign policy are its military security and macroeconomic prosperity or, in other words, its national self-interest. George Kennan, an advocate of the Nationalist position as it is defined here, argues that these interests arise from the very existence of the nation-state system and, therefore, are so basic they should not even be classified as morally good or bad.[8] Leaders who adopt a purely Nationalist position will tend to manipulate less powerful states to achieve purely national purposes, to emphasize strongly the advancement of national ideals and the national interest, and to give little or no weight to other international responsibilities that do not directly contribute to the attainment of these goals.

Unlike Nationalists, Exceptionalists accept greater moral responsibility for the fate of people living outside their own nation's borders. But, like Nationalists, they do not recognize the existence of any clear and generally accepted values or international code of foreign policy behavior. As a consequence, they believe the United States should advance purely American values in the Third World. When the governments of other nations fail to conform with these principles, the United States has a moral obligation to take actions designed to help bring them into compliance. Exceptionalists view the institutions, values, and ideology dominant in their own country as superior and as best for all nations. They therefore have a moral responsibility to proselytize, so that the political, social, and economic systems of other nations increasingly come to resemble the U.S. model. Leaders of stable, economically prosperous, militarily powerful nations are especially prone to view their own nations as exceptional and to adopt the Exceptionalist position in foreign affairs.

In the United States, both Nationalists and Exceptionalists seek to maximize values derived from the U.S. political experience through foreign policy, but there is a fundamental difference in their approach. Whereas Nationalists require foreign compliance with those values only when fundamental U.S. national interests are threatened, Exceptionalists advocate international activism and interventionism in a much wider variety of situations. The rhetoric and actions of Presidents Woodrow Wilson, William McKinley, and Theodore Roosevelt seem to place them squarely in the Exceptionalist camp.

Progressives and Radical Progressives attempt to distinguish national ideals (which may be accepted by the people in some cultures but not in others) from universal ones and then give relatively greater weight to universal ideals in the making of foreign policy. Rulers who adopt the Progressive as opposed to the Radical Progressive moral position place greater emphasis on achieving the national self-interest and, once assured it is protected, will seek to advance the welfare of humankind. Unlike Nationalists and Exceptionalists, Progressives find clear and generally accepted moral values in international agreements such as the United Nations Charter and the Universal Declaration of Human Rights. They pay special attention to the moral claims of government leaders and intellectuals in the poorest, least powerful nations of the world, whose voices are most easily ignored. With this perspective, Progressives and Radical Progressives tend to be more concerned about obtaining world-wide access to adequate health care, housing, and education than about advancing world capitalism as the best way of achieving these ends. They tend to be more absorbed with the principle of self-determination than with the particular institutional forms self-determination can take. They are also more likely to advocate multilateral rather than unilateral action in world affairs.

Radical Progressives believe that the welfare of humankind is the "good" all national leaders should advance through their foreign policies, even when the pursuit of that good is detrimental to particular national interests. According to this view, world peace, human rights, social justice, and ecological harmony are far more important than any purely national concern. Some advocates of world government (as a replacement for the existing nation state system), many neo-Marxist scholars, and most Third World leaders have embraced the Radical Progressive position. Third World leaders, for example, have urged the redistribution of the world's wealth and power over international affairs from the rich to the poor nations. No U.S. president has ever adopted the Radical Progressive moral position on First World–Third World relations, and the Radical Progressive voice is rarely, if ever, heard within the mainstream foreign policy debate in the United States. Nonetheless, it provides a valuable critical perspective on the morality of U.S. foreign policy.

The mainstream debate in the United States over what moral principles should guide American foreign policy has been mainly a discourse among Nationalists, Exceptionalists, and Progressives. Generally, the American people have supported their presidents who justify unilateral military interventions in the Third World on the basis of Nationalist or Exceptionalist principles. That public support provides considerable solace for those who advocate those positions. Cynics often note that elites create public opinion as often as they follow it.

The typology depicted in Figure 1.1 does not exhaust all the dimensions of moral conflict relevant to U.S. behavior toward the Third World, but the positions individuals take on the two dimensions highlighted – the values they should advance and to whom they should be responsible – strongly predict their resolutions for many moral dilemmas. (A "moral dilemma" in foreign policy-making occurs when resolving a policy problem requires trading off two or more moral values.) For example, based on whether an individual is categorized as either Nationalist or Radical Progressive, we could guess that individual's views about whether the United States should expand or contract its foreign aid program, whether the United States should assume an activist role in international affairs, whether it is morally right to negotiate with the leaders of other governments whose primary interests are not their own people, and whether covert or overt intervention into the domestic affairs of other nations is ever morally justified.

APPLICATIONS

The four positions identified in the typology above are sometimes difficult for observers to distinguish in practice because the public rhetoric can be misleading, compromise positions are common, and a single presidential administration may employ policies of more than one type. For example, the Bush administration justified the U.S. role in the Gulf War partly on the basis of the need to create a New (and better) World Order, but for some the United States' role was better explained by its desire to protect its supply of inexpensive oil. In fact, there were almost certainly multiple goals at work, some Progressive, some Nationalist. Indeed, most real examples of American foreign policy toward the Third World do not fit any of the four ideal types perfectly. Remember, the two dimensions of the typology represent continuums rather than dichotomies; therefore, hybrid or compromise positions are possible. Categorizing individual foreign policy actions or the collective policies of administrations according to the typology almost always amounts to classifying these policies as *mainly* of one type or another. Consider the following hybrid argument for making the United Nations more democratic:

As governments around the world open their doors to democratic ideals, perhaps it is time for our world government, the United Nations, to do the same. Currently, the Security Council and especially the five permanent members — the United States, China, France, the United Kingdom, and, now, the Russian Federation — exercise too much power. The U.N. Charter allows the Security Council to make final decisions on all of the most important issues coming before the United Nations, with each permanent member exercising a binding veto. This distribution of power is unfair and should not stand. It makes the United Nations an undemocratic and, ultimately, ineffective body for maintaining world peace, encouraging the promotion of human rights, protecting the global environment, and promoting world economic development.

The 175 members of the General Assembly who are not permanently represented on the Security Council have no voice in many significant decisions, nor do they have much incentive to support those decisions. Because of their lack of effective representation, it is not easy to gain their cooperation in solving the massive problems of our day: regional conflicts; international terrorism; drug trafficking; nuclear, chemical, and biological weapons proliferation; and environmental degradation. All nations must have a voice on such issues; all must cooperate; and all must be held responsible.

What steps can be taken to redress the current inequitable distribution of power within the United Nations? It would be neither politically feasible nor wise to give the General Assembly, which operates according to the one-nation/one-vote principle, substantially more power. Third World nations would benefit, but the United States and the other industrialized nations would lose too much power. The best way to imbue the United Nations with greater moral force would be to abolish the Security Council, while at the same time reforming the General Assembly, thereby ensuring that power and responsibility are widely shared among the members and distributed on a more equitable basis.

The first step toward democratic reform of the United Nations, then, is to ensure that all members have some say in making all global policies, with each member's "voice" proportional to the power each should exercise in resolving important international conflicts. This could be accomplished through a weighted voting system in which out of, say, 2,000 votes, the United States might be allotted 200, while some less developed country might cast 5. A second, equally important step, is to require all nations to contribute funds in support of U.N. functions in proportion to their voices in U.N. decisions. Thus, the extent to which each nation would affect the outcomes of global decisions and the degree of its financial responsibility for implementing those decisions would be proportionately the same.

The main stumbling block to this proposal is the difficulty members will have in determining an acceptable formula for establishing vote weights. There are many possible tactics, but the important point is that the formula should be performance-based; that is, vote and contribution weights should be based on the following three fundamental principles.

First, nations with larger and more rapidly expanding economies would be assigned greater weights, proportional to the size of each nation's gross domestic product and rate of economic growth. This principle would ensure that nations with permanent Security Council seats will continue to exercise substantial control over U.N. policies for at least the next decade even under the reformed system, giving the plan some chance of gaining the support of the current Security Council.

Second, governments respecting the human rights of their citizens would be given greater weight. International human rights agreements established since the Second World War have encouraged all governments to be open to popular participation; provide for the rule of law; and ensure respect for the exercise of basic civil liberties such as freedom of speech, religion, and the press. These accords have also urged governments to promote the welfare of the least advantaged members of their societies and to protect their citizens from torture, arbitrary imprisonment, and cruel and unusual punishment. For the past two years, the United Nations Development Programme (UNDP) has generated two measures of governmental respect for human rights that could be used in developing the vote weights. The Human Development Index measures the extent to which a nation has made socioeconomic progress. This index is made up of three components: longevity, knowledge, and decent living standards. In 1990 the United States ranked seventh; Japan ranked first; China ranked eighty-second. The UNDP also computed a Human Freedom Index, measuring respect for the other human rights noted above. In 1990, the United States ranked thirteenth, tied with Australia. Japan ranked fourteenth. China was tied with Ethiopia in next-to-last place.

Third, nations whose domestic policies improved the quality of the global environment would be weighted more heavily. Since protection of the world's environment is necessary for the survival and prosperity of all the world's people, global ecological welfare requires international cooperation. Two commonly accepted measures of each nation's contribution to global pollution are (1) per capita and (2) total annual greenhouse gas emissions, as reported by the World Resource Institute in collaboration with the UNDP and the U.N. Environment Programme. Using the total emissions indicator, the United States ranked highest in 1987, with Japan ranking sixth, and China ranking fourth. Vote weight would be inversely proportional to the amount of pollution produced.

Based on these three criteria, Japan, Germany and the current permanent members of the Security Council would become the most influential and responsible members of the United Nations. China would no longer be ranked among the top five because of its poor human rights record. Voice and contribution weights would not be assigned permanently, however; they would be recalculated every year or two. Nations that progressed on any or all of these three dimensions would be rewarded with greater voice, whereas those losing ground in these areas would have their voices reduced. The promise of periodic adjustments could actually motivate government leaders to improve human rights practices and environmental policies.

An additional advantage is that nations such as Japan and Germany, which are now demanding more power in the international political arena, would automatically acquire more influence, and they would do so without necessitating a destructive and acrimonious debate that would dredge up their past misdeeds. However, these and other relatively rich nations would pay a price for their increased voices by assuming greater financial responsibility for implementing international policies. Since the peacemaking and peacekeeping role of the United Nations is likely to grow in the post–Cold War period, this redistribution of financial responsibility could result in significant savings for the United States. The United States has assumed too much moral and financial responsibility for setting and implementing international policies, impairing its ability to compete in the international marketplace. By sharing international power and financial responsibility with developing nations, the United Nations could be made more democratic and, thus, more effective; by redistributing power and financial responsibility among economic rivals, an equitable economic competition could be ensured for all global players of the twenty-first century.

This argument that the U.S. government should support reforms making the United Nations more democratic clearly does not fit the Nationalist or Exceptionalist type. Rather, it is located somewhere between the Progressive and Radical Progressive ideal types, but in the final analysis, fits the Progressive type best. It is Progressive in the sense that the proposal would encourage the governments of all nations to respect the human rights of their citizens, which is a universal value; it would encourage the U.S. government to develop more stringent policies to protect the global environment, something the Reagan and Bush administrations have resisted so far; and it would emphasize the need for coordinated political action and responsibility.

The argument comes close to the Radical Progressive position, because it would shift some political power from the permanent Security Council members to other members of the United Nations, including Third World nations. The Third World would benefit immediately from the elimination of the present two-tiered decision-making process that shuts them out entirely from the most important United Nations decisions. Their governments would go from having no say on important matters to having a limited voice. The specific amount of voice would be based on their economic performance, human rights practices, and environmental policies. Major oil-producing nations such as Iran and Saudi Arabia would receive the most benefit from this formula right away, as would the better human rights performers such as Costa Rica, Jordan, and India. All Third World countries would also benefit from a principle distributing power in international affairs that is fluid and based on explicit performance criteria rather than one that is fixed and based on the power balance that resulted from the last world war.

Unfortunately, but characteristically, what Progressives see as a step in the right direction, others would view as either insufficient or detrimental. Radical Progressives would reject this proposal on at least two grounds, either of which would be sufficient for them. First, adoption of this plan would cause too little distribution of power in international affairs; it would be at least a decade before Third World governments would account for even a quarter of the vote in U.N. decisions. Second, they would reject the notion that the size of a nation's economy has anything to do with performance. Nationalists would view the same proposal as detrimental to U.S. interests, because it would redistribute too much power away from the United States. And Exceptionalists would be likely to view this proposal as a misguided diversion from America's real mission in the world.

Because rhetoric can be misleading and because, as in the case of the example above, actual policies often represent compromises among two or more ideal type positions, particular foreign policy actions can be difficult to categorize. Using the typology to characterize the policies of a particular presidential administration is even harder because developing a summary evaluation of a foreign policy that, by its very nature, is conducted in many places, in many ways, and with many goals is not easily accomplished. Consider the Reagan and Bush administration's choice to use "constructive engagement" and "quiet diplomacy" to gently urge human rights reforms by repressive Third World regimes. Following this strategy, the United States should not sever relations or publicly embarrass governments that violate the human rights of their citizens, but it should continue to work closely with them to encourage them to make improvements. By itself, it represents a cautiously Progressive approach to improving respect for human rights around the world. Spokespersons for both administrations stressed the importance of "targets of opportunity" to make substantial gains in respect for human rights without seriously risking the national self-interest. During the Reagan administration, targets of opportunity occurred in such places as the Philippines, South Korea, Haiti, and Chile. The victory of the National Opposition Union (U.N.O.) in Nicaragua presented a similar target of opportunity for the Bush administration in that country.

On most other foreign policy issues, however, especially those most relevant to the Third World, both administrations have taken Nationalist positions (see Chapter 11). Thus, overall the Reagan and Bush administrations should be categorized as mainly Nationalist, but closer to the Progressive position than either the Johnson or Nixon administrations were. The Truman, Kennedy, and Carter administrations were more explicitly Progressive in the sense that they gave more consistent voice to a wider range of Progressive objectives; pursued those objectives more consistently, even when they seemed to conflict with the short-term national interest; and were faithful to those objectives, at least in part, because they viewed universal values as having intrinsic as well as instrumental importance. My own evaluations concerning the moral positions of the full set of U.S. presidents in the twentieth century are depicted in Figure 1.2 and are explained in later chapters.

A PROGRESSIVE TREND

This work maintains that U.S. foreign policy toward the Third World has "evolved." The evolutionary metaphor is appropriate, because each administration has built on the policies of its predecessors; each has reacted to environmental stimuli or action-forcing events, and, as indicated in Figure 1.2, since World War II there has been a slight but perceptible shift away from Nationalist and Exceptionalist principles toward Progressive and even Radical Progressive doctrines, especially during Democratic administrations. With the easing of tensions between the United States and the former Soviet Union, this shift is likely to accelerate. This viewpoint, which holds that U.S. foreign policy is trending toward Progressive values, stands in sharp contrast to the view held by many scholars that the United States is bent on manipulating and exploiting Third World governments and peoples.[9]

As a particularly provocative recent example of this alternative point of view, Michael Hunt argues that history reveals three core ideas relevant to the conduct of foreign affairs. Comprising what he calls the United States' foreign policy ideology, these ideas have wielded great influence over U.S. foreign policy toward the Third World throughout the twentieth

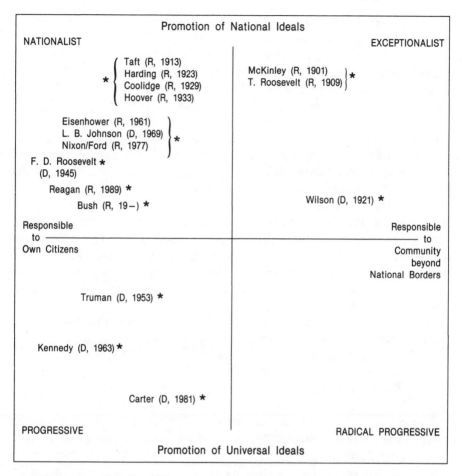

FIGURE 1.2   The Positions of Twentieth-Century U.S. Presidents on Morality and Foreign Policy toward the Third World (political party and last year of presidency in parentheses; asterisks indicate exact position within the continuums)

century. One idea is that the greatness of the American nation can be maintained through international activism, coupled with the promotion of liberty as a foreign policy value. A second element in the American ideology, as described by Hunt, is the superiority of white people in a racial hierarchy. The third is that revolutions elsewhere in the world could easily be dangerous to U.S. interests.[10]

In the present work, ideas and values are portrayed as less homogeneous and as ever-changing. Hunt's first idea would be strongly associated with what is portrayed here as the Exceptionalist position but not with any of the others. The second and third ideas would, almost by definition, be rejected by Progressives and Radical Progressives. On a more fundamental level, contrary to Hunt's thesis that a more or less homogeneous U.S. foreign policy ideology guides U.S.-Third World relations, at least four competing sets of views can be delineated. Moreover, as noted above, the historical record suggests that over time, and especially since World War II, U.S. policymakers have increasingly recognized the importance of universal as opposed to American values and of duties beyond borders.

Although this trend has not been monotonic, it has been at least perceptible in the changing rhetoric, actions, and consequences of U.S. foreign policy toward the Third World over the past two hundred years. The Progressive evolution in U.S. foreign policy has been caused mainly by the United States' changing place within the international power structure, by the longstanding rivalry with the former Soviet Union over alternative conceptions of the "good society," by a shift in American values, by the lessons learned from the Vietnam War, and, most importantly, by the institutional changes in foreign policy decision-making structures and processes wrought by Progressive administrations.

The international power structure is a significant attribute of any nation's foreign policy.[11] During the first 75 years or so of the United States' existence as a nation, its military and economic weakness relative to the major powers of Europe and the opportunity to gain strength at the expense of weaker neighboring states motivated its imperialistic foreign policy behavior, first toward the Indian nations and then toward Mexico. As its economic and military power grew, its needs for more land and population, essential building blocks of national power, diminished.

As time passed, the United States' position continued to rise relative to that of other states in the power hierarchy. All states at or near the top of the distribution of economic or military power have a stake in the stability of that distribution. Some U.S. policymakers have recognized that poverty and political oppression in the Third World are important causes of political instability there. Reforms removing the causes of revolution in the Third World, therefore, are both humanitarian and in the long-term self-interest of the United States.

Congressman Don Bonker, an advocate of a Progressive U.S. foreign policy and chairman of the House Subcommittee on Human Rights and International Organizations, recently expressed this view:

> It has never been a lack of weapons but rather internal discord and disregard of basic rights that threaten repressive governments allied with us and often threaten our strategic interests. As recent history has shown it was not our human rights policy that brought about the downfall of

several dictators allied with us. Rather, it was the lack of even a minimal level of decency and justice in those nations and our uncritical support of such governments that has estranged us from successor regimes.[12]

Once Soviet communism had emerged as an ideological counterpoint to the dominant political and economic ideas of the West, the superpower conflict became a contest over conceptions of good government, good economics, and social justice. American foreign policy toward the Third World was transformed into a struggle between the moral values of capitalism and those of socialism, between the values of authoritarianism and those of democracy, and between unalienable human rights and citizen rights to be granted or withheld by the state. American leaders had a stake in that struggle as it occurred in weaker states, because the spread of one set of moral values to some extent damages the others and because most Third World states had modeled their economic and political systems on the United States. In most instances, when those governments collapsed, the U.S. model of politics and economics was discredited. In contrast, the Soviet Union was less committed to the success of Third World governments, and, when they collapsed, the Soviet model became more attractive, by default.

Because the United States generally has been more committed to the survival of existing Third World governments than has the former Soviet Union, it has had a greater interest in promoting viable Third World societies. The necessary conditions for the existence of a viable society include a reasonably high rate of economic growth; political development founded on reasonably competent government and legitimate political institutions permitting widespread participation as well as responsive decisions; and social reforms addressing the grievances of disadvantaged groups.[13]

As the United States has become more affluent, the values held by its public have become less materialistic, making exploitation of Third World peoples even less likely. In other words, the moral evolution that is occurring in U.S. foreign policy toward the Third World can be traced in part to the American public's changing values. Inglehart has documented a gradual change in the values of the mass publics of all Western democracies since the great depression. He sees a shift away from the acquisitive values of those deeply affected by the economic depression from 1929 to 1936 toward more altruistic, less materialistic values of those who were not.[14] It follows that the emphasis of Progressive foreign policy objectives will become more pronounced as new age cohorts, ever less exposed to economic deprivation, assume power in the United States. Today, many of those who occupy important foreign policy-making roles or exercise substantial influence over policymakers were not deeply affected by the great depression.

As an illustration of the effect of Progressive values on foreign policy, consider recent U.S. policy toward South Africa. Since the early 1970s, public pressure has been put on U.S.-based multinational corporations and on the U.S. government to stop doing business with the South African government until it ended apartheid. The pressure became so strong that many corporations with enterprises in South Africa either left or reduced the size of their operations, and several companies that were considering opening new facilities there decided against it. Many investment funds divested holdings in South African companies, and some investment firms have set up funds using standards of social responsibility when making investment decisions. These funds have attracted hundreds of millions of dollars. Not only has the U.S. government joined this movement by instituting progressively more severe economic sanctions, but more than 50 states and cities have adopted "selective purchasing" policies that bar purchases from companies with objectionable practices in South Africa.[15]

In the 1960s and early 1970s, support for Progressive values and principles were strengthened by the lessons many Americans drew from the Vietnam War experience. Although the issue is still a highly contentious one, some lessons seem clear. One is that the United States should not become involved in long-term ground combat except as a last resort. Another is that the U.S. economy cannot support both a concerted effort to solve social problems at home and a prolonged, expensive war abroad. The attempt to do so during the Vietnam War contributed significantly to the massive foreign debt the United States still labors under today. Still another lesson is that, no matter how appealing the economic and political organization of the United States is to American citizens, it is dangerous and often destructive to impose that organization on people from a very different cultural tradition.

Perhaps, most important, even when particular presidents have not been personally committed to Progressive foreign policy goals set by their predecessors, members of Congress and interest groups have continued to advocate and advance these goals, keeping the ideas alive. This continued advocacy is virtually guaranteed, since many of the foreign policy goals have become law, and the institutions of governance have been modified to ensure their continued consideration. For example, during the Kennedy administration, the Peace Corps was established, and it continues to perform its Progressive foreign policy mission even today. Then, in the 1970s Congress created a Bureau of Human Rights and Humanitarian Affairs and added a Subcommittee on Human Rights and International Organizations to its Committee on Foreign Affairs. Congress also stipulated procedures that would guarantee the consideration of human rights practices of foreign governments when foreign aid decisions were made. Once organizations are created to pursue specific goals, whether or not they are Progressive, they are exceedingly difficult to dismantle. Herbert Kaufman found that, out of a sample of 421 national government organizations, only 27 had been terminated since 1923.[16] Even the House Un-American Activities Committee, which was largely discredited by 1955, was not officially abolished until 1975.[17]

Thus, several factors have pushed the United States government toward the pursuit of a more Progressive foreign policy since the Second World War. Some are less important today than they were forty years ago, while others are gaining in importance. The main point is that the continuation of a Progressive trend does not depend on any one factor, since it is pushed ahead by a variety of factors and sustained, even in the face of opposing pressures, by the institutionalization of new rules, roles, and structures.

CYCLES OF POLITICAL PARTY CONTROL

The historical record since World War II also illustrates the difference between the ways Republican and Democratic administrations in the United States have conducted relations with Third World states. Democrats generally have expanded the Progressive foreign policy agenda rhetorically and have made more efforts to follow through on that rhetoric. They have been more willing to use tax dollars to finance Third World development, to give economic rather than military aid, to provide grants rather than loans, to move resources from bilateral to multilateral aid programs, to seek regional or other kinds of international solutions to problems of instability, and to use methods other than unilateral military intervention and covert action to solve problems in relations with less developed countries. Although Democrats have not accepted the argument that the United States and other developed states are responsible for poverty in the Third World, they have tended to advocate helping Third World peoples improve their standard of living as a moral responsibility of a great and wealthy nation.[18]

In contrast, Republican administrations have tended to be more Nationalist in their approach to foreign policy. They have also been more inclined to see private sector initiatives as solutions to problems in the Third World. Foreign aid, on the other hand, is viewed as a bottomless pit of handouts, having short-term beneficial effects both for the United States and for the recipient regimes, but no long-term consequences for enhancing the well-being of Third World people. Unlike Democrats, Republicans rarely admit to any moral obligation to help the governments of less developed countries (LDCs) raise the standard of living of the abject poor segments of their societies. Republican administrations also have been quicker to resort to military intervention and to use covert action to achieve U.S. objectives in Third World states.

These systematic political party differences in foreign policy are consistent with the longstanding differences between the domestic policy agendas of the two major parties. In domestic policy, at least since the 1930s (when the present coalitions supporting the two major parties were formed), Democrats have been more willing than Republicans to rely on government intervention instead of the private sector to achieve policy goals, to support individual rights even when they conflict with majority preferences, to emphasize spending on health, education, and welfare over spending on defense, and generally to encourage policies that redistribute wealth and well-being from the rich to the poor. From these domestic policy positions, it has required a very short leap to emphases on human rights and other programs designed to benefit the least advantaged in the Third World.

These party differences are also logical extensions of the stated agendas of the two parties in their respective national platforms and the actions of the representatives of the two parties in Congress. Democratic candidates for the presidency since the 1930s have tended to embrace the Progressive foreign policy agenda toward the Third World more eagerly than have their Republican counterparts. For example, the 1988 Democratic party platform plank on South Africa promised strong action to encourage the establishment of black majority rule there:

> We believe that the time has come to end all vestiges of the failed policy of constructive engagement, to declare South Africa a terrorist state, to impose comprehensive sanctions upon its economy, to lead the international community in participation in these actions, and to determine a date certain by which United States corporations must leave South Africa.

Contrast this position with the much milder platform plank issued by the Republican party:

> Republicans deplore the apartheid system of South Africa and consider it morally repugnant. . . . We believe firmly that one element in the evolution of black political progress must be black economic progress; actions designed to pressure the government of South Africa must not have the effect of adversely affecting the rising aspirations and achieve-

ments of black South African entrepreneurs and workers and their families.

Similarly, in Congress, it has been mainly the Democrats who have championed the Progressive cause, especially since the mid-1960s when many powerful Southern Democrats left Congress. It is no accident that all of the most significant human rights laws now on the books were introduced by Democrats in Congress, and most were passed soon after the election of a large influx of Democrats to the House of Representatives in 1974. Today Republican-Democrat splits on foreign policy votes routinely reflect the tension between Republicans who generally prefer either a Nationalist or Exceptionalist approach and Democrats who usually prefer a more Progressive one.

As a recent example, on February 25, 1992, the U.S. Senate voted to impose conditions on the renewal of China's most-favored-nation trade status. The bill would condition the renewal on the Chinese government's accounting for and releasing from prison all citizens accused of expressing their political beliefs nonviolently. Among other conditions, it would also require that the president certify to Congress that China had made substantial progress in respect for the human rights of its citizens. Only five Democrats voted against the bill, but a large majority of Republicans opposed it. It passed by a 59–34 margin, not enough to override the subsequent veto by President Bush.

If Michael Dukakis had been elected president in 1988, this bill would have become law. Indeed, when Democrats have controlled the U.S. government, there has been a ratchet effect on the place of Progressive moral principles in the making of foreign policy toward less developed countries. If progress is measured as the addition of new foreign policy objectives related to improving the welfare of the poorest people in the Third World or as a willingness to take greater risks in the attainment of Nationalist objectives to achieve Progressive objectives, then Democrats have tended to ratchet the policy toward Progressivism during their tenures in terms of both rhetoric and actions. Republicans have tended to allow that upward progress to erode somewhat during their terms of office, but they are unable to turn the clock back completely. President Bush might wish that the furor over promoting international human rights would go away, but it will not.

Progressive principles became a higher priority during the Truman and Kennedy administrations, reaching their zenith during the Carter years. Then, except for the promotion of democracy, their importance as guides for foreign policy-making declined under the stewardship of Presidents Reagan and Bush. However, both Reagan and Bush have had to contend with a more established Progressive foreign policy agenda and, as a consequence, probably have given more weight to Progressive principles than Nixon or Ford did. Thus, despite the current cycle away from the trajectory set by Carter, Progressive foreign policy principles continue to receive higher priority as guides for the conduct of U.S.-Third World relations, a trend that began at the end of World War II.

THE THIRD WORLD

As is the common practice elsewhere, the terms *Third World, less developed, developing, less industrialized,* and *underdeveloped* are used interchangeably in this work mainly for linguistic convenience. Similarly, the term *American foreign policy* is used quite often instead of the more accurate *U.S. foreign policy,* not out of arrogance, but rather because of a desire to produce better sounding prose. Some find the term *Third World* objectionable, but most agree that it refers to an analytically meaningful category of nation-states.[19] George Kurian defines the Third World as "the politically nonaligned and economically developing and less industrialized nations of the world."[20] Unlike many First World States, these nations have relatively little ability to determine the outcomes of international conflicts through the use of force. The overwhelming majority of Third World states were formerly colonies; this common history helps us understand the positions their leaders take on most issues of international relations.[21] Applying his definition to the world's current stock of states, Kurian concludes that there are now 118 Third World countries comprising 49 percent of the world's land surface and 51 percent of the world's population.[22] Besides relative economic and military weakness and a history of exploitation by a former colonial power, most Third World states share the disadvantages of a tremendous income inequality, a very small middle class, a predominantly nonwhite population, an adverse climate, little industry, heavy reliance on the production of only one or two commodities for export, a primarily peasant agriculture, low capital per worker, poor communications facilities, limited educational opportunities, poor health services, and a relatively fluid political and economic structure.[23] The great majority also have a predominant religion other than Christianity or Judaism.

Estimates of the extent of poverty in the Third World vary somewhat depending on the particular measure of poverty used. According to one calculation, of the people living in the noncommunist developing countries in 1987, two thirds were seriously poor and two fifths were destitute.[24] The division between the world's rich and poor generally conforms with the equator, with the rich in the Northern Hemisphere and the poor in the

Southern, but several Third World nations in Asia and the Middle East are exceptions to this rule. The nations of the Third World are located mainly in Latin America, Africa, and Asia. Most have economic systems characterized by a predominance of free enterprise, but intellectual support for socialist doctrines is substantial. Approximately half of all Third World countries also have authoritarian forms of government.[25] In recent years, many Third World states have organized and presented demands for a New International Economic Order. Its net effect would be to shift significant amounts of the world's wealth and the power to control the world's economy away from those states that now have it to those that do not.

Besides providing a context highlighting moral and ethical issues, U.S.-Third World relations merit a thorough reexamination for compelling practical reasons. Most of the major foreign policy crises since World War II have occurred in the Third World: in Korea, Cuba, Vietnam, Panama, Iran, and Iraq, for example. In the last few decades power over policy outcomes in the Third World has shifted away from major national powers such as the United States and toward multinational corporations (MNCs) and international financial institutions. This shift is occurring at a geometric rate and is likely to continue for the foreseeable future.

The world continues to become smaller, and all states are increasingly interdependent. As the war in the Gulf vividly demonstrated, more states than ever before, including many in the Third World, now have the power to destroy or significantly damage the world's environment, economy, and people. Although some Third World countries are more important to the United States than others, it is becoming increasingly difficult to name any Third World country that is unimportant to U.S. interests. In his 1985 book, Donald Neuchterlein compiled a list of Third World countries where developments and their outcomes could have significant impact on the military security and economic prosperity of the United States.[26] The list did not include Iraq or Kuwait, countries that now certainly should be added. And in the years to come, the list will get longer. For this reason, a "fortress America" mentality—even one restricted to isolation from Third World affairs—is less viable today than ever before.

With the ending of the Cold War, the importance of East-West relations has declined and the significance of North-South relations has increased. Recognizing the increased relevance of U.S.-Third World relations to the national self-interest, a 1989 report commissioned by the Arms Control and Foreign Policy Caucus of Congress discussed five key problems confronting the leaders of most developing countries, noting that an inability to solve these problems would seriously threaten U.S. interests.[27] The five problems cited were economic stagnation and excessive foreign debt, environmental damage, the threat of the military sector to democracy and civilian control of government, weapons proliferation and militarization, and drug trafficking. Many developing countries have become important trading partners with the United States. Some have become competitors in manufactured goods such as steel and automobiles. Many have borrowed heavily from the multilateral development banks and from the commercial banking systems of the industrialized world. As a result, Third World conditions and policies are more central to U.S. economic prosperity today than was ever the case in earlier periods.[28]

PLAN OF THIS BOOK

One caveat: it is not my purpose here to argue that any particular position on morality and foreign policy is best. Although my own position is generally Progressive and I do not attempt to hide it, my main goal was to conduct an objective, analytical, descriptive, and historical inquiry into what intentions have guided actual American foreign policies toward the Third World. The typology of positions presented in this chapter provides an analytical reference point for that inquiry. Chapter 2 explores in greater detail the mainstream debate among Nationalists, Exceptionalists, and Progressives. Chapter 3 is devoted to a similar in-depth exploration of the Marxist position, which is one important stream of thought that often leads to a Radical Progressive position on U.S. behavior toward the Third World. Taken together, these two chapters provide a fairly complete picture of alternative moral reasonings about foreign policy, that is, which "good" should be maximized and why.

Most of the remainder of the book examines different historical periods of U.S. foreign relations with the Third World, identifying the most significant goals during each period, with special emphasis on the post–World War II era. In each chapter, the rhetoric of U.S. policymakers is compared with actual U.S. foreign policy during their terms of office. Military interventions, known covert operations, and U.S. government responses to action-forcing events in the Third World are described.

The methodology employed is historical analysis, because history provides real examples of how U.S. leaders have responded to real moral dilemmas in the making of foreign policy. This approach allows us to identify the hierarchy of values and objectives that U.S. leaders have expressed in public statements on U.S. foreign policy toward the Third World, to look for patterns of congruence and divergence between public statements and foreign policy as actually implemented, and, based on this evidence, to draw conclusions about changes in the hierarchy of foreign policy values. An understanding of notable developments in U.S.-Third World relations also enhances our sensitivity to differences between other historical times and our own, increases our ability to perceive and explain significant changes over time, and heightens our awareness of basic continuities in policy.

Identifying foreign policy goals is an important and intellectually challenging task, but one that is also fraught with danger. The evidence is indirect, fragmentary, and open to alternative interpretation. Because motives can never be observed directly, they must be inferred from public statements and government actions. Since the foreign policy decision-making process itself tends to be secret (for good and obvious reasons), even the factual record about what actions were taken is incomplete. Moreover, the available facts never speak for themselves. Thus, different analysis viewing the same facts may draw different conclusions from them about the motives of the decision maker. These problems are discussed in greater detail in Chapter 4. If these problems are not overcome, discussions of the morality of foreign policies must be avoided altogether.

Chapters 5 and 6, which make up Part II of the book, briefly discuss the early history of U.S. foreign policy toward weaker nations. Chapter 5 begins at the beginning by briefly examining the relations between the U.S. government and the American Indians and Mexico between 1776 and the end of the nineteenth century. Chapter 6 focuses on the first half of the twentieth century, with special emphasis on U.S. involvement in the Philippines and Latin America. The term *Third World,* though of recent origin, is applied in chapters 5 and 6 retrospectively to countries that would have fit the definition in earlier times. Part III (chapters 7–9) provides a more detailed account of significant developments in U.S.-Third World relations between the end of World War II and the beginning of the Reagan and Bush era. As noted, this was a period of fairly rapid movement toward Progressive principles, especially during the Truman, Kennedy, and Carter administrations.

Part IV (Chapters 10 and 11) focuses on the Reagan and Bush administrations and the future. Chapter 10 in this section examines the most recent U.S. foreign policy choices and directions on North-South issues. It presents a snapshot of the present at a time in history when many of the rules of international relations are being rewritten. The final chapter is both retrospective and predictive. First, it reviews the evidence showing that there has been a long-term trend toward Progressivism in U.S. foreign policy rhetoric and behavior toward the Third World. Then, it examines three possible scenarios for U.S. foreign policy toward the Third World in the twenty-first century.

NOTES

1. Kenneth N. Waltz, *Theory of International Politics* (New York: Random House, 1979).

2. Interpretations of U.S. foreign policy stressing societal forces include Robert Dallick, *The American Style of Foreign Policy: Cultural Politics and Foreign Affairs* (New York: Alfred A. Knopf, 1983) and Loren Baritz, *Backfire: A History of How American Culture Led Us into Vietnam and Made Us Fight the Way We Did* (New York: William Morrow, 1985).

3. Alexander L. George, "The Operational Code: A Neglected Approach to the Study of Political Decision-Making," *International Studies Quarterly* 12 (June 1969): 190–122.

4. Henry Kissinger, *The White House Years* (Boston: Little, Brown, 1979), p. 54.

5. Terry Nardin, "Moral Renewal: The Lessons of Eastern Europe," *Ethics and International Affairs* 5 (1991): 3, and Alan Donagan, *The Theory of Morality* (Chicago: University of Chicago Press, 1977).

6. Although one can imagine a hypothetical situation where maintaining national sovereignty is not consistent with the best interests of citizens, real examples are hard to find.

7. Stanley Hoffmann, *Duties Beyond Borders* (Syracuse, N.Y.: Syracuse University Press, 1981), p. xiii.

8. George F. Kennan, "Morality and Foreign Policy," *Foreign Affairs* 64, No. 2 (Winter 1985–1986): 205–218.

9. Recent examples of this scholarship include Gabriel Kolko, *Confronting the Third World: United States Foreign Policy, 1945–1980* (New York: Pantheon, 1980), Melvin Gurtov and Ray Maghroori, *Roots of Failure: United States Policy and the Third World* (Westport, Conn.: Greenwood Press, 1984), and Michael Parenti, *The Sword and the Dollar: Imperialism, Revolution, and the Arms Race* (New York: St. Martin's Press, 1989).

10. Michael H. Hunt, *Ideology and U.S. Foreign Policy* (New Haven, Conn.: Yale University Press, 1987).

11. The argument that the international power structure and each state's place within it impose constraints on state actions is made most eloquently by Waltz, *Theory of International Politics.*

12. Prepared statement submitted for the record of the Hearings on "Reconciling Human Rights and Security Interests in Asia," August 10–December 15, 1982 (Washington, D.C.: U.S. Government Printing Office, 1983), p. 3.

13. This argument concerning the U.S. interest in creating viable societies in the Third World has been developed best by Jacob J. Kaplan, *The Challenge of Foreign Aid* (New York: Praeger Publishers, 1967), pp. 120–131.

14. Ronald Inglehart, *The Silent Revolution* (Princeton, N.J.: Princeton University Press, 1977).

15. See Gary C. Hufbauer and Jeffrey J. Schott, *Economic Sanctions Reconsidered* (Washington, D.C.: Institute for International Economics, 1985) for a history of U.S. economic sanctions on South Africa. For a report on the impact of public concern on the private sector, see Steven Mufson, "The Long March from College Campuses to Corporate Boardrooms," *Washington Post National Weekly Edition,* February 19–25, 1990, p. 8.

16. Herbert Kaufman, *Are Government Organizations Immortal?* (Washington, D.C.: Brookings Institution, 1976), p. 65.

17. It was renamed the Committee on Internal Security in 1969. In 1975 it was abolished, and its jurisdiction was given to the Judicial Committee.

18. Arguably, Lyndon Johnson was a notable exception to this pattern of foreign policy orientations by Democratic presidents.

19. See the debate over the use of the term *Third World* in *Third World Quarterly* 1, No. 1 (January 1979), pp. 105–115.

20. George Thomas Kurian, *Encyclopedia of the Third World,* 3rd ed. (New York: Facts on File, 1987), Vol. 1, ix.

21. See Caroline Thomas, *In Search of Security: The Third World in International Relations* (Boulder, Colo.: Rienner, 1987). She considers status as an ex-colony to be a necessary criterion for inclusion in the category of Third World states. However, application of this criterion as a necessary condition excludes from the Third World category such states as Afghanistan, Bhutan, Ethiopia, Haiti, Iran, Lebanon, Liberia, Nepal, Thailand, and Turkey.

22. Ibid., p. ix.

23. For a very readable description of economic, social, and political conditions in the Third World, see Paul Harrison, *Inside the Third World* (Middlesex, England: Penguin Books, 1987).

24. Ibid., pp. 405–407.

25. Raymond D. Gastil, "The Comparative Survey of Freedom 1986," *Freedom at Issue* (January–February 1986); 15.

26. Donald E. Neuchterlein, *America Overcommitted: United States National Interests in the 1980s* (Lexington: University Press of Kentucky, 1985), pp. 208–209.

27. U.S. Congress, Arms Control and Foreign Policy Caucus, *The Developing World: Danger Point for U.S. Security* (Washington, D.C.: U.S. Congress, August 1989). Earlier significant government reports relevant to this subject include the report produced by the Gordon Gray Commission, *Report to the President on Foreign Economic Policies* (Washington, D.C.: U.S. Government Printing Office, 1950) and the Rockefeller Report, U.S. International Advisory Board, *Partners in Progress: A Report to President Truman* (New York: Simon and Schuster, 1951).

28. John W. Sewell, "The Metamorphosis of the Third World: U.S. Interests in the 1990s," in William Brock and Robert Hormats, eds., *The Global Economy* (New York: W. W. Norton, 1990), pp. 120–146.

CHAPTER 2

The Contemporary Debate

It is widely agreed that the conduct of foreign policy should be moral, but there is a lively debate over which moral principles should be used. Each of the four schools of thought, Nationalism, Exceptionalism, Progressivism, and Radical Progressivism, provides a different answer to this question. This chapter discusses the relative merits of each position and shows that each has a consistent logical underpinning. No attempt is made, however, to present every logical argument that might lead to the adoption of one rather than another position. This chapter also fleshes out these four ideal positions, providing information necessary to assess the thesis that since World War II the trend among U.S. leaders has been toward Progressivism and away from both Nationalism and Exceptionalism.

NATIONALISM

There is a close relationship between a person's view of how things really work in the world (or one's empirical theory) and that person's policy prescriptions (which reflect moral reasoning). In *The Federalist,* James Madison argued that since human beings were by nature corruptible, particular institutional arrangements for making collective choices in society were necessary to prevent the abuse of power by government officials. Similarly, the usual Nationalist reading of history indicates that humankind is by nature sinful and evil and that the international system is an anarchy in which the strong survive and the weak perish. In this hostile environment, the principal moral responsibility of every government is to advance the interests of its citizens and to direct all efforts to their survival and prosperity. If all states base their foreign affairs on these principles, peace will result through the operation of a balance of power.

Avoiding the debate over what a moral foreign policy should be, Kenneth Waltz contends that the structure of the international system propels all leaders toward policies designed to expand economic and military power, simply because increased power is in every state's interest.

Power provides the means for maintaining autonomy in the face of force wielded by other states. It also permits a wider range of options for action. Moreover, the powerful have a larger margin of safety in their dealings with less powerful states and greater control over the outcomes of interactions with them.[1]

Hans Morgenthau makes a more explicit moral argument. He asserts that, because states operate within an anarchy, the inevitable immediate objective of foreign policy is to accumulate power: "Foreign policy, like all politics, is in its essence a struggle for power, waged by sovereign nations for national advantage. The struggle is never ending, because the lust for power is insatiable and the fear of it in others is never stilled."[2] Machiavelli was even more explicit, stressing that foreign policy-making should be free from humanitarian considerations. He noted that "where the well-being of one's country is at all in question, no consideration of justice or injustice, of mercy or cruelty, of honor or shame must be allowed to enter in at all."[3]

Nations struggle for power in both the economic and military spheres, because winning in both spheres is essential to national survival. The United States is the most powerful nation in the international system, because it is the only nation that is a world leader in both spheres. The linkage between economic and military power was never more dramatically demonstrated than during World War II when the United States used its massive industrial capacity to rebuild its navy after the disastrous Pearl Harbor attack. The necessity for economic resources to back up military commitments is undeniable. Robert Gilpin's analysis of the rise and decline of great powers underscores this relationship between economic and military power. He argues that decline is inevitable, because the "protection costs" associated with maintaining an empire rise faster than the capacity of a great power to finance them.[4]

Jacob Viner has identified five propositions that summarize the essentials of mercantilist doctrine within international economic thought. These propositions provide some implications of Nationalist thinking for foreign economic policy:

(1) Policy should be framed and executed in strictly nationalistic terms, that is, national advantage alone is to be given weight; (2) in appraising any relevant element of national policy or of foreign trade, great weight is always to be put on its effect, direct or indirect, on the national stock of precious metals; (3) in the absence of domestic gold or silver mines, a primary national goal should be the attainment of as large an excess of exports over imports as is practicable, as the sole means whereby the national stock of precious metals can be augmented; (4) a balance of trade "in favor" of one's country is to be sought through direct promotion by the authorities of exports and restriction of imports or by other measures

which will operate indirectly in these directions; (5) economic foreign policy and political foreign policy are to be pursued with constant attention to both plenty and "power" (including security under this latter term) as coordinate and generally mutually supporting national objectives, each capable of being used as a means to the attainment of the other.[5]

Consistent with this kind of thinking, Nationalists advocate policies ensuring the United States' access to scarce mineral resources and other raw materials, many of which are found only or mainly in Third World states. They also support policies that encourage Third World states to adopt market economies and to maintain free trade policies. These arrangements make it easier for U.S.-based multinational corporations (MNCs) to operate profitably on foreign soil and to find foreign markets for the goods they produce. Nationalists believe that there is a positive relationship between the profitability of U.S.-based multinationals and the economic well-being of American citizens.

Morgenthau argued that a general goal for foreign policy should be to preserve the balance of power between the United States and the other great powers and, within limits, to increase the weight on the U.S. side of the fulcrum. He portrayed Third World states as prizes to be won by more powerful states or, at a minimum, as prizes to be denied adversaries. Nationalist thinking tends to be explicitly utilitarian in the sense that what is best depends entirely on what outcome would be expected. When confronted by action-forcing events in the international environment, the United States' leaders should determine which outcome would either preserve the present balance of power or marginally shift the balance in its favor. Then they should determine whether the United States has the power to achieve that outcome, and, if so, how much of its limited resources, diplomatic, financial, and military, would have to be expended. Preserving or enhancing the United States' position in the prevailing balance of power is the benefit, and expending resources is the cost. Nationalists would prefer the particular course of action that would lead to the most favorable benefit-cost ratio. This is why Morgenthau claimed that the national interest could be discovered through scientific and rational analysis.

As one means of enhancing military power, U.S. foreign policy should be directed toward increasing the number of developing nations willing to help defend the United States against potential external military threats. Depending on the circumstances, a developing country could demonstrate this willingness by signing a mutual defense treaty, by giving the United States permission to establish military bases on its territory, by providing intelligence information necessary for military defense of the United

States, and by maintaining peaceful relations with its own neighbors. Until the end of the Cold War, Nationalists sought to prevent Third World states from developing communist political systems. The fear was that such nations might subsequently become allies of the United States' then principal military rival, the Soviet Union. The fears of Nationalists today center on a communist revival or a military coup in the states that now constitute the Commonwealth of Independent States—especially Russia—and on Third World alliances with Communist China, a potentially formidable future military adversary.

The existence of a generally stable international system helps the United States maintain its economic and military power, for the nation now occupies a privileged position. Since any change is more likely to hurt than help the United States, Nationalists advocate the immoral policy of suppressing all revolutionary movements (except those against communist governments), because the outcomes might upset the delicate balance of power among the giants. In the past, however, genuine popular revolutions and Soviet-inspired revolutions often were difficult to distinguish in practice. As a result, those who placed a high priority on the value of anti-communism frequently advocated counterrevolution.

The United States has supported many Third World governments ruled at one time or another by dictators even against popular revolutions. There is an abundance of examples in the twentieth century: the authoritarian governments of Spain, Portugal, Paraguay, Argentina, the Dominican Republic, Guatemala, Brazil, Haiti, Greece, Cuba, South Korea, Taiwan, Vietnam, Nicaragua, and the Philippines all received U.S. support in the face of popular revolutions. Charles Kegley and Eugene Wittkopf note that in these and many other cases, "the United States has armed and otherwise supported some of the most ruthless tyrannies in the modern world (while referring to their governments as members of 'the Free World'!)."[6] In truth, their common position against communism was the only characteristic of these dictatorships that was important to U.S. Nationalists.

President Kennedy's foreign policy toward the Third World is not characterized in this work as mainly Nationalist, but his explanation of the U.S. response to the assassination of Rafael Trujillo, an anti-communist Dominican dictator, showed the power of Nationalist principles even over his thinking:

There are three possibilities in descending order of preference: a decent democratic regime, a continuation of the Trujillo regime [a dictatorship], or a Castro regime [a communist government]. We ought to aim at the first, but we really can't renounce the second until we are sure we can avoid the third.

Of course, U.S. leaders are rarely *sure* that they can avoid this third possibility in the aftermath of a popular revolution, because they are seldom in a position to control or even to predict what the people will decide. The question, then, really comes down to the relative importance of contending values and the willingness to risk loss on some to achieve possible gains in others.

Nationalists place a very high value on maintaining and expanding economic and military power relative to other goals. They are unwilling to risk losses in these areas in order to achieve such goals as greater democracy in the Third World. Whether the U.S. pursuit of those interests helps or hurts the people of developing countries is not particularly relevant, because the chief purpose of U.S. foreign policy is to promote the interests of the American people — not to interfere in the internal domestic affairs of other states.[7] Therefore, leaders should consider themselves virtuous when they have advanced the national interest of the United States without inflicting injuries on others. Any other pretensions about moral purposes in the conduct of foreign policy are at best irrelevant and at worst hypocritical, because leaders, when faced with the choice between adherence to an idealistic principle and a gain in power, will and should choose power. Table 2.1 summarizes Nationalist thinking on the proper ends and means of U.S. foreign policy toward the Third World.

Among the members of the American public and the policy-making elite, Nationalism constitutes the dominant position on proper U.S. foreign policy toward the Third World. All opinion polls show that U.S. public attitudes support a mainly Nationalist foreign policy. For example, a 1986 public opinion survey sponsored by the Chicago Council on Foreign Relations showed that the public supported those military interventions in the Third World and foreign policies that promoted the general economic prosperity of the United States. The survey also revealed that the desire to protect American jobs and to secure access to raw materials took priority over such altruistic objectives as promoting democracy, improving human rights, or improving the standard of living for the mass publics of Third World states. Forty-two percent of the public even went so far as to oppose all forms of foreign aid. Leaders in the Reagan administration, though still mainly Nationalist in orientation, generally professed more support for more humanitarian objectives and for foreign aid than did the general public.[8] A 1989 public opinion poll sponsored by the Carnegie Foundation illustrated the tensions and contradictions in public opinion on foreign policy. Seventy-two percent of the 1,000 respondents felt that it was

TABLE 2.1
Attributes of the Nationalist Ideal Type

Perspective:
Instability and poverty in the Third World result from East-West conflict.
Human nature is evil.
The international system is an anarchy.

Foreign Policy Ends:
Maintain security from external threat.
Secure economic prosperity for U.S. citizens.
Strengthen and extend the scope of the world capitalist system.
Influence the foreign policies of other governments.

Objectives:
Support anti-communist/pro-United States regimes even against popular revolutions.
Encourage Third World governments to assist in the military defense of the United
    States.
Assure access to strategic raw materials.
Aid U.S.-based MNCs operating in foreign countries.
Encourage Third World states to adopt market economies.
Advocate free trade rules.

Policy Targets:
Emphasize East-West relations.
Gain cooperation of Third World governments.

Acceptable Means Include:
Unilateral military intervention and covert action.

extremely important that the United States play a leading role in the
advancement of human rights internationally, but only 31 percent thought
it was important to support the economic needs of underdeveloped
nations.[9]

EXCEPTIONALISM

As a world view, Exceptionalists assume that humankind is essentially
good and capable of altruism, that all people want basically the same
things, no matter where they may live. Evil behavior is the result not of bad
people but of bad institutions. An oppressive Third World government
would be less so if it adopted democratic institutions and processes.
American values and institutions are best for all times, for all places, and
for all people. Therefore, one important purpose of foreign policy is to

help other nations adopt the U.S. model. The roots of Exceptionalism are the ideas of American superiority and Manifest Destiny discussed in greater detail in Chapter 5. Although it is still a very real part of the mainstream debate over U.S. foreign policy in the Third World, the Exceptionalist point of view is probably the best understood, so it is not discussed at length in this chapter.

Edward Banfield explains why a democratic nation is so strongly compelled to express the moral principles held by its citizens in its foreign policy:

> A public . . . cannot deliberately transgress the principles of its morality. Societies are held together by attachment to common values, especially ones that are held sacred. To call such values publicly into question, to consider openly the expediency of transgressing them, and then actually to do so (even though in order to realize other values) would profane and destroy the values and so weaken the mystic bonds that hold the society together. Such a thing could happen only if the values of the society had already lost their sacredness, and if, therefore, the society was in the process of disintegration.[10]

One of the strongest contemporary advocates of Exceptionalism in U.S.–Third World relations is Joshua Muravchik. This scholar argues that the goals of advancing the democratic cause and encouraging "freemarket strategies for economic development" should be at the center of U.S. foreign policy throughout the world, even if that strategy offends the leaders of friendly authoritarian governments. These goals are so crucial that he believes U.S. leaders should use all means including covert action and military occupation, if necessary, to ensure their attainment.[11]

In contrast, Howard Wiarda believes that U.S. leaders should resist the temptation to help the people of other nations. Like Banfield, he recognizes the United States' strong missionary spirit of bringing the benefits of Western civilization to the developing nations. However, this spirit too often leads to a lack of respect for institutions and to procedures different from those adopted in the United States, to an insistence that other nations do it the American way or do it without U.S. assistance. He warns that the United States should not change its policy toward particular Third World states based on the degree to which each achieves U.S.-government defined reforms. With regard to U.S. foreign policy toward El Salvador, he writes:

> If democracy [in El Salvador] should fail or be overthrown, we might still have to support the succeeding government, however undemocratic, because our nation's interests are affected. . . . My own view is that we can favor a strong human rights policy in support of democracy, but that

we must be very sure of what we are doing, accept the requirement to adapt our categories and prescriptions to particular Third World situations, and recognize the need to exercise restraint, prudence, and considerable forbearance in these matters.[12]

There is some wisdom in the views of those who argue in favor of ethical relativism. The administrations of Theodore Roosevelt, McKinley, and Wilson are often cited as offending examples of administrations whose treatment of Third World states was patronizing and ethnocentric. Each was quick to use force to impose U.S. ideals on weaker states. The Exceptionalist foreign policies of these presidents, though popular at the time, are seldom praised today. Still, carried too far, ethical relativism can be a prescription for paralysis and the abdication of any moral responsibilities extending beyond national borders. Table 2.2 summarizes Exceptionalist thinking on the proper ends and means of U.S. foreign policy toward the Third World.

TABLE 2.2
Attributes of the Exceptionalist Ideal Type

Perspective:

Instability and poverty in the Third World and oppression by Third World governments are all caused by the absence of U.S.-style political, social, and economic institutions.

All human beings have the same needs and wants, no matter where they live.

Foreign Policy Ends:

Maintain security from external threat.

Secure economic prosperity for U.S. citizens.

Strengthen and extend the scope of the world capitalist system.

Influence the foreign and domestic policies of other governments.

Help other nations of the world become more like the United States.

Objectives:

All the Nationalist objectives listed in Table 2.1 plus:

Encourage Third World governments to adopt democratic political institutions similar to those used in the United States and to adopt capitalist economic principles.

Influence Third World peoples to adopt values, attitudes, and beliefs just like those in the popular U.S. culture (e.g., individualism and materialism).

Policy Targets:

All Third World governments and their peoples.

Emphasize nations in Latin America and communist nations everywhere.

Acceptable Means Include:

Unilateral military intervention and covert action.

PROGRESSIVISM

Progressives differ from Exceptionalists mainly in the degree of respect they accord Third World cultures, in the importance they place on the achievement of distributive justice in Third World societies, and in their reluctance to resort to unilateral intervention or covert action as the means to their ends. As a world view, Progressivism, like Exceptionalism, assumes that humankind is essentially good and capable of altruism. Progressives, too, believe that evil behavior derives not from bad people but from bad institutions and that the adoption of democratic processes would lead an oppressive Third World government to become less so. Power politics would be less prevalent in international affairs if only the enforcement powers of international institutions like the United Nations were strengthened. Whereas the Nationalist prescription for foreign policy is that each situation should be treated as unique and be handled only in terms of calculating the U.S. national interest, the Progressive thinker prefers the statement of principles to be applied as consistently as possible across cases. Whereas Nationalism views national leaders as the only representatives of a nation's interests, Progressivism suggests that U.S. foreign policy should give greater weight to the needs and wants of the poorest citizens of other nations.

Progressives believe that U.S. foreign policymakers should carefully examine the U.S. national interest along with the needs and aspirations of the peoples of developing countries. In this way, it is possible to develop principles to guide U.S. foreign policy actions toward those countries that are consistent with both considerations. Over the years, Progressive thinkers have proposed at least four foreign policy values that have been justified on these grounds. U.S. foreign policy, they state, ought to (1) aid fledgling democracies; (2) stimulate economic and social development; (3) foster an equitable distribution of wealth; and (4) promote the human rights of all people, especially the poorest. If achieved, these goals would improve the level of economic well-being and political empowerment of the masses in less developed countries, in particular, the peoples occupying the bottom fifth of the income distribution within their own countries.

Some argue that encouraging the adoption of market economies in the Third World also is a Progressive end in the sense that a market economy would improve the condition of the least well off. However, many Third World intellectuals and government leaders reject this idea. Moreover, encouraging market economies in Third World states also is considered to be central to the United States' ability to maintain its economic power within the international system. Accordingly, in this book spreading capitalism is treated as a Nationalist foreign policy goal. The remainder of this analysis will be consistent with this usual treatment. But the crucial question is whether the encouragement of market economies in the Third World is more effective than alternative economic arrangements in advancing the well-being of the poorest segment of societies. That remains an unsettled empirical question. Progressives would accord greater weight to the preferences of Third World peoples on this point than would either Nationalists or Exceptionalists.

One of the most important aspects of a state's interest in foreign affairs should be the needs and aspirations of its own people, but Progressives and Radical Progressives believe that the interests of the poorest people sometimes are ignored or even suppressed by their own leaders. When U.S. foreign policymakers lose sight of those mass interests, however, they risk serious miscalculation of the long-term consequences of their policies. Progressives believe that eventually those needs and aspirations will be espoused by future Third World leaders who will not quickly forget the United States' past cynical and expedient policies toward their nations. A Progressive U.S. foreign policy would focus attention and resources on the pursuit of those policies that enhance security from external threats and the economic prosperity of its people, but that also are consistent with both the ideals of the American people and with Third World aspirations. Progressives believe that showing benevolence toward the common people in less developed countries usually is the best way to serve the long-term U.S. national interest. They also embrace the principle of nonintervention, or at least of multilateral rather than unilateral intervention. Progressive ideas are often included within the mainstream debate over proper U.S. foreign policy toward the Third World, because few advocates of Progressivism would argue against the Nationalist principle that foreign policy should be designed primarily to promote national security. Where many Progressives part company from Nationalists is over the notion that "national security" primarily means the pursuit of ever greater military power for the U.S. government. Richard Ullman, for example, criticizing the Reagan administration's overemphasis on building military capacity, argued that the United States could gain greater national security by promoting self-sustaining development in poor countries and by minimizing its military reliance on repressive governments.[13]

From a Progressive perspective, a nation is more than a territory containing people. Therefore, national survival and security consist of more than the continued governance of that territory and those people by a particular government. Security from external threat and the economic well-being of citizens are necessary, but not sufficient, conditions for national success. This is because every great nation represents a set of ideas, a character, a philosophy, a morality; these are the essence of the nation. Beyond survival, the function of government is to advance this conception of nationhood through public policy, both domestic and foreign. A foreign policy divorced from those ideas, alienated from the national character, cannot serve the long-term national interest. Indeed, the pursuit of some foreign policy ends and the use of bad means toward those ends may adversely affect other things the American people value including their own rights, freedoms, and ideals.

A foreign policy ultimately designed to control the destinies of other nations could not be further from the values of the American public. The long-term national interest is served best by the existence of a world system of nations whose important values and beliefs, at least as expressed through their foreign policies, are compatible with those held by the American people. The only effective way to achieve or approach that end is to act as an example for other nations. The goal should not be cultural imperialism, whereby the U.S. government expects every nation to mirror the dominant values and beliefs of the American people. Rather, it should be international peace and mutual respect for differences that do no harm to others. The most important value of the United States' own liberal democratic political system is the freedom and fulfillment of the individual consistent with the welfare of the larger community. Progressives believe that respect for individual rights and liberties at home should translate into an analogous respect for the rights of other nations to govern in their own ways providing they do not harm the international community and do not oppress their own people. Thus, the norm against intervention, especially unilateral intervention, is essential to the Progressive perspective.

Frequent unilateral interventions by the United States such as those that have occurred in recent years in Libya, Grenada, and Panama are disturbing evidence to Progressives that U.S. foreign policymakers are too willing to risk the long-range national interest to achieve short-range Nationalist objectives. Progressives urge a more consistent focus on long-term consequences when making foreign policy, even if doing so requires risking or even sacrificing the attainment of nearer term objectives. A tribe of Native American Indians believes that all policy decisions for their tribe should be made according to the impacts of those decisions in seven generations. This is a good rule for all public policy-making, especially for foreign policy-making toward the Third World, because the institutions in most of those countries are still developing and are therefore malleable. Thus, U.S. policies toward them should be based more on longer term needs than on the needs of the moment or on the preservation of a particular friendly regime in a Third World state. More specifically, they should be based on whether that long-term course is helpful or harmful to U.S. military security, to the macroeconomic prosperity of the American people, to the core ideals of the majority of the American people, and to the welfare of the least advantaged members of Third World societies.

In this context, most Progressives also accept the norm against counterrevolution. For example, the late Senator Frank Church, as chairman of the Senate Foreign Relations Committee, saw the counterrevolutionary thrust in foreign policy toward the Third World as immoral and counterproductive, even in terms of Nationalist ends.[14] Counterrevolution may be counterproductive, because there may be a positive feedback system wherein U.S. efforts to suppress revolutions in less developed countries (LDCs) increase the probability and frequency of future violent political insurrections. It might work as follows: The more the United States works against popular revolutions in the Third World, the less responsive Third World regimes are likely to be, the less likely democratic reforms will take place, and the more likely further revolutions will occur.[15] Table 2.3 summarizes Progressive thinking on the proper ends and means of U.S. foreign policy toward the Third World.

As noted above, Wiarda, who is probably best categorized as a Nationalist thinker, strongly warned against both Exceptionalism and Progressivism in foreign policy. He believes, for example, that the United States should not set ambitious Progressive goals for foreign policy toward Third World states such as helping them become more democratic or aiding in their economic development, because the U.S. government does not yet know how to accomplish these goals. Indeed, no consensus has been reached as to how democracy and economic development can be stimulated in the developing nations. Even the less developed countries have exhibited serious difficulties over which economic development model they should follow. But to Progressive thinkers these are not serious obstacles for developed nations that truly want to be helpful. In the past, all the developed nations set their own ambitious goals and either accomplished them or made great progress toward them. Among these goals were the exploration of space, the cure of serious diseases, universal literacy, and the development of weapons of destruction. Having experienced its own period of industrialization, the United States and other developed nations can certainly help other nations that wish to go down that path. The United States can also be tolerant and helpful to the ends of Third World leaders as long as those ends reasonably conform with the people's needs and do not seriously threaten U.S. military security or economic well-being.

Progressives also repudiate the notion that a statement of principle ties the hands of U.S. leaders by preventing the achievement of other foreign policy goals or makes U.S. leaders look hypocritical when they pursue those other goals. This criticism was raised most forcefully against

TABLE 2.3
Attributes of the Progressive Ideal Type

Perspective:

Instability and poverty in the Third World result from the low priority placed on the value of distributive justice by Third World governments, by the governments of economically developed states, and by international financial institutions like the World Bank.

Human nature is good.

Foreign Policy Ends:

Maintain long-term security from external threat.

Secure long-term economic prosperity for U.S. citizens.

Influence the foreign and domestic policies of other governments.

Help other nations of the world develop economically.

Improve the economic, political, and social well-being of people within the bottom fifth of the income distribution in Third World societies.

Objectives:

Encourage improved human rights practices by Third World governments.

Respect the right of Third World peoples to self-determination and autonomy. Do not oppose popular revolutions, even when they are waged against governments that cooperate with the U.S. foreign policy.

Give more foreign aid. Give a higher proportion of economic aid. Give more multilateral aid as a percentage of the total.

Policy Targets:

Emphasize North-South relations.

Gain the respect of all Third World governments and their peoples.

Acceptable Means Include:

Unilateral military intervention and covert action, as methods of last resort.

Strong preference for multilateral mechanisms of dispute resolution.

President Carter's promotion of human rights in the Third World. Every national foreign policy has multiple goals, and some will naturally take precedence over others as conflicts arise among them. Although no single moral principle can guide all foreign policy behavior, this does not mean that there are no basic moral values. There may be considerable discrepancy between ideals and their practices, but the existence of the discrepancies does not diminish the importance of the ideals.

In an address before a group contemplating careers in foreign service, former Secretary of State Dean Acheson leveled yet another common criticism of the Progressive agenda when he observed that "Generally speaking, morality often imposes upon those who exercise the powers of government, standards of conduct quite different from what might seem right to them as private citizens."[16] By this statement, he apparently meant that moral principles affecting personal conduct could be set aside when the national interest was at stake. But why should the national interest exclude moral ideals? Pursuit of national self-interest may sometimes cause U.S. leaders to ignore important moral principles. But those occasions can be rare isolated events or become an accepted way of doing business. As noted above, the real questions should revolve around how narrow the definition of the national interest should be and how long a time frame should be used when calculating it. Progressive thinkers do not believe that the kind of world most Americans want can be created through the power politics advocated by the Nationalists. Policies inspired by Nationalist principles give short shrift to the needs and wants of the powerless, and so create widespread resentment among the masses. In the process, the ideas and philosophy Americans hold so dear become mere hypocrisy in the eyes of others. As a result, the United States' attempts to influence international affairs lose moral force and become less effective.

This is enough reason to deemphasize power politics in foreign policy, but other recent developments make it clear to Progressives that the old rules of the game which maintained the balance of power among nations are changing.[17] A delicate countervailing balance of nations with mixes of economic and military capacities may no longer be sufficient to maintain world peace and to preserve the United States' security from external threats. Coercion alone will not be sufficient to preserve international peace and to ensure progress toward greater material and spiritual well-being. Instead, cooperation based on widely accepted moral principles will be necessary.

RADICAL PROGRESSIVISM

The Radical Progressive is unique in advocating a significant redistribution of the world's wealth and political power from the haves to the have nots. Most Third World leaders hold to this position, and some Americans support their moral claims. As a moral philosophy, it is rarely, if ever, included in the mainstream foreign policy debate in the United States. The reason is simple: if the U.S. government maintained a Radical Progressive position and if Radical Progressive goals were achieved, the United States would sacrifice control over international affairs and would have to transfer much of its accumulated wealth to those living in poverty beyond its national borders. Moreover, these reallocations would be unconditional rather than contingent on meeting U.S.-defined performance criteria such as adopting U.S.-style political institutions and implementing a capitalist economy.

American leaders have trouble accepting these foreign policy prescriptions, but Third World leaders see them as perfectly reasonable. Many, if not most, Third World leaders believe that the United States and other developed states are themselves responsible for their countries' underdevelopment and, consequently, have an obligation to assist future economic development efforts there. Some like Muammar al-Qadhafi of Libya, Saddam Hussein of Iraq, and Fidel Castro of Cuba even see the policies of the United States as the main reason for the poverty of the masses in the Third World. The leaders of the industrialized nations are unwilling to concede this point, and so structural conflict between the North and South has become an important feature of international relations.[18]

Radical Progressives view much of the official U.S. government foreign policy rhetoric as hypocritical or, at the least, disingenuous. For example, many Third World leaders view America's refusal to embrace a popular Islamic movement in Algeria as inconsistent with its support of democratic movements elsewhere. They also view the United States' justification of its invasion of Panama as inconsistent with the war America fought with Iraq over that country's invasion of Kuwait. They do not understand why the U.S. government was ready to block the shipment of Scud-C missiles to Iran in 1992, but prepared to sell advanced fighter planes to Saudi Arabia. Nor do they understand the continued U.S. military presence in the Persian Gulf, particularly now that the Soviet Union no longer exists. The leaders of Latin American nations are skeptical, and often cynical, about the supply-side emphasis in the U.S. war against drugs, pointing out that demand for a product usually creates supply, not the other way around. They see the war against drugs as the new excuse for an interventionist foreign policy in the Western hemisphere now that the fight against communism no longer provides a plausible excuse.

The main goal of the foreign policies of less developed nations is autonomy or at least freedom from foreign control.[19] Achieving this goal requires a strong economy. In order to attain economic independence, they must secure capital to establish new industries and public utility services, to build more roads and housing, and to improve education and health services. Directly or indirectly, that capital must come mainly from the richer nations. The challenge each Third World leader faces, therefore, is how to attract capital from richer states without falling too far within their spheres of influence. Since World War II, such nations have resorted to: nonalignment in the competition between the United States and the Soviet Union, attracting investments from many rich states, not just one or two; buildup of relatively large indigenous military and police forces; use of international lending agencies as sources of capital and technical assistance; pursuit of investments from multinational corporations (which are increasingly independent of the control of any nation-state); and formation of regional associations.[20]

At a minimum, Third World leaders insist that U.S. foreign policy toward their nations should not interfere with their internal economic and political affairs and should not involve them in major power conflicts. As noted, most also advocate measures that would redistribute the world's wealth. They do not believe that a sense of manifest destiny or a missionary spirit is an excuse for imperialism of any kind, economic, political, or cultural, no matter how much a society or its leaders think their own way of life is superior. Most Third World leaders even object to the practice of making rewards such as foreign aid, loans, and favorable trade provisions contingent on the adoption of Western-style political and economic institutions. Radical Progressives do not believe any nation has the right to impose its way of life on others.

It naturally follows then that Radical Progressives do not believe that unilateral strong-arm tactics such as covert action, military intervention, or any form of coercion are justified by any ends, no matter how noble they may seem. Strong nations like the United States have no right to use their power to dictate the outcomes of international events. The United States should never respond unilaterally to what its public and leaders perceive as action-forcing events in the international environment, but should always act in concert with other nations and within the bounds of international law.

In a speech delivered during his May 1992 visit to the United States, Mikhail S. Gorbachev, former leader of the former Soviet Union and prime mover behind the end of the Cold War, became a leading First World proponent of the Radical Progressive position in international affairs. He noted that much had been accomplished to improve the international system in the late 1980s and early 1990s, but that the leadership of the United States and the Soviet Union had not given enough attention to their moral responsibilities, to "the rights and interests of other states and peoples." This inability to overcome nationalism even with the ending of superpower conflict, he said, had made more visible today's major contradictions between the rich and the poor countries, between the North and the South. He concluded by arguing for a stronger, reformed United Nations government, with a greatly enlarged Security Council that included such nations as India, Mexico, Brazil, Indonesia, and Egypt as permanent members. As a much strengthened and more democratic world government, the United Nations could then eliminate nuclear weapons and could ensure that all governments around the world respected the human rights of their citizens.

Stephen Krasner, in his book, *Structural Conflict,* provides a provocative portrait of the Third World viewpoint on some important economic and political issues.[21] He notes that many Third World leaders see problems with the capitalist world system since it is based on the idea that global utility is maximized by the free flow of goods and services. The basic norm of what is sometimes called the "liberal international regime for trade" is that tariff and other barriers to free trade should be eliminated. Specific rules for trade and decision-making procedures for the international economic system are spelled out and periodically revised in the General Agreement on Tariffs and Trade (GATT). At that forum, U.S. representatives have consistently advanced free trade principles.

Krasner's thesis is that the leaders of most developing countries consider central economic planning more attractive because it provides more local control over the economy and results in more rapid economic development. In 1964 Third World leaders formed the United Nations Conference on Trade and Development (UNCTAD) to provide a counterposition to the GATT. They also formed the Group of 77, which has pressed for debt relief. Free market orientations have dominated the U.S. position on these issues during the postwar period. In the United States, Democrats have been more receptive to the Third World positions on economic issues, whereas Republicans have leaned more toward the orthodox liberal perspective.[22]

The Third World's position in favor of central economic planning may be changing, however. Most Third World countries are capitalist or predominantly capitalist and, especially in the aftermath of recent developments in the former Soviet Union and Eastern Europe, are showing even greater inclination to embrace free market principles. In 1990 when Rafael Angel Calderon assumed the presidency of Costa Rica, Latin America's most stable democracy, he promised a government in which private enterprise would be the motor of his so-called economic democracy. Perhaps the most surprising recent convert is President Hashemi Rafsanjani of Iran. He has recently won support in his own country for a five-year plan for economic development, the linchpin of which is $27 billion in foreign loans. If the plan is implemented, economic interdependence with the West and acceptance of World Bank and International Monetary Fund (IMF) conditions are inevitable.[23] What most Third World leaders really want from North-South economic relations, therefore, are financial assistance and the freedom to develop indigenous plans for economic development, which may or may not incorporate some degree of central planning and control.

According to the Group of 77, a New International Economic Order is needed in which the rules should favor the historically exploited states of the Third World. The new economic arrangements should be designed to provide Third World states with reparations from their former oppressors in the First World. Fidel Castro, in a declaration before the United Nations in October 1979, demanded that the developed states of the North distribute $300 billion over the next decade, about ten times what was actually distributed during the 1980s.[24] Third World leaders continue to voice the demand for reparations. Evidence on the U.S. response to this appeal is mixed. Table 2.4 demonstrates that, although the United States ranked second among all states in the absolute level of official development assistance provided to the Third World in 1989, it ranked near the bottom when rankings were determined on the basis of aid as a percentage of GNP. On this criterion, Saudi Arabia ranks first in the world. In 1989 Japan surpassed the United States as the leading provider of economic assistance to the Third World even in absolute terms.

Many Third World leaders are also dissatisfied with the way the United States provides aid to LDCs. To increase the value of the monetary transfer to the recipient, they want all foreign aid to be given in the form of outright grants. (In 1990 approximately one third was given in the form of loans.) To increase their economic and political autonomy, they prefer that aid be provided through multilateral rather than bilateral channels, and they want foreign aid to be given with no strings attached. But the

TABLE 2.4
Official Development Assistance in 1989 from Selected OECD and
OPEC Countries

	Millions of U.S. Dollars	As % of Donor GNP
OECD		
United States	7,676	0.15
United Kingdom	2,587	0.31
Norway	917	1.04
France	7,450	0.78
Japan	8,959	0.32
Canada	2,320	0.44
OPEC		
Iraq	none	—
Kuwait	316	.10
Saudi Arabia	2,888	1.46
Libya	76	0.52

Source: World Bank, *World Development Report 1991* (New York: Oxford University Press, 1991).

United States only provides about one fourth of its economic aid through multilateral institutions, and most bilateral foreign aid is now tied to conditions limiting the ways the recipient can spend it. Perhaps as much as 70 percent of U.S. bilateral economic development aid is given under the condition that it be used to purchase U.S.-made goods and services.[25] Moreover, in 1990 approximately 30 percent of all U.S. foreign aid was given under the condition that it be used only for military purposes.[26]

As another tactic to increase political control and autonomy, Third World leaders support one-nation/one-vote decision rules in international organizations and oppose departures from that rule. They advocate the supremacy and sanctity of the sovereign nation-state, seeking to bring more decisions into the sphere of unilateral state control. Many Latin American states as well as Libya have attempted to extend national sovereignty further into the oceans. In some LDCs, the influence of transnational corporations over the economic welfare of the state and, indirectly, over its political system has been so great that they have established laws restricting the amount and types of foreign investment and limiting the options available to existing foreign firms.

Therefore, beyond increasing and liberalizing the foreign aid program, the Group of 77 has put forward other proposals which, if adopted, would begin to institutionalize the New International Economic Order. The proposals call for

1. Trade preferences. The Group of 77 wants preferential and nonreciprocal treatment, including the removal of all tariff and nontariff barriers that impede their exports to more industrialized states. The group also seeks more attractive terms of trade between advanced and less developed countries.

2. Price controls for raw material exports. The leaders of Third World states want the right to nationalize foreign raw materials production corporations and the right of establishing, without outside interference, adequate compensation to nationalized companies. The Group of 77 also wants LDCs to have the right to form price-fixing commodity cartels that are not subject to retaliation and to create a fund to stabilize and increase the prices of commodities produced in the South and exported to the North.

3. More foreign aid. The Group of 77 emphasizes more foreign aid and less restricted foreign aid.

4. Technology transfers. Currently, some multinational corporations (MNCs) restrict the export of certain products produced with particularly advanced technology. The Third World wants these restrictions dropped, arguing that technology is part of the common heritage of humankind, not the exclusive property of the company that develops it.

5. Cancellation of the foreign debt of Third World states or at least substantial reductions in their interest payments.

6. Measures to promote industrial production in the Third World.

7. A greater voice for Third World governments in the decisions of multilateral lending agencies. The Group of 77 wants to move away from decision making based on the size of the economic contribution each state makes to development funds. Instead of weighting votes on this basis, the Group wants a one-nation/one-vote system in order to improve the access of the poor to economic opportunities.[27]

Some of these steps would improve the power of the LDCs in relation to richer states like the United States. Many would require the expenditure of additional resources by richer states. Since resources are limited, the leaders of richer states would have to make some difficult choices among worthy contenders. Should they give every Third World state an equal amount of direct aid and price concessions? Or should the value of the subsidy be in proportion to the population of the country or its need for assistance? Radical Progressives rarely directly address the question of which LDCs should receive greater benefits and why. But, consistent with the socialist philosophy and the concerns expressed by the Group of 77, level of need probably should be the primary criterion for distributing scarce resources from the North to competing states in the Third World.

Other criteria like progress toward true democracy and respect for human rights might come into play, but only if the larger community of nations agreed on them. In general, however, Third World leaders have been skeptical about proposals that would make favorable U.S. aid, trade, investment, and military policies contingent on "good" performance. Forcing conditionality on them, as often is done via World Bank and IMF lending policies, causes resentment within target countries.[28] Leaders of target nations tend to resent U.S. human rights policies, whether conditional or not. But rather than taking the uncomfortable position of challenging human rights policies frontally, they have tried to alter U.S. conceptions by emphasizing economic and social rather than civil and political rights and by emphasizing group rights rather than the inalienable rights of individuals.[29] This has led some to wonder whether democracy is valued cross-culturally and whether there is a universal conception of human rights. Ending apartheid is a Third World human rights issue that combines concern for individual and group rights. The leaders of African countries have been able to use the apartheid issue to turn the tables, putting pressure on South Africa's First World allies, including the United States, to sever their ties with South Africa in the name of promoting human rights.

Table 2.5 summarizes the Radical Progressive perspective on the proper course of U.S. foreign policy toward the Third World.

TABLE 2.5
Attributes of the Radical Progressive Ideal Type

Perspective:

Poverty in the Third World is due mainly to the long history of colonization. Industrialized nations owe less developed countries reparations to make amends for previous exploitation. Poverty in the Third World continues to be reinforced by the policies of international financial institutions and industrialized countries such as the United States.

Extreme disparities in economic well-being among nations and between the upper and lower classes within Third World countries cause instability.

Human nature is neither good nor evil. Capitalism brings out the worst in human beings (Marxists; see Chapter 3).

Foreign Policy Ends:

Highest priority should be placed on respect for the sovereignty of every state and on obeying the strictures of international law (especially the principle of nonintervention).

Third World states should have more control over important international economic and political decisions.

The United States should help LDCs create economically and politically viable, autonomous societies consistent with indigenous cultures and values.

Objectives:

The United States should provide massive resources to aid development efforts in the Third World with no strings attached.

Multilateral aid and grants rather than loans are preferred.

Important international decisions should be made on a majority rule, one-state/one-vote basis.

The United States should assist the establishment of a New International Economic Order.

Policy Targets:

Greater emphasis should be placed on North-South relations.

Acceptable Means Include:

U.S. leaders should consult with Third World leaders on appropriate U.S. policy, encourage regional resolutions to conflicts, and respect regional agreements.

Only military attack justifies a powerful state's use of military force or covert operations against a much weaker one.

Short of a military attack, the United States should never use force unilaterally to achieve its objectives in international relations.

SUMMARY

Actual U.S. foreign policy toward the Third World since World War II has represented a blend of Nationalist, Exceptionalist, and Progressive principles. These principles are closely related to perspectives on human nature, the international system, the most important targets of foreign policy, and the causes of poverty and instability in less developed countries. These different premises lead to different conclusions about the larger ends, concrete objectives, and acceptable means of foreign policy.

Although there is a lively debate over the proper ends and means of U.S. foreign policy toward the Third World, few Americans argue against the preeminence of national economic prosperity and military power goals. Since economic and military power are inextricably linked, both must be maintained at a minimum threshold. Nationalist and Progressive thinkers argue about the location of that minimum threshold, the definition of the national interest, the intrinsic value of some Progressive objectives, the morality of unilateral intervention and counterrevolutionary policies, and the consistency of Nationalist and Progressive objectives. The Exceptionalist voice within the mainstream debate emphasizes the responsibilities of the United States to people living beyond its borders and urges a foreign policy that would make the world over in the U.S. image. The main thrust of the Radical Progressive position is to oppose unilateral intervention in the Third World under any circumstances; to support the implementation of a New International Economic Order; and to advance other reforms that would reduce poverty in the Third World and increase the voice of Third World nations in international affairs.

NOTES

1. Kenneth N. Waltz, *Theory of International Politics* (New York: Random House, 1979).

2. Hans J. Morgenthau, *In Defense of the National Interest* (New York: Alfred A. Knopf, 1951), p. 92.

3. Daniel Donno, ed., *The Prince and Selected Discourses: Machiavelli* (New York: Bantam Books, 1966), p. 121.

4. Robert Gilpin, "Equilibrium and Decline," in Robert Gilpin, ed., *War and Change in World Politics* (Cambridge: Cambridge University Press, 1981).

5. Jacob Viner, "Economic Thought: Mercantilist Thought," in *International Encyclopedia of the Social Sciences,* vol. 4 (New York: Free Press, 1968), p. 436.

6. Charles W. Kegley, Jr., and Eugene R. Wittkopf, *American Foreign Policy: Pattern and Process,* 3rd ed. (New York: St. Martin's Press, 1987), p. 70.

7. See Michael J. Smith, "Ethics and Intervention," *Ethics and International Affairs,* vol. 3, 1989, pp. 1–26 for an excellent discussion of different schools of thought on the ethics of U.S. intervention into the domestic affairs of other states.

8. John E. Rielly, "America's State of Mind: Trends in Public Attitudes Toward Foreign Policy," in Charles W. Kegley and Eugene R. Wittkopf, *The Domestic Sources of American Foreign Policy: An Introduction* (New York: St. Martin's Press, 1988), pp. 54–56.

9. Robert J. Meyers, "The Carnegie Poll on Values in American Foreign Policy," *Ethics and International Affairs,* vol. 3, 1989, pp. 297–302.

10. Edward C. Banfield, *American Foreign Aid Doctrines* (Washington, D.C.: American Enterprise Institute, 1963), pp. 63–64.

11. Joshua Muravchik, *Exporting Democracy: Fulfilling America's Destiny* (Washington, D.C.: AEI Press, 1991), especially chapters 8 and 9.

12. Howard J. Wiarda, *Enthnocentrism in Foreign Policy: Can We Understand the Third World?* (Washington, D.C.: American Enterprise Institute, 1985), p. 7.

13. Richard H. Ullman, "Redefining Security," *International Security* 8, No. 1 (Summer 1983).

14. David A. Broder, "Frank Church's Challenge," *The Washington Post National Weekly Edition,* February 6, 1984, p. 4.

15. Walter LaFeber, *Inevitable Revolutions: The United States in Central America* (New York: W. W. Norton, 1983).

16. Quoted in Sidney Hook, *Philosophy and Public Policy* (Carbondale, IL: Southern Illinois University Press, 1980), 57.

17. For an elaboration of this argument about the need for increased public attention to nonmilitary threats to national security, see Ullman, "Redefining Security," pp. 129–153.

18. Stephen D. Krasner, *Structural Conflict: The Third World Against Global Liberalism* (Berkeley: University of California Press, 1985).

19. Most are probably more concerned about dominating or being dominated by neighbors than they are about intervention by a major power. But the leaders of Third World states that are geographically proximate to a major military power have had to be concerned about both.

20. Jacob J. Kaplan, *The Challenge of Foreign Aid* (New York: Praeger Publishers, 1967), pp. 14–16. See also Peter Calvert, *The Foreign Policy of New States* (Brighton, G.B.: Wheatsheaf, 1986).

21. Ibid.

22. Krasner, *Structural Conflict,* p. 23.

23. Steve Coll, "What Should Be Done When the Great Satan Spews Forth Money?" *Washington Post National Weekly Edition,* July 2–8, 1990, p. 17.

24. Castro's speech is reprinted in United Nations, *Proceedings of the United Nations Conference on Trade and Development* (Nairobi), vol. 1, annex 5, 1977, p. 110.

25. Judith Tendler, *Inside Foreign Aid* (Baltimore, Md.: Johns Hopkins University Press, 1975).

26. Agency for International Development, Statistics and Reports Division, Office of Financial Management, *U.S. Overseas Loans and Grants and Assistance from International Organizations, July 1, 1945–June 30, 1987* (Washington, D.C.: U.S. Government Printing Office, 1988).

27. These proposals are reviewed in Stephen D. Krasner, "North-South Economic Relations," in Kenneth A. Oye, Donald Rothchild, and Robert J. Lieber, *Eagle Entangled* (New York: Longman, 1979), pp. 123–146.

28. Louise G. White, *Implementing Policy Reforms in LDCs* (Boulder, Colo.: Lynne Rienner Publishers, 1990), pp. 28–29.

29. Rajni Kothari, "Human Rights as a North-South Issue," *Bulletin of Peace Proposals* 11, No. 4 (1980): 331–338. See also Krasner, *Structural Conflict,* pp. 278–279.

CHAPTER 3

The Marxists

Those who believe in Marx's theory of how capitalist society is organized, how it works, and who it benefits would probably adopt a Radical Progressive position on U.S. foreign policy toward the Third World. The Marxist's moral position flows naturally from a theory about how international wealth and power came to be concentrated in the industrialized nations in the first place. Others, including those who advocate world government for idealistic reasons, and many Third World leaders, who do not necessarily subscribe to Marxist theory, sometimes reach the same conclusions from different premises. Indeed, anyone who favors a radical redistribution of global wealth and power in order to achieve universal ideals (such as peace, social justice, and human rights) and is willing to do so even at some considerable loss to one's own government and people is a Radical Progressive.

Marxist theory is important because it represents the most severe critique of mainstream thinking about the United States' Third World policy. This chapter describes some of the recurrent themes found in Marxism regarding U.S. policy.[1] Marxist theory on the forces driving U.S. foreign policy toward the Third World is examined briefly, followed by an equally brief mainstream response to Marxist explanations of foreign policy.

THE EMPIRICAL ARGUMENT

Marxism makes three assumptions. First, Marxists believe that economic classes are the most important actors in society, and they identify two main classes—the ruling class consisting of the owners of the means of production and labor, or workers. Second, they assume that the classes maximize their own economic interests, so the real conflicts in society are class conflicts. Their reading of history indicates that humankind is neither good nor evil by nature. Instead the human character depends on the nature and structure of the environment. If that structure brings out the

53

better qualities of human beings, the society will be a good and moral one. If it brings out the worst qualities of human beings, the society will be evil and immoral. Their third assumption—that capitalism is the dominant characteristic of the international system—is crucial to understanding why most contemporary advanced industrial societies are evil. Thus, counteracting the effects of capitalism becomes the driving force behind their position on morality and U.S. foreign policy.

According to Marxists, capitalism allows and encourages the exploitation of labor by the ruling class. This fact is the key to understanding the nature of domestic politics within the United States and the nature of U.S. foreign policy. The basic characteristics of a capitalist economic system are private ownership of property, including the means of production, reliance on markets and prices to allocate resources and to distribute income, and the predominance of profit or economic gain as motivators. As an economic system, it plays upon human greed, which is one of humankind's worst qualities, and it thereby causes human beings to behave in unjust, evil ways. The world capitalist system causes social, political, and economic inequities within American society, within LDCs, and between the First and Third Worlds.

Rejecting mainstream arguments about morality and U.S. foreign policy as largely irrelevant, Marxists have advanced another set of propositions explaining U.S. foreign policy toward the Third World—economic and cultural imperialism. Although Karl Marx wrote primarily about conflicts between classes within countries, Vladimir Ilyich Lenin extended his ideas to international political economy to explain economic imperialism and war.[2] According to Lenin, the foreign policies of industrialized, capitalist states toward the Third World are designed to enable them to build and maintain their empires. Following this theme, the purposes of U.S. foreign policy toward the Third World are to expropriate the land, labor, markets, and natural resources of weaker nations and to build a military security system to safeguard the international social order that ensures further capital accumulation by U.S.-based interests.[3]

Some contemporary Marxist thinkers contend that preserving economic prosperity at home through foreign trade and investment is the primary objective of U.S. foreign policy. Others portray U.S. foreign policy as serving the interests of multinational corporations (MNCs) and international banks first, and the American public second, if at all. Not only are the ends of foreign policy morally questionable, but also the means are usually unscrupulous. Because capitalism creates tremendous inequalities both within and between societies, force is necessary to maintain a world capitalist system. Thus, an interventionist or "globalist" foreign policy is inevitable.

As noted in Chapter 2, most Third World leaders agree with Marxist theorists on the fundamental point that underdevelopment and development do not simply coexist; one is a function of the other. According to Franz Fanon, a Marxist theorist, U.S. and European opulence

> is literally scandalous, for it has been founded on slavery, it has been nourished from the blood of slaves, and it comes directly from the soil and from the subsoil of that underdeveloped world. The well-being and progress of Europe have been built up with the sweat and dead bodies of Negroes, Arabs, Indians, and the yellow races.[4]

Similarly, Tony Smith contends that "imperialism set in place an international division of labor whose consequence in normal operation has been to delay and distort the economic development of the South, thus breeding the manifold miseries we see today in underdevelopment, including the prevalence of authoritarian-military governments in this region."[5] Under the current rules of the international economic and political order, Marxists see the continued underdevelopment of Third World societies as inevitable.

Almost all observers of American foreign policy, mainstream or otherwise, agree that amassing wealth and economic advantage has been an important objective of U.S. foreign policy. They disagree over how dominant this objective has been relative to others, and they argue over the morality of economic gain as a foreign policy goal. Most Nationalist thinkers openly advocate the pursuit of some expansionist economic policies as serving the national interest by maintaining the general economic prosperity of American citizens. Striving for economic prosperity is morally justifiable, from a mainstream perspective, first, because it serves the interests of Americans by enhancing their economic well-being — a moral obligation of all U.S. elected officials — and second, because an economically powerful state has greater security from external threat. Beyond these moral considerations is a practical one: in a democratic state economic prosperity enables leaders to maintain the electoral support of followers. Thus, even Progressive thinkers rarely attack economic foreign policy goals in principle, although they often attack the too high priority these goals sometimes are accorded.

Marxist theorists contend that economic gain has been, by far, the most important U.S. foreign policy objective in the Third World and that the use of power to achieve economic objectives through foreign policy is immoral. The Marxist view of U.S. foreign policy can be analyzed on at least three levels. In its mildest form of the critique, its adherents simply express displeasure about the strong voice of big business in the policy-making process, because that voice supports an emphasis on the accumulation of capital as a goal of foreign policy and effectively prevents the pursuit of other worthy objectives. In its moderate form, the critique contends that there is no true "national interest" in the accumulation of capital by U.S.-based corporations or economic power by the U.S. government. In its most damning variety, its adherents argue that U.S. foreign policy is motivated almost entirely by the avarice of political and private elites and is actually designed to oppress the masses in the Third World as a means of maximizing the profits of a privileged class. Several lines of reasoning have been developed to explain why world capitalism causes economic imperialism in U.S. foreign policy, alternatively underscoring the need to develop new markets for U.S. exports, the demand for investment opportunities by U.S.-based MNCs, the appetite for raw materials, and the hunger to make a profit.[6]

The connection between imperialism and the need for markets is derived from the classical theory of underconsumption and is associated with the work of J. A. Hobson and Rosa Luxemburg.[7] They state that capitalist nations generate insufficient demand to consume all that the nation produces; consequently, there is a need to find new markets for surplus production. Other nations represent important potential markets for excess production, and an imperialist foreign policy provides access to those markets.

Other analysts emphasize the connection between the needs of U.S.-based MNCs and imperialism. According to this argument, transnational corporations need overseas investments because of the limited availability of profitable investment opportunities at home. The costs of labor and the amount of government regulation are much lower in most Third World countries than in the United States. American officials are motivated to help MNCs become more profitable because corporations are an important source of election campaign contributions. Moreover, the activities of MNCs are essential to maintaining the existing liberal international economic order from which the United States benefits, and some officials wrongly believe that helping U.S.-based corporations increases the macroeconomic prosperity of the nation. For some or all of these reasons, U.S. leaders make policy decisions that help MNCs by increasing the range of investment options, subsidizing the cost of foreign investments, and making foreign investments safer.

Still another explanation for the United States' economic imperialism in the Third World stresses the importance of raw materials for an industrialized economy. No industrialized nation has an adequate domestic supply of all the raw materials it needs to sustain the home economy. For a military superpower like the United States, the problem is exacerbated by the need to maintain an adequate supply of strategic minerals like uranium and titanium required for military purposes. The United States imports most of its raw materials from Third World states, especially the mineral-rich states of Africa and the oil-producing states of the Middle East. An imperialist foreign policy assures continued access to those important raw material imports.[8]

A related but more general line of reasoning suggests that imperialism may simply be motivated by greed or the desire to increase the "aggregate economic gains" of the imperialist nation from its economic relations with other states. To the extent to which one nation has power over another, it may be able to extract greater economic gains for its nationals than would be possible if the economic transactions took place among equals. For example, MNCs may be able to manipulate the terms of trade, so that they pay less for commodities imported from the Third World than they should.[9] Third World countries are vulnerable because they often have a limited number of trading partners (partner concentration) and a limited number of products to export (commodity concentration). The unfair terms of trade between industrialized and Third World countries result partly from the structure of the market and ensure the continued political and economic subordination of the Third World.[10] Although it is not surprising when greed tempts a private entrepreneur to take advantage of a vulnerable trading partner, it is unconscionable when militarily powerful states like the United States back this kind of fleecing.[11]

Today, most Third World leaders are less concerned about the role of transnational corporations in their countries than they are about the influence of international lending agencies, especially the World Bank and the International Monetary Fund (IMF). These agencies have become the major source of external capital for most Third World states, and their lending policies are strongly influenced by the preferences of U.S. leaders. Both institutions use a weighted system of voting to decide which states will receive loans, the size of those loans, and the conditions attached to the loans. The largest contributors to the funds have the most votes, and the United States has always been the largest single contributor to both funds.

Under current World Bank and IMF policies, Third World nations with large debts must agree to "stabilization" terms before loans are given. These terms usually include an agreement to cut back on spending for education, health, and welfare while producing more for export, encouraging more foreign investment, and introducing more free enterprise principles into the economy.[12] Imposition of austerity measures places severe short-term burdens on the poor and the middle classes in LDCs, sometimes resulting in rioting and political instability.[13] Most mainstream thinkers accept the World Bank and IMF rationale that these measures are necessary if LDCs are to establish healthy, self-sustaining economies. Critical theorists maintain that these same lending policies cause hardships for the poorest people in the Third World in order to provide advantages for capitalists.[14]

Some Marxists do not even concede that expansionist economic policies serve a legitimate national interest. The real interests served, they contend, are not those of the masses of U.S. citizens but those of the "ruling class"—the rich and powerful members of the society who own most of the land and capital, employ most of the people, and can translate their immense economic power into political influence. It is foolish to believe that capitalists pursue the national interest; they do not even have national loyalties. As even Thomas Jefferson observed, "Merchants have no country. The mere spot they stand on does not constitute so strong an attachment as that from which they draw their gains."[15]

Cooperation between economic and political elites is therefore dangerous to the national interest because such cooperation is usually designed to promote mutual interests, not a larger public interest. Even the Carter administration, which pursued a generally Progressive approach to foreign policy toward the Third World, has been criticized by Michael Parenti as an example of a regime pursuing narrow elite interests. He notes that 17 top members of Carter's administration were participants in the Trilateral Commission, including Carter himself and Vice President Walter Mondale. The Trilateral Commission was established in 1972 through the efforts of David Rockefeller, then chairman of the board of Chase Manhattan Bank, and the Council on Foreign Relations and the Rockefeller Foundation. This group of public officials and representatives of MNCs meets periodically to discuss the economic policies of the United States, Western Europe, and Japan.[16] Among the group's objectives, Parenti implies, are the advancement of the interests of the world's economic elites and the concurrent exploitation of Third World peoples and their leaders.

Many Marxist theorists see Third World leaders as the victims of a capitalist world system. According to one strand of Marxist thinking on this topic, dependency theory, the global system is stratified into an area of autonomous self-sustaining growth, called the core or First World, and an area of underdevelopment called the periphery. International capitalism allows the nations of the core to exploit economically the nations of the periphery through the policies of MNCs, international markets and financial organizations, and trade. Some dependency theorists also emphasize the importance of cultural imperialism, or the domination of ideas and values by First World countries, as essential to maintaining the underdevelopment of Third World societies.[17] According to the dependency theory perspective, leaders of Third World peripheral states are generally powerless to stop the exploitation.[18] In order to survive, they accept the raw deals they are offered by powerful countries like the United States, by major international financial institutions like the World Bank, and by large MNCs.

According to the most extreme variety of Marxist thinking on the subject of First World–Third World relations, the agents of capitalism and the leaders of many Third World countries are engaged in a conspiracy. This conspiracy serves the interests of corrupt Third World leaders by allowing them to profit personally from arrangements that hurt their own citizens. Parenti reminds us that nations as such do not make the decisions to borrow money, buy armaments, and raise large armies; their leaders do.[19] As a result of such decisions, former Third World leaders such as the Shah of Iran, Luis and Anastasio Somoza of Nicaragua, and Ferdinand Marcos of the Philippines reaped huge profits, while the general public was left with the bills.

In essence, Parenti portrays U.S. and Third World leaders as working together like organized criminals, scheming in secret, ignoring national and international laws, and taking whatever measures are necessary to turn a profit. Violence by governments against the masses in the Third World is a common byproduct of this brand of international collusion, because it is often required to protect foreign investors and the ruling elites of LDCs from their own potentially rebellious populations. Human rights abuses and other forms of oppression are actually encouraged, because the repression of labor generally improves the investment climate for MNCs.[20] As extreme examples of capitalists oppressing the powerless, critics point to instances when large numbers of people were exterminated, as happened when the United States spread westward at the expense of Native American Indians. (This period of American history is reviewed in the next chapter.) They also note instances of enslavement of native peoples for profit as more evidence supporting their argument. Since the United States is a predominantly white nation and most Third World states are not, some, like Michael Hunt, have even speculated that U.S. foreign policy is not only imperialistic but racist as well.[21]

Just as organized criminals seek to stay out of the limelight, exploitation of the masses in the Third World also is muted. As a result, the moral indignation of the public within the "colonizing nation" is rarely aroused. Much of the U.S. foreign policy effort in the Third World is designed to keep right-wing regimes in power, critics claim, because this arrangement allows the U.S. corporations' exploitation of the people to continue without the direct involvement of the U.S. government. Through this arrangement, Parenti notes, it is highly unlikely that the American mass

public will ever realize that atrocities committed by Third World governments are the direct, intended result of U.S. government policies.

Those who subscribe to this extremely critical perspective also do not
believe that American foreign policy is designed to advance the national
interests of the United States. They do not believe that leaders whose
rhetoric reflects Nationalist moral principles are sincere when they argue
that the United States should pursue an objective only if the aggregate
benefits to U.S. society outweigh the costs. Instead, they contend that the
United States will expend tremendous amounts of resources to ensure
future opportunities for corporate profit and to guarantee continued
access by corporations to relatively inexpensive and abundant labor in less
industrialized foreign economies. Even when there is no rational national
interest in an imperialist activity, the U.S. government may still undertake
it if a particular class has an interest in the activity and the power of that
class is sufficiently disproportionate.

Maintaining the world capitalist system has become a primary objective of U.S. foreign policy, not because capitalism is the best or even a
good way to organize economic relations, but because the United States is
one of the leaders and prime beneficiaries of that system. Mainstream
thinkers have often advocated a counterrevolutionary foreign policy in the
Third World in the name of anti-communism, or in the cause of maintaining world stability and the consequent balance of power. Marxist
theorists, on the other hand, see these efforts as having nothing to do with
preserving security from external military threats and having everything to
do with maintaining the existing exploitative world capitalist system.[22]

A MAINSTREAM RESPONSE

There is some truth to the Marxist critique of U.S. foreign policy. The
question is: how much truth? In its less vitriolic forms, many mainstream
thinkers would concede some point to the Marxists. Especially since World
War II, the United States has supported numerous oppressive dictators in
the fight against genuine popularly supported revolutions in their own
countries. The Nationalist defense of this strategy was explained in the last
chapter. Progressives have fairly consistently opposed the United States'
counterrevolutionary role in the Third World as a violation of America's
own values. To some extent, U.S. foreign policy also has been motivated
by commercial goals. America's leaders have taken actions to protect the
foreign investments of U.S.-based MNCs. "Dollar diplomacy" has been a
recurrent theme.[23] Aid, trade, tax, and loan policies have been affected
somewhat by the desire to serve U.S. overseas business interests and to
safeguard domestic markets from foreign penetration.[24]

Moreover, the Marxist critique is very important because it forces us to pay attention to the potential corrupting influence of capitalism on democracy. Capitalism and democracy exist in an uneasy balance in American society. Capitalism creates disparities of resources among individuals, and those with more resources have more ability to influence the outcomes of political processes. Individuals or corporations with extensive resources tend to use their influence within the political system to create a policy environment that allows them to accumulate even more resources and, as a consequence, even more influence. Over time, in the absence of corrective measures, the inequalities tend to become entrenched. Beyond a certain point, the inequality of resources endangers a fundamental prerequisite of democracy—that there be equal opportunity for all to participate meaningfully in the political process.

Capitalism presents an additional challenge to true democracy in the United States: how to deal with a relatively new, important, and ominous actor in international politics, the multinational corporation. Some MNCs such as Exxon, General Motors, and IBM are literally as large and as influential as modern sovereign states. Although many are headquartered in the United States, their interests are separate from the interests of any one nation. Moreover, they are difficult to control, for onerous regulations promulgated by one state can be avoided by changing the base of operations to another.

From a mainstream perspective, the problem with most Marxist critiques of U.S. foreign policy is that they venture too far from these telling criticisms. This is not the place for an extensive critical evaluation of the Marxist perspective; only a brief overview of main points is possible here.[25] Marxists are often portrayed as missing the mark by overstating the "problem of capitalism," the degree of business influence on U.S. public policy, the extent to which U.S. macroeconomic prosperity depends on the exercise of economic dominion over developing countries, the deviousness of U.S. leaders, and the impact of U.S. foreign policy on Third World societies. The result, from a mainstream viewpoint, is an allegedly distorted picture of U.S. foreign policy toward the Third World.

The American people generally support their economic system. Of course, there is much public anguish over the influence of money on policy outcomes, but a solution continues to be elusive. Among the proposals to decrease the influence of business on U.S. public policy are those severely restricting the size of private financial contributions to political campaigns, limiting the number of consecutive terms of office for a member of Congress, placing greater controls on the behavior of MNCs based in the United States, and establishing quotas for representation of groups now underrepresented in Congress such as women, blacks, and Hispanics.

One obstacle to fundamental change is that most Americans are wary of the potential effects of such reforms. They do not agree that every gain that the owners of the means of production make is accompanied by a corresponding loss of equal size suffered by the masses. Instead, overwhelming majorities believe that the free enterprise system is a necessary condition for the existence of democracy, is generally fair and efficient, and gives everyone a chance at success. Both rich and poor in the United States hold these views in about the same degree.[26] Large proportions of the American public even seem to subscribe to some version of the idea that "What's good for General Motors is good for the country."[27] This attachment to capitalism has been noted by every major commentator on the nation for over two centuries. Marxists either ignore this point or believe the attachment is the product of a relentless propaganda campaign designed to produce a false consciousness in the minds of the mass public.

Marxists commonly ignore other information when they argue that U.S. foreign policy toward the Third World is driven by the need for new markets, the desire to help U.S.-based MNCs invest in foreign countries, the appetite for raw materials, and the desire to produce favorable terms of trade with weaker states.

1. Reduction of the large and growing budget deficit in the United States would be facilitated by the creation of new markets for goods and services produced by U.S. corporations, but almost no one thinks that much of that demand can come from less developed countries.

2. More than two thirds of the United States' foreign investment assets are in other developed countries. The level of direct foreign investment in the Third World is very low, and the proportion is dropping. Investment by U.S.-based transnational corporations in LDCs is concentrated in the relatively industrialized states. At present, just five countries—Brazil, Mexico, China, Singapore, and Hong Kong—account for more than half of all investment flows from developed to less developed countries.[28] Although the profits from direct foreign investments in the Third World are relatively high, so are the risks.

3. The United States is highly dependent on imported raw materials and gets most of them from Third World states, but raw material substitutes are available and new ones are being created all the time. Even when alternatives are not available, Third World states are unlikely to deny the United States the imports it wants, because they have little to gain from doing so and much to lose economically.

4. Embargoes designed to deny access by some states to the raw material exports of others have not proven to be particularly effective.[29] The workings of the free market assure access without special attention from U.S. leaders. The Organization of Petroleum Exporting Countries (OPEC) is noteworthy in this context. The members of OPEC are

Algeria, Ecuador, Gabon, Indonesia, Iran, Iraq, Kuwait, Libya, Nigeria, Qatar, Saudi Arabia, the United Arab Emirates, and Venezuela. Its purpose is to coordinate the petroleum production and pricing policies of member countries in order to ensure stable prices and avoid harmful price and supply fluctuations.[30] But even OPEC, arguably the most successful of all Third World efforts of this type, has failed to achieve these objectives.

In the early 1970s the OPEC countries agreed to limit oil production and, as a result, oil prices rose faster than the rate of inflation for a few years in the mid-1970s. This success was short-lived. Since 1979 OPEC has been plagued by disputes over production quotas and prices. Partly as a result of a dispute over oil production quotas, in August 1990 one member of OPEC, Iraq, invaded another, Kuwait. Even if the members of OPEC were more cohesive, their strategy would still meet with very limited success, because most of the major consumers of oil have diversified their sources of supply, stockpiled petroleum, shifted to other energy sources, or taken other steps to lessen their dependence on OPEC. As a result, oil has been plentiful and prices have dropped. By 1990 OPEC's share of the oil market, 66 percent in 1979, had fallen below 30 percent and oil prices had plunged to their lowest level since 1978.[31] Prices rose during the War in the Gulf but fell quickly when it ended. OPEC's price-fixing efforts have failed, not because the colluding states are weak, but because collusion to fix prices for any product in a relatively free market that has many producers and suppliers is difficult. Even the U.S. government efforts to limit variations in domestic prices paid for farm products, so that farmers and their families will not be hurt too much by oversupplies and declining prices, have been expensive and have met with very limited success.

5. The United States and most other states are able to distort the working of the free market by establishing tariffs that artificially increase the costs of imports. Tariffs protect home suppliers from foreign competition and, therefore, hurt foreign suppliers including some in Third World states. Argentina and Costa Rica, for example, would like the United States to remove or lower the tariff on imported beef. But domestic beef producers lobby to keep that tariff high. The debate is public and heated, not backroom and conspiratorial. Perhaps the United States should remove tariffs on all products produced in the Third World to help stimulate economic development there. But no one should expect domestic competitors to be happy about such a proposal.[32]

6. Capitalism is not necessary to explain U.S. economic expansionism in the Third World. Robert Tucker suggests that the interests of all states expand roughly in line with their economic and military power, and the United States has been no exception to this experience.[33] Similarly, Mancur Olson provides one of many mainstream explanations for why business groups often get their way in the legislative process. He

suggests that business groups tend to be better organized, because they have better control over the distribution of benefits resulting from legislative victories.[34]

PROPER ENDS AND MEANS OF AMERICAN FOREIGN POLICY

Marxist theorists generally agree about what is wrong and why, but they are less unanimous and have less to say about what the proper ends and means of foreign policy should be. A few of these theorists imply that the United States and other former colonial powers should stay out of Third World affairs, so that LDCs can make their own way without Western influence.[35] A few, like Parenti, advance an organized crime model of U.S.–Third World relations. Therefore, they imply that the United States should not even consult with Third World leaders for their views about the proper course for U.S. foreign policy toward the Third World. Most, however, endorse the moral perspective of Third World leaders in the North-South dialogue. A central element of that perspective is that all people have obligations that extend beyond the borders of their own state. Moreover, these duties are analogous to the ones they have to other citizens of their own nation. Another central element is that the distinction between negative prohibitions and positive commands is a false one. Consequently, citizens of relatively affluent societies have obligations not only *to avoid* depriving the citizens of other societies, but also *to protect* them from deprivation and *to help* them escape deprivation. The most noble foreign policy, from their perspective, would be to pursue the positive commands of its morality even if doing so would require considerable sacrifice of the national self-interest. Of course, a person does not have to be a Marxist to reach such moral conclusions. Idealists such as Charles Beitz and Henry Shue offer these moral prescriptions based on non-Marxist notions of social justice and rights, respectively.[36]

Since the vast majority of Third World countries were once colonies of the now-developed countries in Western Europe, it is not surprising that the intellectual community and political leadership in the Third World are attracted to Marxist ideas. Although there was substantial domestic public support in the United States for recent interventions in Libya, Grenada, Panama, and Iraq, neither the leaders of Third World states nor their peoples expressed much enthusiasm. In fact, most members of the Organization of American States condemned the interventions into Grenada and Panama as unwarranted. Several Third World leaders made statements, and several large popular demonstrations were held in Third World states supporting Iraq's position in the War in the Gulf.

SUMMARY

According to Marxists, throughout its history the United States has been guilty of bad motives when making foreign policy toward weaker states, because it has been concerned primarily with promoting its economic interests. Indeed, the United States' foreign policy has been an extension of and a more subtle form of colonialism, ensuring that most Third World states remain fragile, repressive, and dependent on the developed world for manufactured products, national security, and a substandard level of well-being. Poverty in the Third World is no accident; it is the direct result of activities orchestrated by the U.S. government. The Third World is not underdeveloped; it is overexploited. Capital investment in the Third World has not brought prosperity; it has brought deeper and deeper debt and ever greater inequality in the distribution of wealth and well-being within Third World societies.

Marxist theorists and Third World leaders would prefer a U.S. foreign policy that was based more on multilateralism and noninterventionism. They would also prefer a policy in which the U.S. leaders cared equally about the welfare of all the world's people, making no distinction between the people within U.S. territorial boundaries and people residing elsewhere. Marxists often argue that such a foreign policy would emerge as a natural consequence of world socialism.

The moral imperative behind Progressivism, the mainstream school of thought closest to Marxism, is "when it is in your power to do good for another who needs it at no serious risk to yourself, your duty is to do so." Marxist theorists and Third World leaders reject this standard as too modest. In their view, because the United States and other advanced industrial states bear such great responsibility for the underdevelopment of Third World states, the exploiters must undertake an aggressive program of affirmative action benefiting Third World countries. This program is summed up by the Group of 77's proposals for debt relief and a New International Economic Order that was described in the last chapter.

In contrast, most U.S. leaders have proudly proclaimed the economic foreign policy objectives that Marxist critics and some Third World leaders find so reprehensible. For them, the real issue is not whether the United States has pursued economic interests in the Third World. Of course it has. Mainstream thinkers differ with Marxist theorists mostly over the morality of economic and cultural expansionism, the degree to which economic objectives have motivated U.S. foreign policy, the ethics of unilateralism, covert action and coercion, and how and whether the hierarchy of U.S. foreign policy objectives has changed over time.

NOTES

1. Classic examples of Marxist analyses of U.S.-Third World relations include William Appleman Williams, *The Tragedy of American Diplomacy* (Cleveland: World Publishing Co., 1959); Harry Magdoff, *The Age of Imperialism* (New York: Monthly Review Press, 1969); and Gabriel Kolko, *The Roots of American Foreign Policy* (Boston: Beacon Press, 1971); and Carl Oglesby and Richard Schaull, *Containment and Change* (New York: Macmillan, 1967). A more recent example is Michael Parenti, *The Sword and the Dollar* (New York: St. Martin's Press, 1989) and Lloyd Gardner, *Imperial America* (New York: Harcourt Brace Jovanovich, 1976). All of these authors are more properly referred to as neo-Marxist thinkers, because Marx never explicitly addressed issues of international imperialism.

2. V. I. Lenin, *Imperialism: The Highest Stage of Capitalism* (New York: International Publishers Co., 1939).

3. Parenti, *The Sword and the Dollar*, p. 64.

4. Franz Fanon, *The Wretched of the Earth* (New York: Grove Press, 1966), p. 76.

5. Tony Smith, *The Pattern of Imperialism* (Cambridge: Cambridge University Press, 1981), p. 240.

6. For an overview, see Thomas E. Weisskopf, "Capitalism, Socialism, and the Sources of Imperialism," in Steven Rosen and James Kurth, *Testing Theories of Economic Imperialism* (Lexington, Mass.: D. C. Heath and Co., 1974).

7. J. A. Hobson, *Imperialism: A Study* (Ann Arbor: University of Michigan Press, 1967; first published in 1902). See also Rosa Luxemburg, *The Accumulation of Capital* (London: Routledge Press, 1951; first published in 1913).

8. Williams, *The Tragedy of American Diplomacy*.

9. Steve Chan, *International Relations in Perspective* (New York: Macmillan, 1984), pp. 231–269.

10. Joan Robinson, "Trade in Commodities," in *Aspects of Development and Underdevelopment* (Cambridge: Cambridge University Press, 1979).

11. Williams, *The Tragedy of American Diplomacy*, p. xx.

12. For an overview of World Bank stabilization and adjustment policies, see the World Bank, *World Development Report 1988* (New York: Oxford University Press, 1988), Part II, pp. 43–210.

13. On this point, see Richard E. Feinberg, "The International Monetary Fund and Basic Needs: The Impact of Stand-by Arrangements," in Margaret E. Crahan, ed., *Human Rights and Basic Needs in the Americas* (Washington, D.C.: Georgetown University Press, 1982), especially pp. 190–197.

14. See, for example, Robin Broad and John Cavanagh, "No More NICs," *Foreign Policy* 72 (Fall 1988); and Manuel Pastor, Jr., "Latin America, the Debt Crisis, and the International Monetary Fund," *Latin American Perspectives* 16, Issue 60 (1989): 790–810.

15. Letter to Horatio G. Spafford, March 17, 1914.

16. Parenti, *The Sword and the Dollar*, pp. 196–197.

17. See, for example, Ali Mazrui, *Cultural Forces in World Politics* (Portsmouth: Heineman Educational Books, 1990); Herbert Schiller, *Communication and Cultural Domination* (White Plains, N.Y.: M. E. Sharpe, 1976); and Johan Galtung, "A Structural Theory of Imperialism," *Journal of Peace Research* 8 (1971).

18. Immanuel Wallerstein, *Modern World System* (1974); and Peter Gourevich, "The Second Image Revisited: The International Sources of Domestic Politics," *International Organization* 32, No. 4 (August 1978): 884–891.

19. Parenti, *The Sword and the Dollar,* p. 28.

20. For the argument that U.S. human rights policy is disingenuous, actually serving as a cover for imperialism, see also Issa G. Shivji, *The Concept of Human Rights in Africa* (London: CODESRIA, 1989); and Noam Chomsky and Edward S. Herman, *The Washington Connection and Third World Fascism: The Political Economy of Human Rights* (Boston: South End Press, 1979).

21. See Michael H. Hunt, *Ideology and U.S. Foreign Policy* (New Haven, Conn.: Yale University Press, 1987; Edward Herman, *The Real Terror Network* (Boston: South End Press, 1982); Rubin F. Weston, *Racism in U.S. Imperialism* (Columbia: University of South Carolina Press, 1972); Marian Irish and Elke Frank, *U.S. Foreign Policy: Context, Conduct, Content* (New York: Harcourt Brace Jovanovich, 1975); William D. Coplin, Patrick J. McGowan, and Michael K. O'Leary, *American Foreign Policy* (North Scituate, Mass.: Duxbury Press, 1974); and Minister Louis Farrakhan, *7 Speeches* (Newport News, Va.: United Brothers Communications, 1989).

22. Works emphasizing the counterrevolutionary thrust of U.S. foreign policy in the Third World include Sidney Lens, *The Military-Industrial Complex* (Philadelphia: Pilgrim Press, 1970); Melvin Gurtov, *United Against the Third World* (New York: Praeger Press, 1974); Robert L. Heilbroner, "Counter-Revolutionary America," in Irving Howe, ed., *A Dissenter's Guide to Foreign Policy* (New York: Doubleday-Anchor, 1968); John L.S. Girling, *America and the Third World* (London: Routledge and Kegan Paul, 1980); and Lloyd S. Etheredge, *Can Governments Learn?* (New York: Pergamon Press, 1985).

23. See Dana Munro, *Intervention and Dollar Diplomacy in the Caribbean* (Princeton, N.J.: Princeton University Press, 1964).

24. On this last point, see William Appleton Williams, *Empire as a Way of Life* (New York: Oxford University Press, 1980).

25. Other more extensive evaluations of revisionist theories include John W. Swomley, Jr., *The American Empire: The Political Ethics of Twentieth-Century Conquest* (New York: Macmillan), 1970; and Edmund Stillman and William Pfaff, *Power and Impotence: The Failure of American Foreign Policy* (New York: Random House, 1966).

26. Herbert McClosky and John Zaller, *The American Ethos* (Cambridge, Mass.: Harvard University Press, 1983), pp. 153–156.

27. This quotation usually is attributed to Charles E. Wilson, former chief executive officer of General Motors, who in 1953 made a public statement to this effect.

28. "World Investment Report 1991: The Triad in Foreign Direct Investment" (New York: United Nations Centre on Transnational Corporations, 1991).

29. Shaheen Ayubi, Richard E. Bissell, Nana Amu-Brafih Korsah, and Laurie A. Lerner, *Economic Sanctions in U.S. Foreign Policy* (Philadelphia: Foreign Policy Research Institute, 1982).

30. Arthur S. Banks, ed., *Political Handbook of the World: 1989* (Binghamton, N.Y.: CSA Publications, 1989), p. 792.

31. Ibid., pp. 790–791.

32. For an excellent case study of resistance by the American public and organized interest groups to free trade with developing countries, see Raymond A. Bauer, Itheil de Sola Pool, and Lewis Anthony Dexter, *American Business and Public Policy* (Chicago: Aldine-Atherton, 1963).

33. Robert W. Tucker, "The Radical Critique Assessed," in *The Radical Left and American Foreign Policy.*

34. Mancur Olson, *The Logic of Collective Action* (Cambridge, Mass.: Harvard University Press, 1965).

35. See Stephen D. Krasner, *Structural Conflict: The Third World Against Global Liberalism* (Berkeley: University of California Press, 1985), pp. 301–305, for a review of the literature advocating this position. He contends that "delinking" the North from the South is the most important policy prescription of critical theory.

36. See Henry Shue, *Basic Rights: Subsistence, Affluence, and U.S. Foreign Policy* (Princeton, N.J.: Princeton University Press, 1980). One of Shue's main points is that there is no distinction between negative prohibitions and positive commands relating to a nation's responsibility to promote respect for human rights around the world; See also Charles R. Beitz, *Political Theory and International Relations* (Princeton, N.J.: Princeton University Press, 1979).

CHAPTER 4

Knowing Motives;
Reconciling Means and Ends

Any analysis of the morality of public policy as it actually has been conducted must address two particularly vexing questions — is it possible to know the intentions of policymakers, and do good ends ever justify bad means? The answer to the first question is that no one can ever be sure of the motives of others. One can only know what others say, what they do, and what the consequences of their actions are. Such evidence yields inferences about intentions, but the intentions can never be proven. This chapter discusses two admittedly imperfect procedures for making such inferences about the motives of policymakers — the efforts and impact tests. With regard to the second question — whether good ends can ever justify bad foreign policy methods — the positions taken by Nationalists and Exceptionalists, on the one hand, and Progressives and Radical Progressives, on the other, are fundamentally different. These differences depend mainly on relative degrees of adherence to the internationally recognized principles of nonintervention and multilateralism.

KNOWING THE MOTIVES OF OTHERS

The intentions of leaders can be gleaned in part from the record of their public policy statements. These statements often reveal what objectives they seek, the reasons why those objectives are important, the means appropriate to achieve them, and the circumstances under which different objectives should be pursued and various means should be employed. By sharing this kind of thinking with citizens and with the attentive international public, the leader takes the first necessary step toward formulating a morally justifiable foreign policy. It is a necessary step because a secret moral principle in the field of diplomacy is no principle at all.

Cynical students of the U.S. political system scoff at the notion that the public rhetoric of the nation's elites reflects their basic attitudes and values.

Rather, the cynic might argue, public statements are occasions for carefully staged persuasive appeals, not for honest and revealing expression. Ultimately, however, we must view this extremely cynical view as a bit silly. Even Michael Hunt, who reaches disparaging conclusions about the morality of U.S. foreign policy toward the Third World, does so mainly on the basis of the historical record of public rhetoric. He argues that public rhetoric is mainly a form of communication, and, to be effective, it must appeal to widely shared values and concerns. If public rhetoric does not reflect the speaker's private views, over time it is likely to create false expectations and misunderstanding in the minds of the audience. Hunt notes that deliberate public lies are likely to lead to future inconsistencies, which in turn will lead to diminished persuasiveness. Thus, he concludes that the public rhetoric found in historical records "should be taken with complete seriousness for both the deep-seated attitudes it reveals and the action it may portend."[1] On these points, I believe Hunt is correct, and as a result, the pages that follow frequently cite the rhetoric of leaders. Still, no one should place exclusive reliance on public rhetoric to infer true intentions, primarily because several values are often used to justify a single policy, the relationship between each value and the action taken is unclear, and some values may be unstated. Let us illustrate with two recent incidents.

On December 20, 1989, President Bush, in a televised address to the nation, announced that the United States had intervened militarily in Panama in an operation named "Just Cause." The public was informed that the United States was pursuing three Nationalist objectives: to keep the Panama Canal open, to protect the lives of U.S. citizens living in Panama, and to apprehend the self-proclaimed "Maximum Leader" of Panama, General Manuel Noriega, so that he could be put on trial for alleged violations of U.S. narcotics laws. To this list, President Bush added the Progressive objective of restoring democracy in Panama. Four values had been stated, but the priorities among them were unclear.

Approximately one year later, on January 30, 1991, in his State of the Union Message, President Bush attempted to convince the American public that the War in the Gulf, named "Desert Storm," was morally justified by again appealing to a variety of moral arguments, including the affirmation of a new, seemingly Progressive world order in which naked aggression by strong nations against weaker ones would not be allowed. The administration's stated objectives were to liberate Kuwait, restore its legitimate government, safeguard Americans in the Persian Gulf, stabilize the region, and prevent the unscrupulous national leader of Iraq from controlling too large a portion of one of the world's most important natural resources. Again, multiple foreign policy values had been acknowledged. In neither instance does the rhetoric tell us which individual conditions or what combination less than the full set, if any, would be viewed as sufficient to justify these or future military interventions into Third World states. Neither do we learn whether other conditions, if present, would also have been sufficient to justify military intervention.

In most policy domains, no single goal determines the final action because in almost every real situation more than one goal applies. All of the goals publicly stated in the examples above were consistent with the action taken. In most instances, however, some values will push decision makers in other directions. Even a cursory examination of U.S. history shows that a constellation of values and objectives have sometimes had to be traded off in the contexts of concrete situations. Therefore, in most cases the choice is not between good and bad, but between good and better or between bad and worse.[2] Through long-term observation of such tradeoffs made in many specific situations, it is possible to draw some tentative conclusions about what goals take precedence or serve as trump cards when they come into conflict with other goals and under what circumstances.

Even in the Panama and Gulf War examples presented here, although multiple foreign policy values had been proclaimed, the public rhetoric still may not have revealed the full set of true objectives. Some values, such as nonintervention, might have been somewhat important to the Bush administration but rejected just the same because of some other overriding concerns. It is even possible that there were some truly evil objectives that were never publicly proclaimed in either instance. Critics have variously interpreted the intervention into Panama as an attempt by President Bush to bolster his own public image, as an effort to protect the interests of U.S.-based multinational corporations in Panama, and as another example of the ominous pattern of U.S. attacks against "brown nations" when things are not going well at home. Regarding the Gulf War, the Bush administration's goals were widely reported to include cutting Iraq's military capability down to size, eliminating its ability to produce weapons of mass destruction, and removing Saddam Hussein from power. Although representatives of the Bush administration never publicly acknowledged any of these objectives, it is impossible to prove that such considerations did not indeed enter the minds of U.S. policymakers.

Thus, public rhetoric, though not useless as a source of information about the true intentions of policymakers, does not reveal the whole story. A leader's use of particular moral justifications for different types of foreign policy actions can be observed, and the varying frequency of use over time can be recorded. On this basis alone, we can draw conclusions about the public acceptability of different moral justifications for various foreign policy actions. But the full picture emerges only by assessing the consistency between the goals stated in policy rhetoric, the set of actions pursued by policymakers, and the consequences of those actions.

Two tests can be used to develop stronger circumstantial evidence as to policymaker intent—the efforts and the impacts tests. People use the efforts test informally every day to assess the motives of others. It works as follows: if a leader announces a line of action and a rationale for it, and subsequently takes an action consistent with that statement of intent, then we conclude that the real motives were those that were stated. If a single policymaker makes several decisions that meet the same test, we accept the stated motives even when others occasionally suggest plausible alternative explanations, unless they can produce convincing evidence for these other explanations.

When the stated goal, rationale, and action are all consistent and meet the observer's moral standard, the observer will be tempted to judge the policymaker and action as moral. That judgment may be wrong, however, because the policymaker could have lied about the goal and rationale, and still might have taken the morally correct course of action. In other words, leaders can do morally correct things for the wrong reasons. On the other hand, an apparent inconsistency between stated goals and actions is not always evidence of immorality either, for a leader could do the wrong thing while pursuing morally correct objectives. Moreover, the inevitable trade-offs among foreign policy goals that must be made in the context of real situations sometimes create the appearance of inconsistency between policy statements of intent and actions where none exists.

For example, a 1973 amendment to the Foreign Assistance Act of 1961 prohibits the giving of military aid "to the government of any country which engages in a consistent pattern of gross violations of internationally recognized human rights." Since the passage of that amendment, the U.S. government has denied military aid to several countries (including Argentina, Chile, Guatemala, and Uruguay) because of their poor human rights records. The intent of this legislative provision is that the actual or potential denial of military aid should act as an incentive for oppressive governments to improve their human rights practices. Critics object to this amendment not because its intent is insincere, but because the provision is not implemented often enough or against the governments they view as the worst offenders. Essentially, most Progressive and Radical Progressive critics argue that the U.S. government's effort in pursuit of this and other progressive goals is inadequate, that when human rights objectives conflict with others, they are too easily sacrificed. But the conclusion that human rights concerns are given too low a priority has different moral implications from the conclusion that the stated human rights policy is insincere or, in other words, pure rhetoric.

One way social scientists assess the adequacy of effort to achieve a foreign policy objective is to imagine all plausible goals that may motivate a government policy and then to translate those goals into hypotheses that would be confirmed if government actions were consistent with the pursuit of those goals. Although official policy statements provide a starting point for looking for patterns, other unstated motives such as racism, assistance to multinational corporations (MNCs), and promotion of trade may be equally or even more important. Thus, any investigation of the pattern of foreign policy efforts has to consider both the stated and unstated goals of policymakers. When we consider the full range of potential goals and find that some stated policy objectives consistently affect certain foreign policy decisions as specified in policy statements, then those stated policy objectives may be said to meet the efforts test. If not, they do not meet the test.

In keeping with the earlier example, when U.S. policymakers announce that an important goal of U.S. foreign policy toward developing countries is to encourage them to improve their human rights records, the statement of that goal is expected to change the behavior of the United States toward developing countries in some observable way. Otherwise the goal is symbolic, but not real. Specifically, U.S. foreign policy would be expected to become more favorable toward those governments with better or improving human rights records and less favorable toward oppressive governments. Several studies have been conducted to examine this question, but the results have been mixed.[3] There is general agreement on a few points, but, largely because of differences in research design, the measures of human rights used, the countries selected for study, and the statistical criteria employed, they disagree on many others.

Another way to assess motives based on observation of actions is to compare stated goals with actual impacts on policy targets. For example, since the United States has stated that one of its goals is to persuade oppressive governments to improve their human rights practices, it is legitimate to ask whether the policy has had any effect. Have those oppressive governments with very close relations with the United States improved more than those with more distant relations? The impact test is very stringent, and perhaps unfairly so, inasmuch as governmental intent and outcomes may not agree since government policymakers are unable to make outcomes conform with their intentions. The test is mentioned here because it can produce convincing results and because a utilitarian approach to assessing the morality of public policy must attach strong weight to the consequences of actions.

With regard to assessing the morality of public policy, we can conclude that we have strong evidence that the stated motive was the true motive. If the impact is the opposite of what was expected, then we have somewhat weaker evidence that the stated intent was false. Admittedly, a less conclusive finding of no impact or of morally good *and* bad consequences is not very useful one way or the other. David Forsythe, in a study of the impact of food aid on LDCs, states that U.S. policy can be expected to have little short-term impact on the availability of food in Third World countries that receive food aid. First, the U.S. policy may be of too small a magnitude to affect the status or behavior of the target state. Second, even when some limited impact is observed in the expected direction, it is difficult to decide whether the change was due to the U.S. policy or to other factors.[4] Nonetheless, a systematic research design could be constructed to test whether, other things being equal, U.S. food aid improved or hurt the short-term nutritional status of the target population and the long-term food self-sufficiency of the aid recipients.

Since ethics is more a question of intentions than of results, policy failure is not in itself immoral. An ideal honestly pursued but not achieved, or achieved only in small part; is superior to no ideal at all. On the other hand, a public announcement of a foreign policy objective with no action clause signaling a real change in policy behavior, with no apparent consequences for the targets of the policy, or with consequences very different from those promised may constitute disingenuous, deceptive, and, therefore, immoral policy-making. As noted earlier, some critics contend that the United States' entire publicly proclaimed foreign policy agenda is an exercise in that kind of deception.[5]

MEANS AND ENDS

Leaders achieve their foreign policy objectives through measures ranging from persuasion to coercion. Persuasive actions are those that do not require the use or threat of force. Examples include diplomacy, provision or denial of military or economic aid, symbolic actions (such as honoring dissenters or placing a government on the list of states that sponsor terrorism), economic sanctions, preferential trade agreements, and the establishment or cutoff of diplomatic or trade relations. The ethical debate over proper means has centered on the conditions under which leaders may use bad means such as violence, deception, and broken promises to achieve good ends. Much recent debate in the United States has focused specifically on the question of whether intervention by more powerful states into the affairs of weaker ones is ever justified. The historian, Loren Baritz, in his analysis of U.S. involvement in Vietnam, argues that the cultural distance between Vietnamese and American people facilitated the decision to intervene militarily and massively in Southeast

Asia. Once there, the inability of Americans to understand the Vietnamese impeded the effectiveness of U.S. military and political decisions.[6] If Baritz is correct, then we must be sensitive to a continuing bias in the U.S. foreign policy decision-making process toward military intervention in culturally distant places, many of which are located in the Third World.

Martin Wight defines intervention as the "forcible interference, short of declaring war, by one or more powers in the affairs of another power."[7] Interventions may take several forms and may be undertaken for many different ends. They may be overt (public) or covert (secret), unilateral or multilateral. They may be designed to accomplish an altruistic aim such as preventing genocide or to accomplish a self-interested aim such as seizing resources or enslaving another nation's people.[8]

Perhaps the most basic provision of international law is the principle of nonintervention. This principle is stated as Article 2, Section 4 of the United Nations charter as follows: "All Members shall refrain in their international relations from the threat or use of force against the territorial integrity or political independence of any state, or in any manner inconsistent with the Purposes of the United Nations."[9] This principle, reiterated in many regional compacts, guarantees the continued existence of the state system and the autonomy of its member governments. Adherence to this principle is particularly important to the governments of militarily weak states in the Third World.

The United States and other powerful states have used another principle of international law, the principle of self-defense, to justify the projection of their military power into the Third World. Article 51 of the United Nations charter notes that "Nothing in the present Charter shall impair the inherent right of individual or collective self-defense if an armed attack occurs against a Member of the United Nations . . ."[10] For some analysts, use of the word "inherent" implied that this right preceded the Charter, that it carried with it a long, well-understood tradition of usage, and that it was not even necessary to state it expressly. But this interpretation has been contested on the basis that Article 51 goes on to proscribe the use of force in self-defense except in case of "an armed attack." Powerful nations cling to the broader interpretation of the right of self-defense, whereas weaker ones argue that the principle is highly circumscribed and subordinate to the higher principle of nonintervention. President Bush justified sending a large military force to Saudi Arabia to protect that country from possible invasion by neighboring Iraq, in part, on the basis of the self-defense principle recognized in Article 51 of the United Nations charter.

Of course, the main purpose of the United Nations is to avoid the necessity of resorting to force to settle disputes among nations. Article 33 requires that "The Parties to any dispute, the continuance of which is likely to endanger the maintenance of international peace and security, shall, first of all, seek a solution by negotiation, enquiry, mediation, conciliation, arbitration, judicial settlement, resort to regional agencies or arrangements, or other peaceful means of their own choice."[11] Thus, according to the principles of international law, forcible interference of any kind is morally inferior to the use of other means.

As a last resort, Article 39 allows the use of force to counter threats to world peace, breaches of world peace, or acts of aggression. Under the extraordinary condition of unanimous agreement of the permanent members of the Security Council, the charter allows the members of the United Nations collectively to use demonstrations of force, blockade, and other operations by air, sea, or land forces to counter such threats (Articles 39–51). The Security Council invoked these articles in 1990–1991 to authorize the collective use of force to liberate Kuwait from Iraqi aggression. U.S. leaders often must reconcile the values of nonintervention and multilateralism (regional or global), on the one hand, with self-defense and unilateralism, on the other. In the fights against international terrorism, international drug trafficking, and the proliferation of chemical and nuclear weapons, U.S. leaders are tempted to rely on the principle of self-defense and to resort to unilateral actions to produce preferred outcomes. But serious questions have been raised both about the morality of these foreign policy objectives and, to an even greater extent, about the means U.S. policymakers sometimes use to achieve them.

Most Americans view the fight against international terrorism as a morally defensible foreign policy goal, but one person's terrorist is another's freedom fighter. In other words, depending on how terrorism is defined, the fight against it may be more or less palatable. The U.S. Department of State sees international terrorism as posing a danger to the welfare of the U.S. government and its people. The State Department defines terrorism as "the threat or use of violence for political purposes by individuals or groups acting for, or in opposition to, established governmental authority, when such actions are intended to influence a target group wider than the immediate victim or victims."[12] The problem with most definitions of terrorism, including this one, is that it does not differentiate political, revolutionary violence from terrorism. A political revolution refers to an action that results in a radical change in the way a society makes its collective choices. Since revolutions usually change the distribution of benefits from government policies, they are often accompanied by some level of violence. Those who have no power but seek it through revolutionary activity may resort to terrorist tactics. Thus, some see the fight against international terrorism as a cornerstone of the United

States' counterrevolutionary policy in the Third World. In addition, the State Department definition does not exclude states as sponsors of terrorism, but it does seem to preclude the notion of "state terrorism," or states acting as terrorist organizations against their own people, which Radical Progressives and some Progressives see as an even greater problem. Thus, the definition itself seems to position the United States against popular revolutions and in favor of oppressive governments.

Even if there was agreement about what terrorism meant, there would still be disagreement over the proper means of combatting it. The existence of terrorist activities that cross national boundaries tempts the leaders of democratic states to abandon fundamental principles of due process and nonintervention. Existing United Nations protocols require states apprehending terrorists to prosecute them or extradite them for prosecution.[13] But this stricture has not been effective, because, as noted, there are different views of what constitutes a terrorist act and the apprehending state is sometimes concerned that prosecuting perpetrators will provoke attacks to free the alleged terrorists and to punish the government(s) responsible for their prosecution. In the face of these difficulties, Paul Bremer, former U.S. Department of State ambassador-at-large for counterterrorism, is among those who argue that the United States should be willing to conduct covert operations designed to apprehend suspected terrorists residing in other countries with the purpose of returning them to the United States to face prosecution. If evidence of criminality was strong enough, if the terrorist crime was heinous enough, and if extradition or covert abduction was not possible, he would not rule out the option of a covert operation designed to assassinate suspected terrorists. Under extraordinary circumstances, he would even approve covert operations against the leaders of states sponsoring terrorism.[14] Nationalists and Exceptionalists would be likely to support this position; Progressives and Radical Progressives would not.

The United Nations may play a stronger role in the fight against international terrorism now that the Cold War is over. In 1992 the United Nations Security Council voted to impose a ban on air travel and arms sales (as well as other sanctions) against Libya, because its government refused to surrender agents implicated in the bombings of a Pan Am flight over Scotland in 1988 and a French airliner over West Africa the next year. The vote was ten in favor of the air embargo with five abstentions, but, of the six temporary Third World members on the Security Council, four (Morocco, India, Cape Verde, and Zimbabwe) abstained. These four, joined by China, preferred an approach relying more on negotiation and less on ultimatum.

Drug lords are not terrorists in the strict sense, but, like terrorists, they often reside in foreign countries and conduct activities harmful to U.S. national interests. In 1989 the Bush administration proposed stationing the navy off the coast of Colombia in order to interdict the transportation of cocaine from that country to the United States. When the leaders of several Latin American nations, including Colombia, protested that this action would violate their sovereignty, President Bush promised that no such steps would be taken without the prior agreement of all governments affected. Though most Third World leaders are cynical about the U.S. government's war against drug suppliers, they still have powerful reasons to cooperate. If they do, they may receive more foreign aid or at least their levels of aid will probably not be cut. If they do not cooperate, the United States may decide to intervene to apprehend suspected drug lords for prosecution in the United States. Apprehending General Noriega so that he could be tried in the United States on drug-related charges was one of the reasons President Bush gave for the military intervention into Panama in 1990, proving that the threat of intervention to capture drug lords is real, not empty. Progressives and Radical Progressives would not support either the blockade or the intervention; Nationalists and Exceptionalists would support both.

As a final example of a moral dilemma the United States faces, consider the goal of preventing the spread of chemical weapons — the poor nations' nuclear bomb — and nuclear and biological weapons in the Third World. Since the United States has all three types of weapons in its arsenal, many leaders of less militarized states view the U.S.-led effort to stop weapons proliferation as hypocritical and entirely self-serving. Treaties proscribing the development and storage of such weapons by states that currently do not have them are also probably futile, since it will be very easy for "outlaw" states to develop chemical and biological weapons in secret. When U.S. officials discover such secret development activities, as allegedly was the case in Libya in 1989 and in Iraq in 1990 and again in 1991, does the U.S. government have any moral right to use threats, covert action, or overt military intervention to stop such development? To this last question, Kenneth Adelman, a former high-level U.S. arms treaty negotiator, says "yes."[15]

In contrast, Michael Walzer argues that forcible interference by one state into the affairs of another is almost never ethical. In his view, national self-determination is the highest value in international affairs, and intervention by strong states into weaker ones undermines that value. People have a right to form communities of their own, and others should not transcend the boundaries of those communities for at least two good reasons. First, the existence of diverse states ensures "political alternatives," each of which serves as a potential refuge from oppression. That is, the existence of diverse states provides multiple places for individuals to go if they are unhappy with the treatment they receive from their own government. Second, individuals want governments to respect their rights, but rights do not exist apart from their location in states. Thus, states must be preserved if rights are to be protected. Walzer supports the right of citizens to revolt against their own government, because that right is implied by the preeminent position of the value of self-determination. But the right to revolt does not confer on other states the right to intervene. People must create their own revolutions without the aid of outsiders. According to his perspective, intervention is morally justifiable only if the purpose is to aid a victim of aggression or to prevent the enslavement or massacre of people by their own government. In the latter instance, Walzer notes that the notion of self-determination is irrelevant.[16]

Covert action, or secretly exerting influence on a foreign situation, presents a different set of ethical problems. Use of covert action enables a powerful state to minimize the risk of provoking a response from another major power, since one of the guiding principles in planning such actions is "plausible deniability."[17] Partly for this reason, despite severe moral reservations, numerous congressional committees have decided that covert action must be available as a weapon in the nation's arsenal. Not surprisingly, then, the United States' use of covert action has become common, especially against weaker states that have little capacity to resist or retaliate. All the same, there are good reasons for moral reservations: covert actions stifle public debate, ignore the democratic process, subvert democratic values, and violate international law against intervention.

Recognizing these problems, in 1978 Secretary of State Cyrus Vance recommended that covert action be used only when "absolutely essential to the national security" of the United States and when "no other means" would do.[18] Viewing this standard as still too ambiguous, Gregory Treverton believes that a proposed covert action should not be conducted if the president believes the majority of the American people would not approve of it (e.g., the Bay of Pigs invasion, 1961); it would contradict publicly stated U.S. foreign policy statements (e.g., the Iran-Contra affair, 1985–1986); it would have a harmful effect on U.S. relations with other countries in the region where it would take place (e.g., U.S. aid to the Contras in Nicaragua, 1980–1990, aid to the Angolan rebels, 1985–present); or it would not have a high probability of success.[19]

This last criterion requires some elaboration. Here Treverton's argument becomes explicitly utilitarian, requiring that policymakers think long and hard about the consequences of proposed covert actions. He notes that many of the most well-known and morally reprehensible covert activities conducted by the U.S. government began as relatively small, even seemingly inconsequential plans with grand objectives. These small-scale plans usually failed, but, once begun, the logic of covert action took on a life of its own. Treverton believes that, in practice, covert actions have gone further on a piecemeal, step-by-step basis than anyone would have approved at the outset. Thus, decision makers, in Treverton's view, should make a judgment about the advisability of only those covert actions that have a realistic chance of success. They should not embark on a series of small, individually inadequate steps that so often lead to ever more ethically suspect actions.

William Colby, former director of the CIA, endorsed Treverton's first criterion of hypothetical public approval. Colby argued that the American people would approve of those covert actions (if they knew about them) that could be shown to have been taken in self-defense of the nation or its citizens abroad (the self-defense test) and that had been proportionate to the threat (the proportionality test).[20] Of these two tests, Colby thought proportionality was the stronger moral argument for allowing the conduct of covert actions, because such actions provide a middle option between the two extremes of diplomatic protest and sending in the marines. He admitted, however, that not all U.S. covert operations have met the proportionality test. As examples of actions that probably did not meet the self-defense test, he cited the covert operations in Guatemala in 1954 and in Indonesia in 1958. Surprisingly, in his view, the widely condemned and abortive Bay of Pigs invasion in 1961 did meet the self-defense test, because shortly after the invasion failed the Soviet Union installed medium-range missiles in Cuba.

Current U.S. legislation under which covert operations are conducted incorporates the self-defense test by requiring the president to approve a "finding" that any proposed covert operation is necessary to the national security of the United States.[21] In recent years, the decision-making process has also facilitated use of Colby's proportionality test, because all covert operations conducted since 1977 have been required by law to be reviewed by special intelligence committees in the House and Senate *before execution*.[22] This allows members of the minority party, who are likely to be more impartial observers of the proposed action, to comment on it. However, neither chamber has received or has requested the responsibility of legislative veto power.

One type of covert action frequently used in the Third World does not involve the use of force. It is electioneering, or the "secret" use of U.S. resources to exert influence on the outcome of democratic elections in other countries. Documented U.S. actions have included making direct contributions to the campaigns of candidates, influencing the media coverage of the campaign, or persuading the leaders of important voting blocs to provide endorsements. Although most such activities are intended to be secret, they often become known to the Third World voting public. Official U.S. active support for particular candidates in recent elections in El Salvador and Nicaragua was widely reported in the U.S. news media. Progressives and Radical Progressives, upholding the principle of noninterference into the purely domestic affairs of other nations, would reject such methods as immoral. These methods are also questionable on the grounds that they are ineffective, since completely open campaigning would probably produce the same consequences and, not requiring deception, would be a morally superior course of action.

Within the mainstream debate over whether ends justify means, almost everyone agrees that a nation has the right to use any means to defend itself against external threat and that, if bad methods are to be used for other purposes, they should be used only as a last resort. However, it is hard to characterize the various schools of thought beyond this point. Exceptionalists, convinced by the moral justness of their causes, tend to be most ready to resort to bad methods to achieve them. On principle, Nationalists do not preclude the use of coercion to achieve other ends associated with the national interest, but in practice many leading contemporary Nationalist thinkers have advised against it in most situations. Progressives generally are against military means to achieve the national self-interest, but a few Progressive thinkers would argue that coercion is justified to achieve humanitarian objectives such as the prevention of genocide.

This kind of Progressive argument was used to urge the U.S. government to take action to protect Kurdish refugees against a vengeful pursuing Iraqi army in the spring of 1991. However, Progressives and Radical Progressives are always suspicious when strong governments use coercion against weaker ones. They tend to doubt that the motives for intervention truly will be humanitarian, however well altruistic rhetoric masks the real motives.[23] Since most cases of military interventionism, like the recent ones in Panama and Iraq, are justified for multiple reasons, some self-interested, some humanitarian, Progressives generally oppose unilateral military interventions except in the most extreme cases. Radical Progressives always oppose them.

Within the mainstream debate over U.S. foreign policy toward the Third World, use of espionage to gather information necessary to protect the United States' military security is widely approved. Nationalists and Exceptionalists seem to be willing to go further: to allow covert action to achieve ends associated with the accumulation of economic or military power by the United States. Progressives, on the other hand, are likely to condemn the use of covert action for these purposes, although some are willing to use covert methods to achieve humanitarian objectives. In general, however, Nationalists and Exceptionalists tend to advocate the use of covert methods in a wider range of situations than Progressives.

Consistent with their position on the use of military force, Radical Progressives oppose all covert activities, including espionage.

Finally, Nationalists and Exceptionalists are much more likely to resort to unilateralism in reaction to action-forcing events in the Third World. Progressives, on the other hand, are much less willing to take unilateral action. They prefer to consult with the leaders of the governments most directly affected and to abide by solutions developed by the United Nations or by regional organizations even if they do not directly reflect the preferences of the U.S. government. Radical Progressives believe that unilateral actions by First World nations in the Third World are always immoral.

SUMMARY

Most political scientists avoid analyzing the motives of policymakers because motives are not directly observable. Instead, they must be inferred from other kinds of information. However, since this book is about the morality, or, at a minimum, the goals of American foreign policy toward the Third World, the problem of inferring motives cannot be avoided in the analysis that follows. The efforts and impact tests described in this chapter, though imperfect, are the best tools available for the task and are loosely applied in the chapters that follow.

Machiavelli's advice to the Prince about foreign policy methods was that "He should not depart from the good if he can hold to it, but he should be ready to enter on evil *if he has to*" (emphasis added). This advice would be sufficient to prohibit the U.S. government from engaging in covert campaign activities abroad, but it is too vague to be of much help in guiding action in other circumstances. Most, if not all, U.S. leaders have recognized that they could not avoid using violence, deception, and broken promises to achieve good ends, but they have differed a great deal in their willingness to resort to such methods. Nationalist and Exceptionalist leaders in the United States, having less respect for the universal value of nonintervention and multilateralism, have been more willing to engage in overt and covert unilateral actions in the Third World. Progressives have been less willing to engage in such actions, and Radical Progressives deem them morally unacceptable.

NOTES

1. Michael H. Hunt, *Ideology and U.S. Foreign Policy* (New Haven, Conn.: Yale University Press, 1987), p. 16.

2. Sidney Hook, *Philosophy and Public Policy* (Carbondale, Ill.: Southern Illinois University Press, 1980), pp. 54–66.

3. See David Carleton and Michael Stohl, "The Role of Human Rights in U.S. Foreign Assistance Policy: A Critique and Reappraisal," *American Journal of Political Science* 31, No. 4 (August 1987): 1002–1018; James M. McCormick and Neil Mitchell, "Is U.S. Aid Really Linked to Human Rights in Latin America?" *American Journal of Political Science* 32, No. 1 (February 1988): 231–239; and Steven C. Poe, "Human Rights and Economic Aid under Ronald Reagan and Jimmy Carter," *American Journal of Political Science* (forthcoming, 1992).

4. David P. Forsythe, "US Economic Assistance and Human Rights: Why the Emperor Has (Almost) No Clothes," in David P. Forsythe, ed., *Human Rights and Development* (London: Macmillan, 1989), pp. 171–195.

5. See, for example, Michael Parenti, *The Sword and the Dollar* (New York: St. Martin's Press, 1989); Edward Herman, *The Real Terror Network* (Boston: South End Press, 1982); and Noam Chomsky and Edward Herman, *After the Cataclysm* (Boston: South End Press, 1979).

6. Loren Baritz, *Backfire* (New York: Ballantine, 1985).

7. Martin Wight, *Power Politics* (New York: Penguin Books, 1979), p. 191.

8. Michael Joseph Smith, "Ethics and Intervention," *Ethics and International Affairs* 3 (1989): 5.

9. Leland M. Goodrich and Edward Hambro, *Charter of the United Nations* (Boston: World Peace Foundation, 1946), p. 67.

10. Ibid., pp. 174–175.

11. Ibid., p. 140.

12. U.S. Department of State, *Patterns of International Terrorism 1982* (Washington, D.C.: U.S. Government Printing Office, 1983).

13. Augustus Richard Norton, "Drawing the Line on Opprobrious Violence," *Ethics and International Affairs* 4 (1990): 129.

14. Bremer presented these views at a conference on "Ethics and International Affairs," Washington, D.C., June 11, 1990.

15. Adelman presented this view at a conference on "Ethics and International Affairs," Washington, D.C., June 12, 1990.

16. Michael Walzer, *Just and Unjust Wars* (New York: Basic Books, 1977).

17. Gregory F. Treverton, *Covert Action* (New York: Basic Books, 1987).

18. Testimony before the Senate Select Committee on Intelligence Activities, December 5, 1975.

19. Gregory F. Treverton, "Imposing a Standard: Covert Action and American Democracy," *Ethics and International Affairs* 3 (1989): 27–44.

20. William E. Colby, "Public Policy, Secret Action," *Ethics and International Affairs* 3 (1989): 61–72.

21. Ibid., p. 64.

22. The Senate created a Select Committee on Intelligence in 1976, and the House followed suit in 1977.

23. See, for example, Leo Kuper, *The Prevention of Genocide* (New Haven, Conn.: Yale University Press, 1985).

PART II

Early History: 1776–1945

CHAPTER 5

Territorial Expansionism: 1777–1900

In September 1981 the Mexican government opened a National Museum of Interventions. In the museum, maps and commentaries describe the determination of the U.S. government to conquer the West at Mexico's expense in the nineteenth century. Many Mexican intellectuals think the existence of a Museum of Interventions is especially appropriate today, because of the recent increase in military interventions by the United States in the Caribbean basin.[1] In September 1991 the Philippine Senate opened debate on a new U.S. lease for the Subic Bay Naval Station and appeared ready to reject the pact, thereby forcing an American withdrawal from Subic, the largest U.S. military base in Asia. Many of the senators opposing renewal of the lease cited the need to remove the last vestiges of U.S. colonial control over the Philippines. To them, events such as the Spanish-American War, the subsequent colonization of the Philippines in 1899 by the United States, and the unsuccessful war of independence against the United States were vivid, unpleasant memories. Although the United States formally granted the Philippines its independence in 1946, many Philippine citizens resent what they see as continuing U.S. dominance. Unable to forge a compromise with the Philippine government, the U.S. government announced in 1992 that it would vacate Subic Bay when the current lease expires.

As the Philippine and Mexican cases illustrate, U.S. relations with many Third World countries cannot be properly understood without considering important developments that occurred long before World War II. This chapter discusses selected early events and themes in U.S. relations with militarily weaker nations in order to shed some light on U.S.–Third World relations today. It does not provide a detailed history of U.S. foreign relations from the inception of the nation to the beginning of the twentieth century.

The major thesis of this chapter is that U.S. foreign policy during this early phase was mainly Nationalist and expansionist in character. Important developments during this period, which will be discussed below and which illustrate the Nationalist thrust in U.S. foreign policy, included wars against Mexico and the American Indian nations, the Monroe Doctrine, the increasing willingness of U.S. policymakers to openly acknowledge economic motives in foreign policy, the slave trade with Africa, and the Spanish-American War.

A related argument developed in this chapter is that U.S. foreign policy toward militarily weaker states has never been isolationist. According to Dexter Perkins, "In the first hundred years and more of the history of American foreign policy the distinctive feature, outside of the expansion of territory, is the crystallization of the tradition of what has come to be called isolationism."[2] Isolationists would prefer that the military defense of the United States begin at its borders. Globalists argue that the survival of the American nation requires that the United States influence developments around the world to conform with the preferences of its leaders.

Isolationist sentiments can be traced back at least as far as the colonial experience. Although the nation had its beginning when the Continental Congress declared the independence of the thirteen colonies of England in 1776, the foreign policy of the new nation rested on a foundation of over 150 years of experience as a colony. Among other things, the colonial experience had taught Americans that, because the nation was geographically isolated from the powerful states of that time, all located in Europe, it was possible and desirable to avoid involvements in their conflicts.[3] This was a prudent course for a weak nation that wished to remain an independent and autonomous actor in the international system. Washington was the first president to state the official U.S. position on involvement in world affairs. In his farewell address in 1796, he said that the United States should "steer clear of permanent alliances with any portion of the foreign world," that it could only "safely trust to temporary alliances for extraordinary emergencies."[4] In his inaugural address in 1801, Thomas Jefferson also saw fit to warn the nation against becoming involved in "entangling alliances."

Powerful states welcome foreign entanglements as opportunities to exercise influence; only weaker ones avoid them, because they have little to gain. Washington and Jefferson feared foreign entanglements, because, for at least the first 50 years of its existence, the United States was itself a militarily weak, economically underdeveloped nation. As in most Third World countries today, its leaders were concerned about maintaining independence and autonomy by resisting the influence of stronger states in the international system. They were also anxious about border disputes with neighbors and attentive to the development of indigenous political and economic institutions. Thus, President Washington feared alliances with powerful European nations, because such entanglements provided a dominant ally numerous opportunities "to tamper with domestic factions, to practice the art of seduction, to mislead public opinion, [and] to influence or awe the public councils! Such an attachment of a small or weak nation toward a great and powerful nation dooms the former to be a satellite of the latter."[5] He also warned that it was folly for any nation "to look for disinterested favors from another; that it must pay with a portion of its independence for whatever it may accept under that character."[6]

As the events recounted in this chapter demonstrate, the United States' isolationism did not prevent the government from immediately becoming entangled with the many Native American Indian nations on the North American continent or, later, with Mexico and, later still, with a much weakened Spain. All militarily weak states are "isolationist" in the Washingtonian and Jeffersonian sense, so the preference for isolationism is not peculiar to the United States at all. It is simply symptomatic of a stage in a nation's development, of its power position in the international system. As the United States' power increased relative to that of other states, the penchant for isolationism declined. After the end of World War II, when the United States emerged as the world's foremost economic and military power, policymakers rarely discussed isolationism as a serious option.

During the first half of the nineteenth century, the United States pursued a policy designed to obtain both formal political and economic control of new territory on the North American continent. During the latter half of the nineteenth century, the expansionism continued and the geographic focus widened, but U.S. policymakers had less interest in obtaining formal political control over new areas. The historian, Walter LaFeber, portrays the U.S. military exuberance in the 1890s, not as an aberration, but as a natural culmination of the expansive foreign policy ideas of most U.S. political and business leaders in the latter half of the nineteenth century. The main objectives of policymakers during this latter period, he argues, was to find trade and investment opportunities in areas where the United States did not want to exert formal political control.[7]

WARS AGAINST WEAKER NEIGHBORS

While America was still a colony of England, a process of relentless westward expansion began which continued until 1853, when the continental boundaries of the contiguous states of the United States assumed their present form. Walter Lippmann divides the expansion into six principal stages.[8] First, by the Louisiana Purchase, Jefferson obtained title from France to a frontier running through what is now Montana, Wyoming, Colorado, Texas, and Louisiana. Second, after prolonged negotiation, Spain ceded to the United States all its lands east of the Mississippi. In return, the United States gave up claims against Spain, including its claim to Texas. Third, in 1846 President James K. Polk negotiated a treaty with Great Britain, leading to the annexation of the Oregon Country including all the states of Washington, Oregon, and Idaho, and substantial portions of Montana and Wyoming. Fourth, also in 1846, Texas, which had seceded from Mexico, was incorporated into the Union. The Texas territory included most of what is New Mexico, parts of Colorado, Wyoming, Kansas, and Oklahoma. Fifth, at the conclusion of the war with Mexico, the United States claimed the territory that now includes California, Nevada, Arizona, Utah, and part of New Mexico, Colorado, and Wyoming. Sixth, in 1853 the Gila River Valley in southern Arizona and New Mexico was purchased from Mexico under the Gadsden Treaty. By 1853 the United States had little additional need for territorial expansion, and, with the technological advances of the industrialization period, that need diminished even further. The other major powers, fearing the growing power of the United States, also combined more effectively to slow it down.

This expansion came at the expense of Native American Indians and the Mexican people. In relations with these less powerful governments, U.S. leaders were at best indifferent to their needs and at worst malevolent. For a time some U.S. leaders hoped that Native American Indians could be assimilated into the culture of the white, European citizen-settlers, but by 1830 a general consensus had been reached that removal of the Indians was the only viable alternative. The policy of removal as an alternative to assimilation was first suggested by Jefferson and was widely hailed as a sensible approach. Henry Clay responded positively to the idea, noting that it was impossible to civilize these "savages," since they were inferior to white men. Even "their disappearance from the human race would be no great loss to the world."[9]

There was little negotiation with the leaders of the Native American Indian nations or with Mexico, and the United States often violated the few agreements that were negotiated. Historians agree that passage of the Indian Removal Act of May 28, 1830, despite some gentle language providing for the exchange of lands Indians occupied in the South for lands west of the Mississippi River, doomed Indians to the dictates of whites. By 1837 Andrew Jackson's administration had concluded 94 "treaties" to obtain Indian land. A few tribes resisted. The most notable of these resistance efforts in the 1830s was the Illinois Black Hawk War of 1832 and the Florida Seminole War from 1835 to 1843. The outcomes of these and other less significant wars between the Indians and the U.S. government demonstrated that the only real choice the Indians had was to sign, then move, or die.

In the 1870s many Indian tribes again rose up in rebellion against the unfair treatment they had received from the U.S. government. One of their spokespersons, Washakie, chief of the Shoshoni, had fought on the side of the U.S. army against other Indian nations in the Southwest. Despite this valuable service, even his tribe was poorly treated by the white government. His speech at an 1878 conference called by the governor of Wyoming on an Indian reservation is a moving condemnation of the United States' barbaric treatment of Native American Indians:

> The whiteman, who possesses this whole vast country from sea to sea, who roams over it at pleasure where he likes, cannot know the cramp we feel in this little spot, with the undying remembrance of the fact, which you know as well as we, that every foot you proudly call America, not very long ago belonged to the red man. The great spirit gave it to us. There was room enough for all his many tribes, and all were happy in their freedom. But the white man had, in ways we know not of, learned some things we had not learned; among them, how to make superior tools and terrible weapons, better for war than bows and arrows; and there seemed no end to hordes of men from other lands beyond the sea. . . .
>
> And your great and mighty government—Oh sir, I hesitate for I cannot tell the half! It does not protect us in our rights. It leaves us without implements for harvesting our crops, without breeding animals better than ours, without the food we still lack after all we can do, without the many comforts we cannot produce, without the schools we so much need for our children.[10]

The hunger for land by white settlers was not satisfied by the Indian Removal Act. Many settlers felt that even the little patches set aside for reservations were too large. Under consideration in Congress was a bill that would allot a certain amount of land to each Indian but would reduce the amount of common Indian property granted in earlier treaties. Congressman Nathaniel Pendleton of Ohio, arguing in favor of the General Allotment Act, said: "they [Indians] must either change their mode of life or they must die. We may regret it, we may wish it were otherwise, our sentiments of humanity may be shocked by the alternative, but we cannot shut our eyes to the fact that it is the alternative.[11] The act did not become law.

The U.S. government's treatment of Mexico was only a little better. After the administrations of Presidents John Quincy Adams and Jackson had tried to purchase Texas from Mexico, the United States aided a rebellion by American settlers against the Mexican government. Mexico's leaders, who had never officially recognized an independent Texas, were infuriated by the formal annexation of Texas into the Union. Border tensions heightened, and U.S. troops invaded after a border incident in 1846. Initial easy victories over Mexico's armed forces fueled a mounting demand for more territory, including conquering and annexing all of Mexico. Despite the existence of a strong "all-Mexico" movement, a peace treaty was signed in 1848, which took about half of Mexico.

MANIFEST DESTINY

The United States is a nation founded upon a creed.[12] This creed, stated in the Declaration of Independence, professes that all men are created equal in the eyes of government, that governments exist to give them justice, and that all people have a right to life, liberty, and the pursuit of happiness. The basic ideals of American political culture—equality, liberty, individualism, constitutionalism, free enterprise, and democracy— are what America stands for as a nation, and, from the very beginning, those ideals have had an impact on U.S. foreign policy, especially toward weaker states. The American creed found expression in foreign policy in the notion of Manifest Destiny, a complex concept encompassing three elements—the conviction of superiority, the idea of "natural" boundaries, and the notion of inevitability.

Many Americans held the conviction that the United States was the best nation in the world. They believed that the ideals of the American creed were right not only for the United States, but for other nations too. Therefore, it was the United States' destiny to extend its creed either by coercing or persuading less fortunate, weaker nations to adopt it. In this way, civilization would be brought to the uncivilized. This is the moral dimension of Manifest Destiny. Since the American creed was a better idea, it was altruistic to share it with others who would also benefit from it.

Many also believed that the United States had a right to expand to fill its natural boundaries, which, in the view of Congressman John Harper of New Hampshire, even encompassed most of what is now Canada. In 1812 he said on the House floor: "To me, sir, it appears that the Author of Nature has marked our limits in the south by the Gulf of Mexico, and on the north by the regions of the eternal frost."[13] If Canada had not been settled and coveted by France and Great Britain, whose leaders were not about to give way to this rapidly expanding upstart, today the United States might have the shape Congressman Harper envisioned.

Others felt that the southern border should be the southernmost tip of

South America. A natural anticolonial spirit, combined with a desire to wrest west Florida from the Spanish, caused strong public sympathy with the independence movements in Latin America in the early 1800s. Speaking of South America, Henry Clay, Speaker of the House, exclaimed:

> Within this vast region we behold the most sublime and interesting objects of creation; the loftiest mountains, the most majestic rivers in the world; the richest mines of the precious metals, and the choicest productions of the earth. We behold there a spectacle still more interesting and sublime — the glorious spectacle of eighteen millions of people, struggling to burst their chains and to be free.[14]

The passing of the American frontier in the middle of the nineteenth century led many Americans to seek a new frontier to absorb their dynamic energies. In the 1890s the philosophy of Social Darwinism, the zeal of American missionaries, and the rise of "Anglo-Saxonism" may have prepared the way for a more aggressive and coercive foreign policy toward Latin America, Asia, the Middle East, and Africa. Social Darwinism spread the message that the world's peoples consisted of superior and inferior breeds and that people and nations were locked in a struggle for survival. If the United States turned soft, it would become the prey of a more warlike state. If weaker states could not fend off the stronger ones, they merely exposed their unfitness in the struggle for existence.[15] Thus, both the failures of weaker, less fit states and the United States' successes were inevitable.

THE MONROE DOCTRINE

As the military power of the United States grew, countering European economic and military power in Latin America (especially Britain's) gradually became a more important goal in U.S. foreign policy. On March 8, 1822, despite Spain's protest, President James Monroe recommended immediate recognition of the newly proclaimed independent Latin American republics. Congress approved the president's request. Embedded in his annual message to Congress in December of 1823 was Monroe's now well-known doctrine warning Europe and Russia that the United States would tolerate no further incursions into the Americas. He wrote:

> The occasion has been judged proper for asserting . . . that the American continents, by the free and independent condition which they have

assumed and maintain, are henceforth not to be considered as subjects for future colonization by any European powers.[16]

Seven pages later, Monroe expanded on this principle of anticolonialism in the Americas. Temporarily forgetting the United States' badgering of Spain to cede its colony in Florida, he continued:

> With the existing colonies or dependencies of any European power we have not interfered and shall not interfere. But with the Governments who have declared their independence . . . we could not view any interposition for the purpose of oppressing them, or controlling in any other manner their destiny, by any European power in any other light than as the manifestation of an unholy disposition toward the United States.

The Monroe Doctrine was not purely or mainly an act of generosity toward the new Latin American republics. Instead, it was rooted in the United States' need to defend itself from repeated and troublesome interventions by the European powers. Especially threatening to the United States was the formation in 1815 of the so-called Holy Alliance by Russia, Austria, Prussia, and England. The purpose of the pact was to stamp out dangerous democratic movements in Europe and elsewhere. Monroe and some leaders in Latin America feared that the new alliance would encourage a new round of colonization in South America. Commercial interests in the United States were afraid that the potentially lucrative markets of South and Central America would be lost if the new republics there did not remain independent. Most leaders in Europe made fun of Monroe's statement, noting that the pretensions of the United States far outstripped the nation's military power.

Despite a great deal of skepticism among South American leaders, many responded eagerly and positively to Monroe's statement. Three of the new republics formally applied to the United States for assistance, and two of them sought formal military alliances. Secretary of State John Quincy Adams rebuffed all these entreaties. False hopes had been created and then dashed, reinforcing the initial view by some Latin American leaders that the motivation behind the doctrine was entirely self-interest. The original meaning of the Monroe Doctrine, lasting until about 1900, was essentially defensive, pledging the United States only to refrain from interfering in Europe's then existing colonies and dependencies and to defend the Western Hemisphere against outside threats. Later versions issued by Monroe's successors imparted a more positive, active, aggressive, and imperialistic meaning.

ECONOMIC EXPANSIONISM

Gradually, U.S. foreign policy began to lean toward economic expansionism. Securing access to valuable raw materials and to new markets for U.S.-made goods became important policy objectives. Commerce with other nations was important, because it increased profits and thereby allowed Americans to enjoy a higher standard of living than would otherwise have been possible. An inability to sell U.S. goods abroad would have a negative effect on the economic well-being of American citizens (even as is happening today). In the 1890s when the United States experienced a severe economic downturn, many believed that foreign commerce might relieve social unrest by increasing employment. It could also lead to influence abroad, including the spread of the American way of life, without the need for military engagement.[17]

Although economic expansionism became a higher priority in U.S. foreign policy toward developing nations in the 1890s, economic goals had always been an important part of foreign policy-making. From the earliest days of the republic, many foreign policy decisions, including all those involving the acquisition of new territory, were argued mainly in terms of economic costs and benefits. For example, in 1867 William Seward contended that the United States should purchase Alaska from Russia largely because of the lumber, furs, and mineral resources that could be extracted from it.[18] Although Congress went along with Seward's proposal, it did so reluctantly, because some thought it cost more that it ever would be worth. The *New York Herald* published this satirical advertisement in response to the proposal:

> CASH! CASH! CASH! Cash paid for cast off territory. Best price given for old colonies, North or South. Any impoverished monarchs retiring from the colonization business may find a good purchaser by addressing W.H.S. (Seward), Post Office, Washington, D.C.[19]

Indeed, after 1848 Congress rejected most opportunities for U.S. territorial expansion mainly on the basis of economic criteria.

In 1870 President Ulysses Grant unsuccessfully tried to convince the Senate to approve a treaty annexing the Dominican Republic, then known as San Domingo. His message to Congress on May 31 gives many economic reasons for his proposal:

> It [San Domingo] possesses the richest soil, best and most capacious harbors, most salubrious climate, and the most valuable products of the

forests, mine[s], and soil of any of the West India Islands. Its possession by us will in a few years build up a coastwise commerce of immense magnitude. . . . San Domingo will become a large consumer of the products of Northern farms and manufactories. . . . This will open to us a still wider market for our products.

In perhaps the most famous of all statements acknowledging U.S. foreign economic goals, Secretary of State John Hay, in an 1899 memorandum to several other European heads of state, announced that the United States expected the other major powers to keep an "open door"—meaning equal commercial opportunity—to a war-weakened China. By insisting on an "open door" policy in China, by inference for the first time free international trade became an officially stated U.S. foreign policy goal.

THE AFRICAN SLAVE TRADE

U.S. involvement outside the hemisphere was very limited until the Spanish-American War; it is therefore difficult to characterize U.S. foreign relations with developing nations in other regions. However, it is easy to imagine what the leaders of African nations thought about the central role of the American people and government as participants in the African slave trade. The problem the early European citizen-settlers faced was that land was plentiful, but workers were not. Labor was needed to clear and plow the fields, harvest the crops, and perform other tasks. Freemen could easily own land for themselves and were generally not interested in working for others. Nor could Native American Indians be enticed to work the land for the white settlers. As a result, some landowners turned to slavery as a practical, though morally reprehensible solution to their problem.[20] Private American citizens, especially but not solely in the South, provided a lucrative market for slave trading companies based in Europe. These companies either captured slaves or purchased them from others. The slaves were then transported to the United States under conditions so harsh that most did not reach their destination alive. M. J. Gujral estimates that for every one slave brought to the United States, five died during capture in Africa or on the high seas during transport.[21]

Slavery was a legal institution in all the colonies at the time of the Revolution. Until Lincoln's Emancipation Proclamation in 1863, the system of slavery was tolerated and recognized in many state and national laws and court decisions. Blacks were denied education by law in all the slave states and even in several Northern states. The penalties for violating this law were harsh for both slaves and their owners. In the landmark Dred

Scott decision in 1857, even the U.S. Supreme Court upheld the slaves' legal status as property that could be bought and sold rather than as human beings with inalienable rights.

By 1840 most European leaders had condemned slavery and, led by Britain, were trying to stop it by interdicting slave traders on the high seas. The British asked the United States to allow the British navy to search suspected slave-trading ships flying the U.S. flag, but the U.S. government, worried over a possible abuse of maritime rights, refused. Not until 1862, after the South seceded from the Union, did the United States relent. Thus, for more than 20 years, the United States was one of a very few nations in the world perceived as acting in support of the slave trade.[22]

This history is repugnant to most Americans today, but it is important to recall here, because it still affects perceptions of the American nation held by the leaders and people of the Third World, most of whom are not white. Some of them suspect that the conditions of slavery were as harsh as they were because the United States is a racist nation. As was discussed in the last chapter, even today some people believe that racism is an unstated motive behind much of the United States' behavior toward the Third World. Certainly, the noble ideals of the American creed and the notion of Manifest Destiny are tainted by the backdrop of slavery. Because of this early history of exploiting African tribes and people, any attempt by the U.S. government to provide moral leadership in resolving the conflict between whites and blacks in South Africa will be viewed by the rest of the world with great skepticism.

THE SPANISH-AMERICAN WAR

The end of the nineteenth century witnessed a revival of a nationalistic and imperialistic mood in the United States. No war had been fought since 1865 and no foreign war since the war with Mexico of 1848. Then, in reaction to what in retrospect appears to have been a minor provocation, the United States went to war with Spain in 1898. According to the joint congressional resolution that was the equivalent of a declaration of war against Spain in 1898, the war was to be fought on the side of Cuban nationals for liberation from their unjust colonial rulers. The joint resolution declared Cuba free of Spain; demanded the withdrawal of Spain; directed the president to use military force to achieve these ends; and disclaimed any intention on the part of the United States to annex Cuba. Reflecting the public sentiment of the times, the *New York Sun* reacted to this last provision by exclaiming: "For human lives and the liberty of human beings, for Cuba Libre; not for an extension of United States territory!"[23]

Historians have pointed to an economic motive for the war. Despite large investments of U.S. capital in Cuba in the 1880s and 1890s, U.S. exports to Cuba lagged far behind imports, because of restrictive Spanish laws. The war, therefore, presented an opportunity to impose new rules for trade that would be more favorable to U.S. businesses.[24] Significantly, the only loud voices heard against the war were raised by business leaders who feared that hostilities would slow economic growth, produce inflation, and unleash Spanish warships on their shipping. "We will have this war for the freedom of Cuba," shouted Theodore Roosevelt, shaking his fist at Senator Mark Hanna of Ohio, "in spite of the timidity of the commercial interests."[25]

But during the war with Spain, other Spanish colonies were attacked and occupied, including present-day Puerto Rico, Guam, the Philippines, and Wake Island. The United States could claim these islands as its own colonies or grant them their independence. A great moral debate ensued, which was even joined by the British poet, Rudyard Kipling, who, in "The White Man's Burden," urged the United States to become a colonial power.[26] Commercial interests within the United States also favored the annexation of former Spanish possessions including the Philippines, for these potential colonies presented many interesting possibilities for Eastern trade. But President William McKinley was not easily convinced. Waging a great moral debate with himself, he described his travail over what to do with the Philippine islands:

> The truth is I didn't want the Philippines and when they came to us as a gift from the gods, I did not know what to do with them. . . . And one night it came to me this way: . . . that we could not give them back to Spain — that would be cowardly and dishonorable; that we could not turn them over to France and Germany — our commercial rivals in the Orient — that would be bad business and discreditable; that we could not leave them to themselves — they were unfit for self-government. . . ; and that there was nothing left for us to do but to take them all, and to educate the Filipinos, and uplift and civilize and Christianize them, and by God's grace do the very best we could by them, as our fellow-men for whom Christ also had died.[27]

Whether the colonization of the Philippines was motivated more by U.S. notions of Manifest Destiny or the desire for an economic and naval base in the Orient is still a matter of debate.[28] McKinley was anxious to save the Filipinos by preparing them for self-government and by imparting to them Christian and American values. Unfortunately, the Filipino people were not so anxious to be saved. They had helped the United States in its war against Spain, expecting independence at its conclusion. When independence was not granted, they rose in revolt on February 4, 1899. For reasons historians cannot agree on, the United States was unwilling to extend the same self-denying guarantee to the Philippines it had given to Cuba.[29]

Even the militry campaign against Spain in the Philippines demonstrates the indecision of America's leaders. On May 2, 1898, President McKinley ordered U.S. forces to land on Manila. Commodore George Dewey of the U.S. navy informally allied his forces with those of the indigenous Filipino revolutionary movement against the Spanish. He did not object when Emilio Aguinaldo, the leader of that movement, proclaimed himself temporary dictator on May 24, announced the independence of the Philippines on June 12, and on June 24 arrogated to himself the position as first president of the new republic.[30] In contrast, General Wesley Merritt, commander of U.S. ground forces, who arrived on July 26, chose to work virtually independently of Aguinaldo in the fight against the Spanish forces. The Philippine War pitting the Americans against the Filipinos under the leadership of Aguinaldo began in February 1899, when it was clear that the Philippines would not be granted independence.

It lasted until 1903, although there were frequent outbreaks of anti-American violence until 1906.[31] From the beginning, U.S. newspapers had reported nasty accounts of American cruelties against the Filipinos, including allegations of torture, indiscriminate killing, and the butchery of entire villages. Congressional investigations into these allegations revealed that there was some barbaric behavior by U.S. soldiers, and some officers were court-martialed. The positions of anti-imperialists in the United States were strengthened by these revelations and by a growing public realization that the economic costs of colonialism exceeded the benefits.[32]

Critics of U.S. foreign policy point to the American experience in the Philippines and Cuba following the Spanish-American War as demonstrating the advantage of pursuing an economic expansionist (sometimes called neocolonial) strategy over a colonial strategy in the Third World. William Pomeroy notes that the neocolonial model fits Cuba where U.S.-based corporations gained a protected sphere of operation masked by a form of independence subject to U.S. intervention or control. Whereas colonialism, or the owning of colonies, required the colonizing country to take on substantial military burdens in return for questionable economic gains, neocolonialism was a strategy of overseas economic expansion maintained through superior U.S. production and competitiveness, through manipulation of tariffs, or, at most, through protectorates that implied less responsibility on the part of the colonizing country.[33]

The annexation of the Philippines as a U.S. colony in 1899 began a sordid period in the history of U.S. foreign relations with less developed countries. Although many scholars tend to shrug off the early U.S. policy toward the Philippines as a misguided, short-lived foray into colonialism, the episode continues to have significance in the making of U.S. foreign policy. The occupation of the Philippines, sometimes in the face of violent opposition from the Filipino people, established a justification for U.S. counterrevolution in the developing world that made future counterrevolutionary activity more palatable to the American people.

As a result of the conquest of Spain, in addition to the Philippines the United States took possession of Puerto Rico and Guam. The Hawaiian Islands also were annexed peacefully in 1898, as was the island of Tutuila in the Samoan archipelago, which contained the excellent Pago harbor, in 1899. Walter LaFeber has argued that U.S. control of these areas was a logical outgrowth of the search for new markets for goods produced ever more efficiently during the period of rapid industrialization and of the need for strategically located military bases.[34] Whether or not the new empire was indeed created reluctantly, by the end of the nineteenth century the United States had assumed "the white man's burden," joining the ranks of the other colonial powers.

THE GOALS: 1776–1900

During the first 125 years of its existence, the United States was a rapidly developing nation. It began its founding period as a weak, former colony, but, by the end of the nineteenth century it was among the ten most powerful countries in the world. The primary goals of U.S. foreign policy were to defend the new nation from external threats and to develop economically. Steady progress toward these goals allowed the United States to increase its power and influence in the world system and thereby to ensure its independence from more powerful states. In this sense, U.S. goals then were not much different from those of most other Third World states today. In order to achieve those goals, however, the U.S. government chose to use force against the Native American Indians, Mexico, Spain, and the Filipino people to impose U.S. control over territory formerly ruled by other weaker governments. The U.S. government then governed that territory over the objections of former governments or, in the case of the Philippines, over the objections of a potentially more legitimate one.

The issuance of the Monroe Doctrine, one of the most significant foreign policy statements ever made by a U.S. president, implied a willingness to use military force against other more formidable states, if provoked. Both the actions and the words served to deter aggression by the European powers of the day and also established the special foreign policy status of all developing countries in the Western Hemisphere. Even today, U.S. leaders place a higher priority on foreign policy outcomes in Latin America than in any other region of the world, with the possible exception of the Middle East.

Although elements of Exceptionalism were present in the notion of Manifest Destiny, U.S. leaders exhibited little concern about the welfare of people who were not citizens of the United States. Except for the debate over the taking of Spain's former colonies, most important foreign policy decisions were argued almost entirely on the basis of the probable costs and benefits to U.S. citizens. During these early years, the United States chose a foreign policy toward weaker states that was both Nationalist and expansionist.

The African slave trade must have raised suspicions in the developing world regarding the sincerity of American ideals. By the end of the nineteenth century, the United States' establishment of its first overseas colonies sent a clear message to developing countries that America wasn't so exceptional after all. By winning the Spanish-American War and by taking the Philippines and other previously Spanish possessions as its own colonies, the United States established itself as a middle-range military power and lost its special pro-revolution, anticolonial status in one stroke.

NOTES

1. George W. Grayson, "Anti-Americanism in Mexico," in Alvin Z. Rubinstein and Donald E. Smith, eds., *Anti-Americanism in the Third World* (New York: Praeger Publishers, 1985), pp. 31–48.

2. Dexter Perkins, *The Evolution of American Foreign Policy,* 2nd ed. (New York: Oxford University Press, 1966), p. 27.

3. See M. H. Savelle, "Colonial Origins of American Diplomatic Principles," *Pacific Historical Review* 3 (1934): 334–350.

4. *Messages and Papers of the Presidents* (New York: Bureau of National Literature, 1912), I, 221–222.

5. Ibid., p. 214.

6. Ibid., p. 215.

7. Walter LaFeber, *The New Empire* (Ithaca, N.Y.: Cornell University Press, 1963).

8. Walter Lippmann, *U.S. Foreign Policy: Shield of the Republic* (Boston: Little, Brown, 1943), pp. 13–15.

9. Quoted in Thomas G. Paterson, ed., *Major Problems in American Foreign Policy Volume I: To 1914* (Lexington, Mass.: D. C. Heath and Co., 1989), p. 238.

10. Reprinted in M. L. Gujral, *U.S. Global Involvement: A Study of American Expansionism* (New Delhi, India: Arnold Heinemann Publishers, 1975), pp. 38–39.

11. Ibid., p. 40.

12. G. K. Chesterton, *What I Saw in America* (Hodder and Stoughton, 1922). See also Samuel P. Huntington, *American Politics: The Promise of Disharmony* (Cambridge, Mass.: Belknap Press, 1981).

13. *Annals of Congress,* 12th Congress, 1st session, I, 657 (January 4, 1812).

14. Calvin Colton, ed., *The Works of Henry Clay* (Federal ed.; New York, 1904), VI, 140 (March 24, 1818).

15. Robert L. Beisner, *From the Old Diplomacy to the New, 1865–1900* (New York: Crowel, 1975).

16. *Messages and Papers of the Presidents* (New York: Bureau of National Literature, 1912), I, 215 (December 2, 1823).

17. Thomas G. Paterson, J. Garry Clifford, and Kenneth J. Hagen, *American Foreign Policy: A History,* 3rd ed. (Lexington, Mass.: D. C. Heath and Co., 1988), I, 156–163, 178–182.

18. Of course, Seward and others also favored the purchase of Alaska because it offered a strategic location for control of the Pacific basin. On this point, see Walter LaFeber, *The New Empire: An Interpretation of American Expansion 1860–1898* (Ithaca, N.Y.: Cornell University Press, 1963), pp. 28–29.

19. *New York Herald* 6:5, April 12, 1867.

20. Gujral, *U.S. Global Involvement,* pp. 46–51.

21. Ibid., p. 48.

22. Thomas A. Bailey, *A Diplomatic History of the American People,* 8th ed. (New York: Appleton-Century-Crofts, 1969), pp. 215–216.

23. *New York Sun,* 6:2, March 25, 1898.

24. David M. Pletcher, "Rhetoric and Results: A Pragmatic View of American Economic Expansion, 1865–1898," *Diplomatic History* 5 (Spring 1981): 93–104.

25. H. F. Pringle, *Theodore Roosevelt* (New York: Harcourt Brace Jovanovich, 1931), p. 179.

26. See Rudyard Kipling, *Rudyard Kipling's Verse* (New York: Doubleday, Page and Co., 1920), pp. 371–372.

27. *Christian Advocate* (New York), January 22, 1903.

28. For an account of that debate in the first part of the twentieth century, see Grayson L. Kirk, *Philippine Independence: Motives, Problems, and Prospects* (New York: Farrar and Rinehart, 1936).

29. Bailey, *A Diplomatic History,* p. 478.

30. Brian McAllister Linn, *The U.S. Army and Counterinsurgency in the Philippine War, 1899–1902* (Chapel Hill: University of North Carolina Press, 1989), p. 7.

31. For an eyewitness account, see James H. Blount, *American Occupation of the Philippines 1898–1912* (New York: G. P. Putnam's Sons, 1913).

32. William J. Pomeroy, *American Neo-Colonialism: Its Emergence in the Philippines and Asia* (New York: International Publishers, 1970).

33. Ibid., pp. 219–228.

34. LaFeber, *The New Empire,* pp. 407–417.

CHAPTER 6

Dominance (and Democracy) in the Western Hemisphere

During the period between the endings of the Spanish-American and Second World wars, American foreign policy toward the Third World focused almost exclusively on developments in Central America and the Caribbean, where U.S. leaders were willing to resort to military intervention to achieve their objectives. Elsewhere in the Third World, the United States mainly engaged in a policy of noninvolvement. The emphasis on relations with Central America and the Caribbean, accompanied as it was by numerous military expeditions, gave new meaning to the Monroe Doctrine of 1823. The two key foreign policy achievements during the period were the establishment of Central America and the Caribbean as a "Europe-free" zone firmly within the U.S. sphere of influence and the building of the Panama Canal.

In the process, the goal of economic expansionism took on greater importance relative to other foreign policy initiatives. Although no further territorial expansion took place and no new colonies were taken, economic foreign policy objectives were proclaimed repeatedly and unabashedly. President William Howard Taft and his secretary of state, Philander C. Knox, took an active role in encouraging the investment of U.S. companies in the Third World, protecting investments already made there, and promoting trade with less developed states. Taft's administration contended that these policies were mutually beneficial to the United States and to the target states as well. Most of his successors have tried to distance themselves from the negative imagery of the Taft administration's "dollar diplomacy," but many have simply pursued similar objectives more quietly.

Significantly, Theodore Roosevelt and some of his successors exercised the right of military intervention to accomplish economic and other U.S. foreign policy goals in the name of morality. He believed that a nation had a right and obligation to act to prevent "chronic wrongdoing" by other states. In Latin America, because of proximity and the Monroe Doctrine, that "international police power" fell to the United States. Elsewhere in the world, preventing chronic wrongdoing was the responsibility of other major powers. Many Central American and Caribbean states must have done wrong, because U.S. military interventions designed to change the behavior of their governments were both frequent and long lasting. Significant troop landings during this period occurred in Cuba, the Dominican Republic, Haiti, Mexico, Nicaragua, and Panama. All these states are geographically proximate to the U.S. mainland. The United States used military force to prevent less developed countries from defaulting on their international debts, to ensure political stability, to support democratic processes, to secure military base rights, to acquire access to seaports, to prevent weaker countries from choosing "unacceptable" leaders, and to stop less powerful countries from expropriating the assets of U.S.-based corporations without adequate compensation to the owners.

Theodore Roosevelt's (1901–1909) "big stick" or "gunboat diplomacy" in Latin America is now legendary. He had a keen interest in international relations and had been an advocate of an interventionist U.S. foreign policy throughout his public life. Roosevelt was succeeded by William Howard Taft (1909–1913), who, coming from a corporate background, shifted the emphasis in foreign policy from military to economic expansionism, still with a focus on developing countries. Woodrow Wilson (1913–1921) found Taft's dollar diplomacy to be repugnant, but he discovered his own moralistic reasons for continued intervention into the internal affairs of Latin American countries. In contrast to the policies pursued by Theodore Roosevelt, Taft, and Wilson, the next three presidents, Warren Harding (1921–1923), Calvin Coolidge (1923–1929), and Herbert Hoover (1929–1933), tried to avoid using military force in the Third World. By the time Franklin Roosevelt captured the presidency (1933–1945), the great depression at home and the onset of the Second World War diverted the attention of his administration away from relations with Third World republics.

THEODORE ROOSEVELT AND BIG STICK DIPLOMACY: 1901–1909

Roosevelt was especially quick to use force to accomplish U.S. foreign policy objectives against weaker states. At the high point of big stick diplomacy in 1907, he sent a fleet of battleships around the world with great fanfare to brandish U.S. naval power. Some historians have criticized Roosevelt for his extreme rhetoric and his penchant for foreign interventionism.[1] However, many presidents of this period shared his morally patronizing view of weaker governments in the Western Hemisphere. In many ways, he and Woodrow Wilson reflected the reform era of American politics, especially the reformer's notion that noble ends sometimes justified the use of ignoble means.

In 1901 Britain, then the world's foremost military power, agreed to permit the United States to build, control, and fortify a canal through the Isthmus of Panama. When Colombia, which then contained the territory currently known as the state of Panama, objected to the terms, the United States encouraged and aided an independence movement by the people in the proposed canal region. Then, in an unprecedented move, the Roosevelt administration recognized the new republic of Panama three days after the revolt began. Negotiations to build the canal then proceeded smoothly with the newly recognized government.[2] A wounded Colombian government repeatedly asked the United States to submit the affair to international arbitration, but the United States refused.

Roosevelt claimed that the United States supported the Panamanian revolution, because Colombia had not honored its obligations under a treaty signed in 1896; had not prevented "revolutions, riots, and factional disturbances of every kind" in the state of Panama, then under its jurisdiction; and could not maintain order in the state of Panama without the assistance of the United States. Furthermore, Roosevelt argued that building an interoceanic canal would advance the national interest of the United States, Colombia, and the rest of the world. The Colombian government, on the other hand, contended that the only reason the United States supported the Panamanian revolution was that it was a quick and easy way to achieve U.S. foreign policy objectives at the expense of a weaker state.[3]

By the time Panama was secured as a site for the new interoceanic canal, the United States already had a good start on establishing its power over other nations in Central America as well. Puerto Rico had become a U.S. protectorate as a result of the treaty ending the Spanish-American War. Although the United States had promised not to annex Cuba, it soon asserted its right to intervene in Cuba under a wide range of circumstances.

The Platt Amendment, placing restrictions on Cuban independence, was passed by the U.S. Senate in 1901 as a rider to an army appropriations bill. In 1903 it was incorporated into a treaty with Cuba. A good example of U.S.-imposed constraints on Cuban independence, it prohibited Cuba from entering into any arrangement with a foreign power that might endanger its independence or from contracting any debt beyond its resources. It also permitted the United States to buy or lease naval stations. Cuba was required to incorporate these provisions into its constitution as a condition for the evacuation of U.S. troops from the island at the end of the Spanish-American War. These stipulations also became part of a U.S. treaty signed in 1903. The provision allowing the United States to establish a naval station was invoked in 1904, when the United States built an important base in Cuba's Guantanamo Bay.[4]

The United States' motives were not entirely selfish. During the military occupation, the United States helped establish a democratic system of government in Cuba and tried to assist the development of the Cuban economy. In 1902, after urging sharply reduced tariffs on Cuban imports to help stimulate U.S.-Cuban trade, Roosevelt explained the special relationship between Cuba and the United States:

> Cuba is so near to us that we can never be indifferent to misgovernment and disaster within its limits. . . . We have rightfully insisted upon Cuba adopting toward us an attitude differing politically from that she adopts toward any other power; and in return, as a matter of right, we must give to Cuba a different—that is, a better—position economically in her relations with us than we give to other powers. . . . We are a wealthy and a powerful country, dealing with a much weaker one; and the contrast in wealth and strength makes it all the more our duty to deal with Cuba, as we already dealt with her, in a spirit of large generosity.[5]

Despite limited U.S. assistance, the Cuban economy continued to deteriorate. In 1905 an insurrection began against the Cuban government headed by President Tomás Estrada Palma. In 1906, after diplomatic efforts to end the conflict had failed, the U.S. military intervened to reestablish order and to support the constitutionally elected government. The insurgents and the government militia quickly surrendered their arms, and order was restored. The U.S. occupation lasted a little over two years.

Many Latin American republics had borrowed heavily from the United States and many European states to wage war, construct railroads and other infrastructure, develop natural resources, build capital-intensive projects, and provide concessions to U.S.-based corporations. Some of these purposes were legitimate, whereas others allowed unscrupulous government leaders to loot, pillage, and exploit their own countries. Defaulting on debts became commonplace. Lending states became impatient and threatened to collect debts by force if necessary. But, if the principle of the Monroe Doctrine was to be maintained, the United States could not permit European intervention in Latin America.

The problem was exacerbated by a decision of the Court of International Justice at the Hague in 1904 which encouraged the use of force by creditor nations. The decision came in response to a 1902 military action by Germany, Great Britain, and Italy to collect debts by force. The action included a blockade of Venezuelan ports for three months, bombardment of coastal forts, and the sinking of some Venezuelan vessels. Roosevelt was instrumental in getting the European powers to submit the issue to the Hague for adjudication. The court decided that Venezuela had to pay its debts and that first claim on Venezuela's assets should go to those states that had sent military expeditions, not to the other creditor states which had not. In this way the court rewarded the use of force by powerful states against a weaker state.

Seeking to prevent more military expeditions of this type in the Western Hemisphere, Roosevelt and later U.S. administrations began to take a keener interest in the financial affairs of Latin American republics. Partly in response to this court decision, Theodore Roosevelt formalized his own position on the circumstances warranting intervention by the United States into Latin American affairs. Expanding the Monroe Doctrine, he argued that the United States was justified when it intervened into the affairs of Latin American states for purposes of righting a long list of things the United States defined as wrong:

> All that this country desires is to see the neighboring countries stable, orderly, and prosperous. Any country whose people conduct themselves well can count upon our hearty friendship. If a nation shows that it knows how to act with reasonable efficiency in social and political matters, if it keeps order and pays its obligations, it need fear no interference from the United States. Chronic wrongdoing, or an impotence which results in a general loosening of the ties of civilized society, may in America, as elsewhere, ultimately require intervention by some civilized nation and in the Western Hemisphere the adherence of the United States to the Monroe Doctrine may force the United States, however reluctantly, in flagrant cases of such wrongdoing or impotence, to the exercise of an international police power.[6]

With this statement, failure to pay debts owed to European states became a sufficient justification for U.S. military intervention into the internal affairs of weaker states in Latin America, not just for Roosevelt but for many of his successors as well.

Roosevelt used these newly asserted powers against the Dominican Republic, which formally recognized a debt to European powers in 1904 totaling $18 million but was in financial ruins and could not pay it.[7] Fearing European intervention and internal insurrection, President Carlos Morales requested that the United States develop a plan for the payment of Santo Domingo's international debts and take control of the country's major revenue source, the customshouses, to ensure that the plan would be implemented. Roosevelt accepted the invitation in January 1905. But there was much opposition to this highly unusual arrangement in the U.S. Senate, and it continued until February 1907 when a formal treaty was finally ratified. For a little over two years, U.S. warships patrolled Dominican waters to prevent European intervention and internal insurrection, and U.S. agents administered the customshouses. By the end of the agreement in July 1907, the financial affairs of the republic were much improved, but the Dominican Republic was well within the United States' orbit of power, answerable for its conduct to its giant northern neighbor.

TAFT AND DOLLAR DIPLOMACY: 1909-1913

Taft was less flamboyant than Roosevelt. He believed that the United States should devote less of its energies to military exploits and more to becoming a world economic power. As noted earlier, his foreign policy became known as dollar diplomacy. It consisted of three parts: protecting existing U.S. financial interests in other nations from threats, encouraging the investment of U.S. capital in developing countries, and establishing foreign markets for U.S.-made goods.

The first part of the policy, protecting the investments made by U.S.-based corporations abroad, is not particularly controversial and can be traced back to other administrations. What is distinctive is the strong emphasis Taft placed on this objective and his administration's acknowledgment of an official U.S. government role in encouraging private investments in less developed countries and in promoting sales for U.S. corporations. Taft was the first president to contend that a partnership between U.S.-based corporations abroad and the national government was necessary to the achievement of U.S. foreign policy objectives.

Taft and Secretary of State Knox may have believed that dollar diplomacy was beneficial to developing nations as well as to the U.S. government and to the private commercial and financial institutions the government represented. Dollar diplomacy was not exploitation, they contended. Knox, in defense of the policy, declared in 1911:

> If the American dollar can aid suffering humanity and lift the burden of financial difficulty from States with which we live on terms of intimate intercourse and earnest friendship, and replace insecurity and devastation by stability and peaceful self-development, all I can say is that it would be hard to find better employment.[8]

On the darker side, however, the policy was used to justify high-pressure salesmanship to induce certain Latin American countries to buy battleships from private American yards and strong-arm tactics to convince certain Central American and Caribbean nations to keep out non-American foreign investments. The Taft administration tried unsuccessfully to develop and implement a plan refinancing the international debts of Honduras and Guatemala. In 1910 Knox met with several New York bankers in a successful attempt to promote greater U.S. investment in Haiti. The leaders and people of almost all Latin American nations deeply resented these maneuvers as unwarranted Yankee interference into their internal affairs.

Although Taft deemphasized the use of force to achieve U.S. goals, his administration did send troops into Nicaragua and continued the financial supervision of the Dominican Republic. Furthermore, perhaps because of the existence of a new, U.S.-built Panama Canal, Taft and Knox embraced the Roosevelt corollary to the Monroe Doctrine. In a New York speech Knox said:

> The logic of political geography and of strategy, and now our tremendous national interest created by the Panama Canal, make the safety, the peace, and the prosperity of Central America and the zone of the Caribbean of paramount interest to the Government of the United States. Thus the malady of revolutions and financial collapse is most acute precisely in the region where it is most dangerous to us.[9]

Following the 1909 revolution in Nicaragua, the country suffered much instability and was in financial ruin. Knox would not tolerate the situation and insisted on a three-part stabilization plan similar to the one the Roosevelt administration had used a few years earlier in the Dominican Republic. First, the finances of the country would be reorganized. Second, the customshouses, traditionally centers of corruption, would be supervised by U.S. officials. Finally, Washington would not recognize the new Nicaraguan government until it had arranged for a large loan from U.S. bankers with which it could pay the debt it owed Britain. When the Nicaraguan public opposed these measures, a U.S. warship arrived on the scene. Compliance with Washington's dictates soon followed.[10]

The United States continued to push for greater control over the financial affairs of the Nicaraguan government, and, partly as a result, widespread disorder erupted again in 1912. Taft ordered 2,500 marines to intervene in order to protect American lives and property. Although most of the troops were withdrawn within a few months, a small force remained until 1925.

THE IDEALISM OF WOODROW WILSON: 1913-1921

Wilson, the first Democrat in the White House since 1897, succeeded Taft in 1913 and promptly disavowed dollar diplomacy as catering to the monied interests in the United States and as immoral. The following passage illustrates his disapproval of the goals of dollar diplomacy:

If American enterprise in foreign countries, particularly in those foreign countries which are not strong enough to resist us, takes the shape of imposing upon and exploiting the mass of the people of that country it ought to be checked and not encouraged. I am willing to get anything for an American that money and enterprise can obtain except the suppression of the rights of other men. I will not help any man buy a power which he ought not to exercise over his fellow-beings.[11]

Instead, Wilson championed a curious strategy of interventionism in developing countries in the name of morality. Wilson was an outspoken critic of imperialism, yet as president he ordered more military actions in Latin America than any other president. He resorted to force against Mexico, Haiti, the Dominican Republic, Cuba, and Panama.[12] He was a self-proclaimed reformer, an advocate of the common man against the rich and the powerful, and he applied this reformist zeal to international affairs. Although his goals were essentially Progressive, his approach was so ethnocentric, blind to the uniqueness of other cultures, and impatient, that his foreign policy initiatives also were deeply resented by the leaders and peoples of Latin America.

He was equally committed to upholding Roosevelt's strong version of the Monroe Doctrine and to lending a helping hand to the revolution-cursed republics of the region. Wilson clarified his Latin American policy in 1913 by asserting:

We dare not turn from the principle that morality and not expediency is the thing that must guide us and that we will never condone iniquity because it is most convenient to do so. . . . It is a very perilous thing to determine the foreign policy of a nation in terms of material interest. It not only is unfair to those with whom you are dealing, but is degrading as regards your own actions.[13]

Although most Latin American nations resented Yankee meddling in their internal affairs, some also responded positively to Wilson's leadership during World War I, the war Wilson said would make the world "safe for democracy." Seven republics remained nominally neutral; eight declared war on Germany; none supported Germany. U.S. prestige in Latin America rose during the war, but it declined there and elsewhere in the developing world when the United States refused to join the League of Nations after the war ended.

Some historians have praised Wilson for elevating considerations of morality and idealism to a more important position in U.S. foreign policy rhetoric. However, his most courageous and morally admirable positions were designed primarily to prevent future wars among the major powers.

Specifically, he is respected for his public pronouncement of Fourteen Points which, he contended, were necessary to ensure a just and lasting peace following the First World War and for his special passion to implement the fourteenth point calling for the formation of a League of Nations. In relations with Latin America, only rhetoric set him apart from Theodore Roosevelt. Roosevelt popularized the African proverb, "speak softly, but carry a big stick." In contrast, Wilson had a penchant for moral castigation first and, then if that did not work, wielding the big stick later.

In an episode reminiscent of recent U.S. policy toward Panama, Wilson refused to recognize General Victoriano Huerta, the leader of a successful revolution in Mexico in 1913, as that country's legitimate leader. Wilson regarded Huerta as having usurped power and as being unprincipled and unworthy. In order to destabilize his regime, Washington adopted a policy toward Mexico of nonrecognition, moral castigation, and diplomatic quarantine. When the Huerta government survived despite this challenge, the Wilson administration stepped up its sanctions, culminating in the military occupation of the port of Veracruz in April 1914. Although the immediate provocation for this intervention was unclear, Wilson, speaking "off the record" at a press conference, later said:

> We got Huerta. That was the end of Huerta. That was what I had in mind. It could not be done without taking Veracruz. It could not be done without taking some decisive step—to show the Mexican people that he was all bluff, . . . Now, Huerta was not the Mexican people. He did not represent any part of them. . . . He was nothing but a "plug ugly," working for himself.[14]

The fall of Huerta set off a power struggle within Mexico.

When Venustiano Carranza emerged as the strongest of several rivals, Washington recognized his government. Pancho Villa, an incensed rival, incited his followers to murder several Americans living in Mexico and led a surprise attack on Columbus, New Mexico, in March 1916. Since the Carranza government did not sanction this raid, it was essentially an act of terrorism against the United States by a political group based in Mexico. Wilson, convinced that the new Carranza government could not respond effectively to this act of terrorism, decided to send in a small military force to pursue Villa, capture him, and disperse his organization.

The Carranza government was outraged by yet another U.S. military intervention. Several minor clashes erupted between Mexican citizens and authorities and the U.S. troops led by General John Pershing during the year-long search for Villa. Pershing requested more troops and the declaration of full-scale war with Mexico. Wilson steadfastly rejected expanding the conflict, finally calling Pershing and his troops home as troubles with Germany increased.

Like Roosevelt before him, Wilson had little patience with instability in Latin America. When the Dominican Republic's president was assassinated in 1911, a prolonged period of violence, economic paralysis, and political instability began, which again strained that patience. His administration threatened economic and diplomatic reprisals if the revolt against the Bordas government, recognized by the United States as the legitimate government of the Dominican Republic, did not end. In negotiations between the Bordas government and its opponents, the U.S. ambassador made an unprecedented promise that U.S. observers would monitor the next election to ensure that it was fair. The elections were held with U.S. observers and with few problems threatening fundamental fairness, but unrest and violence resumed and continued. Support for the Bordas government dropped to a dangerous level. Wilson responded in 1914 with a three-step plan. First, everyone should cease hostilities and disband their forces. Second, he ordered the warring factions to agree on a responsible person to act as provisional president until elections could be held. If the factions could not agree, the United States would select someone. However selected, the provisional president would not be a candidate for the position in the election. The United States would ensure proper elections and would recognize the winner as the leader of the government. If the elections were not properly conducted, they would be held again. Finally, Wilson insisted that all revolutionary movements cease and that future changes in government occur only through peaceful means.[15]

The plan was implemented over President José Bordas's objections, and Juan Isidro Jimenez was elected as the new president. But revolutionary activity against his administration began almost immediately. Problems were compounded when the Dominican Republic encountered new financial difficulties and the Wilson administration insisted on greater control over that nation's finances. This insistence provided a rallying point for forces opposing the Jimenez government and spurred anti-American sentiments. In May 1916, U.S. troops were sent to restore order and put down the revolution. Declaring martial law, U.S. officials managed the country's finances, restored law and order, and attempted to impose proper methods of democratic government. The last of the marines did not leave the Dominican Republic until 1924.

There are many parallels between the action-forcing events in the Dominican Republic and the U.S. response to them and developments in nearby Haiti during the same period. Frederick Calhoun describes U.S. foreign policy goals in Haiti as focusing on maintaining access to a natural harbor on the sea lanes to the Panama Canal, prohibiting foreign powers from gaining influence over the Haitian government, establishing U.S. control over Haitian financial affairs, and promoting the establishment of U.S.-style political institutions.[16]

After a prolonged period of political instability, difficulties in paying international debts, and violence threatening the lives and property of U.S. citizens and other foreigners in Haiti, Wilson insisted on implementing a plan that was very similar to the one he had used in the Dominican Republic. It called for a U.S.-supervised election with no revolutionary activity to be tolerated after its conclusion. The plan did not work. Conditions continued to deteriorate, and in July 1915 Wilson ordered the military to intervene. This was the longest and perhaps the ugliest of all U.S. interventions in Latin America. The occupation lasted until 1934, and there were numerous allegations of wrongdoing by the occupying forces. One of the lessons observers drew from this and other long U.S. occupations in Central America is that they rarely end well. Since Haiti had a higher percentage of blacks than any of the other nations where the United States had intervened militarily, there were even racist overtones to the whole incident.

In 1917 Wilson sent troops to Cuba to protect American lives and property during an insurrection and subsequent unsettled conditions. Some troops remained until 1922. In 1918, facing similar circumstances, he sent troops to Panama to help prevent election disturbances and to maintain order during the subsequent period of unsettled conditions. The troops were brought home in 1920.

REPUDIATION OF INTERVENTIONISM: 1921–1945

In 1921 President Warren Harding assumed office, beginning a 12-year period of Republican control of the White House. By then, Haiti, the Dominican Republic, Panama, and Cuba were firmly within the United States' orbit of influence. Like William Taft, Harding, Coolidge, and Hoover were committed to encouraging U.S. investment in Latin America and to creating markets there for U.S.-made goods. Since 1903, there had been eight major military interventions into Latin American countries, or an average of about one every other year. In addition, between 1901 and 1933 there were 23 minor troop incursions of less than one year.[17] Partly because of adverse public reaction to interventionist policies both in the United States and throughout most of Latin America, the United States made only one more large-scale military intervention in Latin America between 1921 and the end of the Second World War, this time to deal with continuing political instability in Nicaragua.

In 1925 the marines left Nicaragua after a 13-year presence there, but almost immediately after their departure a revolution began against the conservative Diaz government. Coolidge ordered the marines to return in 1926 in order, he claimed, to support the constitutionally elected government of Adolfo Diaz, to maintain stability in the canal region, and to protect the United States from the advance of Bolshevism. Contesting this explanation, Senator Burton Wheeler, in a 1927 speech, claimed that the real reason for the intervention was to allow more profitable investments for U.S.-based banks in Nicaragua. In 1927 the United States convinced both sides to put down their arms and submit the issue to a U.S.-supervised election. That election in 1928 paved the way for General Anastasio Somoza Garcia to assume power. Political power remained in the hands of the Somoza family until 1979 when the Sandinista National Liberation Front forced the last of the Somozas to flee to Paraguay. In 1980 General Anastasio Somoza was killed by unknown assailants in a bazooka attack on his limousine.[18]

Relations with Mexico had been deteriorating since 1917, when a reform Constitution was ratified containing a provision nationalizing subsoil property rights. In 1925 President Plutarco Calles announced that the provision was being applied retroactively to expropriate foreign-owned property in Mexico. U.S. oil companies were alarmed and lobbied hard for forceful U.S. intervention to protect their alleged rights. By 1927 the Coolidge administration had diffused the conflict by negotiating a compromise with the government of Mexico: henceforth only those U.S. companies that had begun to develop their subsoil properties in Mexico before 1917 would retain ownership.[19] Understandably, this whole conflict took on added significance, because some U.S. policymakers viewed developments in Mexico as additional evidence of the relentless advance of Bolshevism, which had begun with the Russian Revolution of 1917.

With the crash of the American stock market in 1929 and the ensuing economic depression, U.S. leaders turned their attention from foreign affairs and toward more pressing domestic problems. Though preoccupied with severe economic problems at home, Hoover took a number of steps designed to soothe U.S.–Latin American relations. Perhaps most importantly, he renounced the use of military force to achieve U.S. objectives in Latin America. He ended the U.S. occupation of Nicaragua ordered by Coolidge by withdrawing the approximately 1,600 marines still there, and he developed a plan for withdrawing 700 marines from Haiti, a plan that was implemented by Franklin D. Roosevelt in 1933. Finally, when faced with a troubled situation in Cuba, Hoover refused to use U.S. military force to restore order.

During his term of office, Hoover also distanced himself from

Wilson's policy of using nonrecognition of a foreign government as a weapon. During his administration, two policies on diplomatic recognition were followed — one for the republics of Central America and one for all other governments in Latin America. With regard to the republics of Central America, Hoover agreed to abide by a Pan-American treaty ratified in 1923. The treaty provided that governments coming into power through a coup d'etat or revolution against a recognized government should not be recognized unless and until freely elected representatives of the people had participated in a constitutional reorganization. It was observed in the case of revolutions in Guatemala in 1930 and El Salvador in 1931, but it was renounced by the signatories in 1934.[20] With regard to other republics in Latin America, Hoover returned to the pre-Wilson policy of recognizing any government that could demonstrate control over the country and an ability and willingness to fulfill the country's international obligations. These new policies of diplomatic recognition effectively halted the use of nonrecognition as a means of interfering in the internal affairs of weaker Latin American states.[21]

Concerned about antagonisms resulting from Taft's dollar diplomacy started by Taft and continued by other presidents, Hoover explained in a public address that it had never been and ought not to be the United States' policy to intervene by force in order to uphold a contract between a U.S. company and a foreign state or between a U.S. company and a foreign citizen.[22] He urged that U.S. government policies guaranteeing foreign economic investments and U.S. bank loans abroad should be restricted to projects that would improve living standards, increase consumer consumption, and contribute to social stability. Hoover discouraged loans designed to increase military expenditures in target states, to balance spendthrift budgets, and to prop up weak currencies.[23] But U.S. corporate interests and important members of his own administration opposed these and other Progressive views. Partly because of opposition from the business community, he vetoed a bill that would have granted independence to the Philippines.

Franklin Roosevelt, the first Democrat to occupy the White House since Woodrow Wilson, assumed office in January 1933. Preoccupied with deepening economic depression at home and increasing conflict among the world's major powers, he paid relatively little attention to relations with Third World states. In 1934 his administration supported a bill that would give the Philippines its independence after a ten-year transition period. The other colonial powers objected to this provision, viewing it as a dangerous precedent. Independence for the Philippines was delayed by the war but was formally granted in 1946. Philippine independence marked the end of the colonial period in U.S. history, begun in 1898.

The second modern war among the world's major powers broke out in 1939, a war that the United States soon joined. During this conflict, many leaders of Latin American republics feared a new round of colonization, this time by the Axis powers. This fear was fueled by Italy's conquest of Ethiopia in 1935, as part of Benito Mussolini's attempt to restore the glories of the Roman Empire.

Delegates of the 21 republics of the Pan-American Union met in Havana in 1940, to discuss Latin American defenses. Two thirds of these delgates signed an agreement pledging mutual defense if any republic was in danger of occupation by an Axis power and allowing individual nations like the United States to intervene unilaterally, if necessary, to prevent such occupation.[24] This remarkable compact can be interpreted as a "multilateralization" of the Monroe Doctrine. At least temporarily, a common external threat helped create better relations between the United States and its neighbors in Latin America.

U.S.-Mexican relations were a notable exception, however. Conflict with Mexico was again inflamed in 1938, when the Mexican government reversed itself and expropriated U.S. oil properties on Mexican soil. The oil companies demanded $260 million in compensation, but the compromise worked out with the active diplomatic assistance of the U.S. government in 1941 only provided for a payment of $42 million. The interests of U.S.-based corporations were protected to some degree, but, even allowing for some exaggeration in the claims of the oil companies, some of their resources were sacrificed. The United States clearly wanted to avoid military intervention and thereby maintain a semblance of good relations with its neighbor.

THE GOALS: 1900–1945

On balance, the record indicates that U.S. foreign policy during this 45-year period was confined mainly to the pursuit of narrowly defined national self-interest, often at the expense of weaker neighbors in Central America. All the presidents during this period were Nationalists except Woodrow Wilson, who, more than any of the others, recognized that the U.S. government had responsibilities to protect the welfare of people living beyond its own borders. He championed the formation of a League of Nations to uphold those responsibilities even at the expense of his own political career. Moreover, according to a majority of the members of the U.S. Senate, Wilson pursued the formation of the League even though, in their opinion, the League damaged the United States' national self-interest. Because of his interventionist proclivities, Wilson is probably best categorized as an Exceptionalist rather than as a Progressive. Franklin Roosevelt, though best categorized as a Nationalist, was also different from the other presidents of this period in that he took the first steps toward recognizing the Philippines as an independent nation.

The granting of independence to the Philippines was one of the most significant developments in U.S.-Third World relations during the first half of the twentieth century. The other important foreign policy achievements during the period were the consolidation of U.S. power over Latin America and the construction of the Panama Canal. The hierarchy of objectives pursued through U.S. foreign policy toward the Third World are perhaps best illustrated by the circumstances under which the United States resorted to the use of force.

Military interventions were frequently used to influence the internal affairs of Central American and Caribbean governments between 1901 and 1933. Table 6.1 lists the reasons given for these military interventions as publicly proclaimed by U.S. presidents or by their secretaries of state or as generally attributed in historical accounts. The ordering of U.S. priorities in Table 6.1 reflects my own estimates after reading several historical accounts of each intervention. The occupation of Cuba is included, even though it occurred before 1901, because U.S. troops remained in Cuba until 1902, when the Roosevelt administration had extracted certain guarantees from the Cuban government safeguarding U.S. economic and military interests.

As shown in Table 6.1, most interventions were preceded by political instability, which was usually caused by a revolution against the constitutionally established government, often a government elected by the people. Several interventions were also preceded by the U.S. leaders' concern that a Central American or Caribbean state would default on its debts to one of the major powers in Europe. Either situation — political instability or default on debt — might have prompted one of the European powers to intervene in Western Hemispherie affairs, a development none of the U.S. presidents during this period would have tolerated. Most of the United States' actions during this period were directed at preventing such interference.

Because of the existence of political instability and volatility, the protection of U.S. lives and property could have been listed in Table 6.1 as a reason for every U.S. intervention, with the possible exceptions of the invasion of Cuba and the Philippines during the Spanish-American War. Revolutions are by definition violent, so, in each case, they create the potential for violence against U.S. citizens and for the destruction of their property. But historical accounts of U.S. interventions during this period generally do not justify the use of this rationale for U.S. military

TABLE 6.1
Significant Military Interventions in Central America, 1901-1945,
and U.S. Policy Priorities

Year	Country	U.S. Priorities
1898-1902	Cuba	(1) Liberate Cuba from Spanish rule. (2) Secure the right to build military bases. (3) Prevent default on foreign debts. (4) Promote democracy.
1903-1914	Panama	(1) Secure an agreement to build the Panama Canal. (2) Protect U.S. lives and property during the war of independence from Colombia and construction of the Panama Canal.
1906-1909	Cuba	(1) Support the constitutionally elected government against a revolution.
1912-1925	Nicaragua	(1) Prevent default on foreign debts. (2) Prevent an attempted revolution. (3) Remain to assure stability.
1914-1919	Mexico	(1) Destabilize the Huerta regime. (2) Retaliate against terrorism and attempt to apprehend the terrorist, Villa.
1915-1934	Haiti	(1) Prevent default on foreign debts. (2) Maintain access to a seaport. (3) Promote the establishment of democracy.
1916-1924	Dominican Republic	(1) Support the constitutionally elected government against a revolution. (2) Maintain democracy. (3) Prevent default on foreign debts.
1917-1922	Cuba	(1) Support the constitutionally elected government against a revolution. (2) Maintain democracy. (3) Protect U.S. lives and the investments of U.S.-based MNCs.
1918-1920	Panama	(1) Support the constitutionally elected government against a revolution. (2) Maintain democracy. (3) Protect U.S. lives and the investments of U.S.-based MNCs.
1926-1933	Nicaragua	(1) Support the constitutionally elected government against a revolution. (2) Maintain democracy. (3) Protect U.S. lives and the investments of U.S.-based MNCs.

intervention in the Third World. In only one case, the U.S. retaliation against Villa's raid on Columbus, New Mexico, in 1916, was a U.S. invasion preceded by a massacre of U.S. citizens or by widespread looting of property owned by U.S. corporations. Even in that one case, the violence against U.S. lives and property was a terrorist act, not one perpetrated by the Mexican government. Almost every other U.S. intervention was preceded by some revolutionary activity and violence directed against the government of a weaker state.

Does this mean that the existence of a genuine revolution in a weaker state where U.S. citizens or U.S.-based corporations are located is sufficient justification for a military intervention? I think not. Third World states are developing both economically and politically, so their political arrangements are often fragile. Revolutions, if not inevitable, are at least likely under these circumstances. Therefore, U.S. citizens ought to be wary about accepting "the protection of American lives and property" as a sufficient condition for U.S. military intervention, lest it be used as a pretext. In fairness, however, this factor has rarely been used as the sole rationale for a U.S. military intervention in the Third World. It has been used often but only as a contributing factor.

Finally, Table 6.1 could be interpreted as providing support for the notion that the main purpose of U.S. foreign policy in the Third World during the first half of the twentieth century was to maintain political stability in the Third World by countering all revolutionary efforts there. But the emphasis all administrations placed on promoting democracy in the Third World during this period runs counter to that perspective. Although establishing or maintaining democratic institutions or processes was never the primary reason for a military intervention, it was often the means U.S. administrations preferred for resolving internal domestic conflicts and, thereby, restoring stability. In no case did the United States intervene for the purpose of permanent territorial expansion, and in no case did the U.S. government simply choose to support one faction against all the others. Rather, the pattern was to support the constitutionally established government until elections could be held to determine which faction had popular support. The U.S. government had its own favorites and undoubtedly made its preferences clear in some cases, but there is no evidence that U.S. leaders either helped to rig any election or did not abide by the results of any they did not like.

One reason for the U.S. emphasis on democracy in the Third World was the 1917 Bolshevik revolution in Russia, an event that seemed threatening to U.S. leaders and the public alike. But some support for elections and other institutions of democracy (e.g., Cuba in 1902, the Dominican Republic in 1916, and Haiti in 1915) was evident even before the Bolshevik revolution took place, and, of course, all occurred before the onset of the Cold War. Thus, the United States' desire to promote democracy in the Third World did not result solely from the need to oppose communism. Instead, the yearning to support democracy was at least in part an attempt to project the dominant cultural values of the American public to other places.

Supporting democracy is the item of longest standing on the Progressive foreign policy agenda. "Democracy" is one possible ethical standard by which the behavior of nation-states and especially their leaders may be judged.[25] Moreover, support for democratic movements in the international arena is the only item on the Progressive agenda that has received bipartisan symbolic support from U.S. leaders and enthusiastic endorsement from the general public throughout U.S. history.

The fact that several U.S. administrations supported the establishment and maintenance of democratic institutions in the Third World during the first half of the twentieth century does not in any way compensate for the generally aggressive and expansionist character of U.S. foreign policy toward the Third World during this period. The pro-democracy thrust was clearly secondary to other motives, but it does differentiate this historical period from the eighteenth and nineteenth centuries, when U.S. leaders showed little concern about the welfare of the masses in weaker nations. In this sense, U.S. policy had become marginally more other-centered, though often in a hopelessly ethnocentric way.

During the first half of the twentieth century, we also can begin to see evidence of a relationship between the political party of the president and the foreign policy orientation of the U.S. government toward the Third World, a pattern that has become even more pronounced since the Second World War. We should note at the outset that there was no apparent difference between the two parties over whether the United States should use coercive force to achieve its objectives in Central America. Of the three most interventionist presidents, Theodore Roosevelt and Taft were Republicans, whereas Wilson was a Democrat. There is little evidence of a significant party control difference there.

But the two parties differed on the extent to which the U.S. government should rely on the private sector to help achieve U.S. foreign policy goals. Of the five Republican presidents, all but Theodore Roosevelt believed that a partnership between U.S.-based corporations, U.S. financial institutions, and Washington was essential if the nation was to attain its foreign policy objectives in the Third World. Although their rationales may have differed somewhat, each of these four presidents acted as though the business of U.S. government, even in foreign policy, was to promote private sector interests. Neither Wilson nor Franklin Roosevelt, the two Democrats, publicly embraced this notion, nor did they give much priority to advancing the concerns of overseas private enterprise in their actions. This particular difference in orientation persists even today. Other differences between the political parties are also apparent in more recent U.S. policies and will be discussed in later chapters.

By the end of the Second World War, the United States had become a global power facing a whole new set of foreign policy challenges. The

Soviet Union had emerged from the war as the United States' major military and ideological rival, and anti-American feelings had taken root and were growing in Latin America and elsewhere in the developing world—largely as a result of the gunboat and dollar diplomacy phases in U.S. foreign policy. Although relations with Latin America remain a very high priority in U.S. foreign policy, once the United States emerged as a superpower after the Second World War, it began to project its influence more aggressively into the Eastern Hemisphere.

NOTES

1. See, for example, Walter LaFeber, *The Panama Canal: The Crisis in Historical Perspective* (Oxford: Oxford University Press, 1978).

2. Thomas A. Bailey, *A Diplomatic History of the American People,* 8th ed. (New York: Appleton-Century-Crofts, 1969), p. 493.

3. Roosevelt's rationale was contained in a message to Congress on December 7, 1903. Both his message and Colombia's response are reprinted in Thomas G. Paterson, *Major Problems in American Foreign Policy Volume I: To 1914* (Lexington, Mass.: D. C. Heath and Co., 1989), pp. 457–460.

4. Howard C. Hill, *Roosevelt and the Caribbean* (Chicago: University of Chicago Press, 1927), pp. 69–105.

5. Theodore Roosevelt, *Addresses and Presidential Messages of Theodore Roosevelt, 1902–1904* (New York: G. P. Putnam's Sons, 1904, pp. 7–8.

6. *Congressional Record,* 58th Congress, 2nd session, p. 19.

7. Hill, *Roosevelt and the Caribbean,* p. 154.

8. S. F. Bemis, ed., *American Secretaries of State and Their Diplomacy* (New York: Pageant Book Co., 1929), IX, 327–328.

9. *Foreign Relations,* 1912 (January 19, 1912), p. 1092.

10. Bailey, *A Diplomatic History,* p. 535.

11. Quoted in William Diamond, *The Economic Thought of Woodrow Wilson* (Baltimore: Johns Hopkins University Press, 1943), p. 142.

12. Detailed historical accounts of each of these interventions are contained in Arthur Link, *Wilson,* 5 vols. (Princeton, N.J.: Princeton University Press, 1947–).

13. *Congressional Record,* 63rd Congress, 1st session, p. 5346.

14. This quotation is from a transcript of Wilson's press conference of November 24, 1914, reprinted in Patterson, ed., *Major Problems in American Foreign Policy,* p. 509.

15. This plan is described in Frederick S. Calhoun, *Power and Principle* (Canton, Ohio: Kent State University Press, 1986), pp. 84–86.

16. Ibid., pp. 86–88.

17. A listing of U.S. military interventions in Latin America was prepared by the U.S. Senate in 1962 and reprinted in C. Ronning, ed., *Intervention in Latin America* (New York: Alfred A. Knopf, 1970), pp. 25–32.

18. Arthur S. Banks, *Political Handbook of the World, 1989* (Binghamton, N.Y.: CSA Publications, 1989), p. 438.

19. Wendell C. Gordon, *The Expropriation of Foreign-Owned Property in Mexico* (Westport, Conn.: Greenwood Press, 1975).

20. L. Ethan Ellis, *Republican Foreign Policy, 1921-1933* (New Brunswick, N.J.: Rutgers University Press, 1968), p. 265.

21. William Starr Myers, *The Foreign Policies of Herbert Hoover* (New York: Charles Scribner's Sons, 1940), pp. 45-47.

22. Ibid., p. 43.

23. Joan Hoff Wilson, *Herbert Hoover: Forgotten Progressive* (Boston: Little, Brown and Co., 1975), pp. 180-181.

24. Bailey, *A Diplomatic History,* p. 689.

25. James Turner Johnson, "Is Democracy an Ethical Standard?," *Ethics and International Affairs* (1990): 1-17.

PART III

Establishing the Progressive Agenda: 1946–1980

CHAPTER 7

Promoting Economic Development to Stop Communism

Despite the specter of advancing Bolshevism that had been raised from time to time since the Russian Revolution of 1917, during the Second World War the United States and the Soviet Union did band together to confront a common threat, Nazi Germany. Relations between the two countries deteriorated rapidly after the end of the war, however, so that by 1946 stopping the spread of communism had become the dominant goal of U.S. foreign policy. This goal was perhaps the preeminent determinant of the character of U.S.–Third World relations until major transformations began occurring in the Soviet Union and in Eastern Europe in 1989. These transformations made the advance of old-style communism into the Third World much less likely and much less threatening.

The Truman and Eisenhower administrations, like the Bush administration today, had to formulate foreign policy at a time when the international system was going through a significant transformation. The United States emerged from World War II as the only major power unscathed by the war, its economy and military machine intact. In 1947 the United States alone accounted for 50 percent of the world's total gross national product (GNP), making its economy the strongest in the world. And the nation's monopoly of the atomic bomb gave it unquestioned military supremacy.[1] So unchallenged was U.S. power during this brief period in history that the distribution of power within the world system may be termed "unipolar."

But American dominance did not last long. China's shift into the communist camp in 1949, the Soviet Union's successful explosion of a nuclear device in that same year, and the outbreak of the Korean War in 1950 fueled and confirmed the reality of the already significant fear of militant communism. These developments and others signaled a transformation in the distribution of power within the world system to a bipolar one in which the Soviet Union and the United States waged a Cold War for preeminence in international affairs. Most Third World states tried to remain neutral, but, in practice, weaker states tended to look to one or the other superpower for protection in international conflicts.

The United States had long played the role of protector in Latin America, but the emergence of a U.S. foreign policy designed, first and foremost, to stop the spread of communism required a major change in the geographic orientation of policy toward the Third World. Since Third World nations like Korea and India provided potentially fertile ground for communist movements promising rapid economic development and a more equitable distribution of wealth and political power, cultivating the friendship of the leaders of Third World countries, even those outside the Western Hemisphere, became a higher priority in U.S. foreign policy.

Presidents Harry S Truman (1945-1953) and Dwight D. Eisenhower (1953-1961) were the pioneers in this new foreign policy effort. Truman led the way in making a significant advance toward a more Progressive foreign policy toward the Third World by announcing new government programs to foster the economic development of the United States' allies in the Third World. Eisenhower did not renounce this objective but retreated to a by now familiar Republican strategy of going more slowly and relying more heavily on private sector initiatives.[2]

TRUMAN

Truman hoped to prevent the spread of communism in the Third World by providing less developed, noncommunist countries that had friendly relations with the United States with: (1) financial assistance; (2) technical assistance; and (3) the protection of U.S. troops, if absolutely necessary. In a significant speech before Congress in 1947, Truman declared his intention to oppose communism everywhere:

> One of the primary objectives of the foreign policy of the United States is the creation of conditions in which we and other nations will be able to work out a way of life free from coercion. . . . We shall not realize our objectives, however, unless we are willing to help free peoples to maintain their free institutions and their national integrity against aggressive movements that seek to impose upon them totalitarian regimes. This is no more than a frank recognition that totalitarian regimes imposed on free peoples, by direct or indirect aggression, undermine the foundations of international peace and hence the security of the United States.[3]

This policy of supporting noncommunist governments everywhere against external threats from communist states and against externally aided leftist movements became known as the Truman Doctrine.

Many believe that the Truman and Monroe doctrines are the two most significant U.S. foreign policy statements ever issued. In terms of relevance to contemporary U.S. foreign policy toward the Third World, the Truman Doctrine is the more important of the two. The Monroe Doctrine, even with the stronger corollary by Theodore Roosevelt, had only obligated the United States to take action in response to specified action-forcing events occurring in Central and South America. In contrast, the more ambitious Truman Doctrine announced the United States' willingness to take forceful action against Soviet expansionism everywhere.

Moreover, the Monroe Doctrine only pledged the United States to take actions to prevent the intervention of foreign — mainly European — powers into the affairs of weaker states in the Western Hemisphere. In contrast, the Truman Doctrine implied that the United States would take action to stop some internal rebellions as well. Indirectly, then, the Truman Doctrine further established a U.S. policy of counterrevolution in the Third World by implying that the United States would oppose revolutionary movements if their goals were communist, at least as U.S. policymakers perceived them, or if the insurrections were supported by the Soviet Union. When viewed in this light, the Truman Doctrine was an extraordinary statement coming from a nation which itself had waged a revolutionary movement to gain its own independence.

After winning a close election in 1948, Truman announced an expansion of the war against communism in the Third World — "Point Four" in his inaugural address. Admitting that past U.S. foreign policy toward the Third World had been largely imperialistic, he promised that his administration would be more concerned about the welfare of Third World peoples:

> More than half the people of the world are living in conditions approaching misery. Their food is inadequate. They are victims of disease. Their economic life is primitive and stagnant. Their poverty is a handicap and a threat both to them and to more prosperous areas.
>
> For the first time in history, humanity possesses the knowledge and the skill to relieve the suffering of these people. . . .
>
> Such new economic developments must be devised and controlled to the benefit of the peoples of the areas in which they are established. Guarantees to the investor must be balanced by guarantees in the interest of the people whose resources and whose labor go into these developments.
>
> The old imperialism — exploitation for foreign profit — has no place in our plans. What we envisage is a program of development based on the concepts of democratic fair dealing. . . .
>
> Democracy alone can supply the vitalizing force to stir the peoples of the world into triumphant action, not only against their human oppressors, but also against their ancient enemies — hunger, misery, and despair.

Other presidents had supported democratization in the Third World and had acknowledged the existence of widespread hunger, misery, and despair, but Truman proposed major new government programs to help the United States' allies in the Third World fight against those enemies. One new initiative was to give them American tax dollars through what has become known as the U.S. foreign aid program.

As a start, Truman recommended that Congress appropriate $400 million for economic and military aid to Greece and Turkey, two nations that had cooperative relations with the United States, were located near the Soviet border, and were threatened by both the Soviet Union and internal communist movements. One objection raised against the Truman Doctrine in Congress was based on principle: the United States was creating a bad precedent by pledging to interfere in the internal affairs of other independent nations. Two other objections were more pragmatic: the United States was embarking on a policy that would prove too costly to maintain; and Greece and Turkey were not worthy recipients of U.S. aid because neither was a democracy.

On this last point, Truman and his advisers were convinced that the democratic ideal existed in both countries and that, if the United States failed to help them, both would fall behind the Iron Curtain and have no chance to become more democratic in the future.[4] The debate over whether U.S. foreign policy toward Third World countries should be based on "past accomplishment" or on "promise for future performance" is still relevant to the making of U.S. foreign policy toward the Third World.

Progressive thinkers tend to favor an approach based on past performance, emphasizing the presence or absence of recent improvements in the living standards and political standing of the poorest people in each country's population. Objective performance criteria might include democratization, income distribution, land and tax reform, and improvements in health, education, and housing.[5] According to this view, the United States should only provide foreign aid, favorable trade agreements, and other foreign policy benefits to Third World nations with reasonable records of performance in these areas or, at a minimum, records of recent improvement. Nationalists generally place a stronger emphasis on the promise for future performance in such areas as the establishment of democracy and other reforms leading to the social and political empowerment of the masses and to advances in the living standards of the poorest segments of Third World societies.

This difference is exacerbated by the fact that Progressive thinkers would place great weight on U.S. foreign policy goals related to improving the condition of the poorest people in the Third World. This would mean that the benefits of U.S. foreign policy such as preferential trade agreements and high levels of economic aid would flow mainly to those Third World regimes that make the greatest efforts toward social and political reform. In contrast, Nationalists propose that greater rewards should go to those countries with a proven track record of helping the United States achieve its own foreign policy goals.[6] Promise of future performance usually is good enough for Nationalists only when it comes to the foreign policy goals on the Progressive agenda.

Walter Rostow defines foreign aid as "the voluntary transfer of resources or technology from one country to another at less than market rates."[7] Bilateral aid is the earliest and still the most prevalent type, involving only two countries, the donor and the recipient. Multilateral aid refers to aid channeled from several donors into some international organization like the United Nations. The international organization then provides the aid to one or more recipient nations. Some observers viewed the fourth point in Truman's inaugural address as evidence of his administration's determination to "go it alone" in a policy to assist Third World development and, therefore, as a snub to the recently created United Nations.

But this criticism ignores other multilateral initiatives of the United States in the conduct of its relations with Third World states. In 1944 the United States had joined with 17 other countries in the Bretton Woods Agreement, which provided the basis for establishing several important public, multilateral lending institutions, including the International Bank for Reconstruction and Development (IBRD), the World Bank, and the International Monetary Fund (IMF). The participants in the Bretton Woods Agreement included seven countries that were then considered underdeveloped — Brazil, Chile, China, Cuba, Greece, India, and Mexico. The IBRD became a specialized agency of the United Nations in 1947.

The idea behind the IBRD was that all developed nations would contribute to a guarantee fund to be used mainly for insuring private investments in less developed countries against loss. Contributors to the guarantee fund were essentially stockholders, with the largest stockholders having the largest voice in bank policies. Since the United States provided most of the funds, and since the Bank was located within U.S. territory, its independent, international status was undermined. However, the agreement stipulated that loans would be made solely on the basis of economic considerations, making it difficult for even the largest contributors to use Bank loan policies to accomplish short-term political objectives.

Multilateral aid of the type provided by the IBRD is almost always given in the form of a concessionary loan requiring repayment by the recipient, and not as an outright grant. The loans are concessionary in the sense that the interest rate is lower than the market rate and other repayment terms are usually generous as well. The value of the loan as a transfer of wealth is equal to the difference between what the loan would have cost to repay if provided under normal market conditions and what it actually costs as a result of preferential concessions by the lender.

The World Bank was created in the late 1950s, pursuant to the Bretton Woods Agreement and within the IBRD framework. Its Board of Governors participates much more directly in loan decisions than did the early IBRD board. Contributors to World Bank funds still make decisions on the grounds of a weighted voting system based on individual country subscriptions, but poorer states are accorded a slightly disproportionate voice. As of mid-1988, the leading subscribers were the United States with 19.6 percent (18.7 percent of the voting power), Japan with 6.9 percent (6.7), the Federal Republic of Germany with 5.4 percent (5.1), the United Kingdom with 5.1 percent (4.9), and France with 5.1 percent (4.9).[8]

By the Articles of Agreement signed at Bretton Woods, the IMF was created to foster international monetary cooperation, facilitate international trade, and promote high levels of world employment and real income and the economic development of all members.[9] The IMF began operations in 1947 and became a specialized agency of the United Nations that same year. Upon joining the fund, each country is assigned a quota determining both the amount of foreign exchange it may borrow or its "drawing rights," and its approximate voting power. As of September 1988, the United States was still the largest contributor to the fund and had 19.1 percent of the voting power.[10]

The giving of nonmilitary foreign aid, whether through bilateral or multilateral channels, is still controversial in the United States. Some justify it on the basis that it will enhance U.S. national security. Others defend it on the grounds that the rich have a moral responsibility to aid the poor. Edward Banfield, taking a Nationalist position, has questioned both justifications.[11] In his view, there is little evidence that foreign aid enhances U.S. national security by changing the cultures and institutions of recipient societies so that they will be more compatible with our own. Aid recipients, he contends, are no more likely to develop economically as the result of receiving aid, because the obstacles to development in the Third World have little to do with the availability of capital. Moreover, even if aid helped recipients to develop economically, there is no obvious relationship between economic development and political stability in the Third World. Seymour Lipset has demonstrated that wealthier Latin American states tend to be more democratic than poorer ones,[12] but Banfield is not convinced that democratic states are more stable than others or that promoting democracy in the Third World is all that important to U.S. national interests anyway.

Of course, foreign aid can be justified in terms of its potential direct effect in advancing the U.S. national interests by encouraging recipients to take desired actions or to refrain from taking undesired ones. However, Banfield contends that using aid to make friendly Third World countries friendlier is of little use, and using aid to make unfriendly Third World states friendly is either impossible or too costly, given the benefits that would accrue to the United States from doing so. Like most other Nationalists, Banfield also does not believe that American foreign policy can or should be justified in terms of doing good for other nations. But he concludes that the widespread misguided public perception that giving economic aid is morally right is, in the final analysis, the main reason why the foreign aid program continues:

> If the American people cannot express their goodness through foreign aid they will doubtless find some other way of expressing it. To the extent that public opinion rules, our policy will reflect goodness. This is a cause for concern because goodness is, by its very nature, incapable of understanding its own inadequacy as a principle by which to govern relations among states.[13]

Besides the transfer of money and equipment, Truman hoped that the war against hunger, disease, and despair in the Third World could be waged through the implementation of a Technical Assistance Program that would teach the leaders and peoples of developing countries how to help themselves. His rationale for such a program was presented to the American people also as part of Point Four of his 1949 inaugural address:

> The United States is preeminent among nations in the development of industrial and scientific techniques. The material resources which we can afford to use for the assistance of other people are limited. But our imponderable resources in technical knowledge are constantly growing and are inexhaustible. . . .
> We invite other countries to pool their technological resources in this undertaking. Their contributions will be warmly welcomed. This should be a cooperative enterprise in which all nations work together through the United Nations and its specialized agencies whenever practicable.

Few in Congress criticized Truman's technical assistance proposal. Perhaps because of the crusading and missionary spirit in the American culture, Congress and the public have always reacted more warmly to proposals for greater technical assistance to the Third World than to proposals for higher levels of foreign aid. By the end of 1951, trainees from more than ten countries had come to the United States in the hopes of benefiting from American knowhow.[14]

Unfortunately, other significant events diverted energy and attention from the humanitarian and progressive aspects of Truman's foreign policy toward the Third World. Resources were transferred into the Marshall Plan, which was designed to help the United States' European allies recover from the devastation of the Second World War and into the military assistance necessary to help South Korea maintain its independence. In domestic politics, Truman also was forced to contend with a period of fanatic anti-communism, shifting much of his administration's energies away from more significant foreign policy concerns. The public hysteria lasted until 1954, when the Senate finally censured Senator Joseph McCarthy, the leader of the domestic anti-communism campaign. These developments, among others, caused less attention to be paid to progressive elements in Truman's foreign policy agenda.

Once the people had accepted the principle of using tax dollars to help other independent nations resist the advance of communism, it was easier to accept Secretary of State George Marshall's proposal for a massive transfer of resources to the United States' allies in war-weakened Europe. Congress approved the administration's so-called Marshall Plan in April 1948, just in time to influence the outcome of the Italian elections, where the Communist party was thought to have a serious chance of capturing control of the government. U.S. officials were so concerned about a communist takeover in Italy that covert funding was provided to help the Christian Democrats and the Social Democrats. Moreover, direct U.S. military intervention was never completely ruled out.[15]

Since, as Truman himself had admitted, the amount of tax dollars the United States was willing to provide other nations for their use was limited, the Marshall Plan itself probably lowered the level of humanitarian aid provided to Third World countries during the early years of the foreign aid program. Over the three years following congressional approval of the Marshall Plan, approximately $6 billion per year was provided to European nations. Over the same period, less than one-half billion dollars per year were provided to less developed countries. The U.S. foreign aid program continued to hover between $4.5 and 6.5 billion per year through 1954, but the allocation of aid among countries began to change dramatically in 1950. By 1950 the European recovery was assured, so, even holding the level of foreign aid constant, more funds were now available to be distributed among the less developed countries.

The Truman administration demonstrated its compassion for a dispossessed people through the strong position it took in favor of the creation of a Jewish state. The Jews, victimized by the Nazis during World War II, pressed for the establishment of their own nation located in their ancestral lands, Palestine. However, the Arabs residing in Palestine outnumbered the Jews about two to one and had established rights of their own to this land, based on centuries of residence. Thus, two sets of reasonable moral claims came into direct conflict. U.S. leaders were torn on this issue. The United States was then dependent on Arab oil and needed military bases in the Middle East, so its leaders did not want to drive the Arab states closer to the Soviet camp. But there was also strong humanitarian sentiment in the United States in favor of establishing a Jewish state.

Throughout the course of the international debate, Truman publicly and strongly supported the Jewish cause. When a plan for partitioning the Holy Land between Arabs and Jews was put before the United Nations Assembly in 1947, the State Department, concerned about the United States' vital strategic interest in maintaining access to Middle Eastern oil, vigorously opposed partition. But Truman applied pressure to help force partition through the United Nations.[16] Whether Truman was motivated mainly by humanitarian concerns or by partisan electoral interests in cultivating the American Jewish vote in the 1948 campaign against the Republican nominee for president, Thomas Dewey, cannot be established conclusively. But, for whatever reason, the obvious Nationalist strategy advocated by the State Department was not pursued.

Jews in Palestine were already locked in combat with their Arab counterparts. In May 1948, they announced the formation of a new state of Israel. Within minutes of this proclamation, Truman extended de facto recognition.[17] U.S. Jews provided massive amounts of financial aid to the cause of Israel, and, largely because of this assistance, the new state was able to defend itself from the onslaught of several Arab armies. Having been beaten by Jews bearing American arms, most Arabs developed strong anti-American feelings. Palestinian Arabs who had been forced to flee Israel as a result of the war of independence were not permitted to return by the Israeli government and were unwilling to resettle permanently elsewhere. Today, nearly 50 years later, the problem of finding a homeland for these displaced, impoverished refugees continues, with no practical resolution in sight.

The Truman administration faced its most serious foreign policy challenge on June 24, 1950, when Communist North Korea attacked South Korea, beginning the Korean War. U.S. leaders perceived the attack as having been mounted, supplied, and instigated by the Soviet Union and Communist China. The conflict was also perceived as a challenge to the United States' internationally recognized position as the protector of South Korea, an area vital to the security of American-occupied Japan. The next day the United Nations Security Council condemned the invasion as a "breach of the peace." The U.S. response to the invasion was closely coordinated with the responses of the other members of the United

Nations. On June 26, Truman ordered U.S. military forces to assist in the defense of South Korea, one day before the United Nations Security Council passed a second resolution, this time calling on U.N. members to give Korea such help as might be needed to repel the armed attack and restore peace in the area.[18] A few days later, Truman reported to Congress that the Soviet-inspired attack on South Korea showed that the United States must provide more military assistance to all "free nations associated with us in common defense."[19]

The initial public and congressional response to U.S. participation in the war was positive, but, as the fighting dragged on, the public mood turned restless. Republican charges that the Democrats had lost China to the communists and had mishandled the Korean conflict helped propel Eisenhower to a victory over Democrat Adlai Stevenson in the 1952 election campaign. The Korean armistice recognizing a military stalemate was finally concluded in July 1953 after three years of fighting, including two years of peace negotiations.

The outbreak of war in Korea had at least one important negative effect on U.S.–Third World relations at a crucial moment in the history of the foreign aid program. Just as the Marshall Plan was coming to a conclusion and a larger share of U.S. foreign aid was still available to assist the economic development of LDCs, fears of communism were fueled by the outbreak of the Korean War. Instead of providing funds for economic development in the Third World, U.S. aid was given mainly in the form of military assistance to strategically located allies such as Morocco, South Korea, Taiwan, Egypt, Greece, India, Iran, Israel, Indonesia, and the Philippines. Most Latin American countries received only token amounts of foreign aid except Brazil and Mexico, which received modest amounts. African countries received almost nothing. In essence, resources that had been provided to Western Europe for economic development were provided to the Third World for a military buildup.

Without the Korean War, more funds would likely have been provided to Third World countries for economic development and less would have been reserved for the exclusive use of strategically located military allies. This would have been an important precedent in U.S. foreign policy toward the Third World. Between 1946 and 1950, about 90 percent of the bilateral aid provided to less developed countries was for economic development. With the outbreak of the Korean War in 1950, military aid began to dominate, accounting for more than two thirds of the total by 1953.[20] So important were the military aspects of the foreign aid program that the statutory basis for all bilateral foreign aid to developing countries between 1953 and 1961 was the Mutual Security Act.

The Korean War not only changed the United States' foreign aid priorities, but it also dominated the Truman administration's foreign policy agenda for the remainder of his term of office, basically preempting other progressive objectives. Thus, the invasion of South Korea by North Korea provides a good example of how action-forcing events can affect the legacy an administration leaves in the foreign policy field. The siege mentality developing at home as a result of McCarthyism provided yet more justification for a shift away from Progressive foreign policy principles and toward greater Nationalism.

EISENHOWER

At least three foreign policy decisions of the Eisenhower administration had great and lasting impact on U.S.-Third World relations. First, Eisenhower quietly, but steadfastly, resisted proposals from within his administration to expand the humanitarian aspects of the U.S. foreign aid program to less developed countries. Instead, he preferred to rely on the stimulation of foreign investment and trade as a way of fostering economic development in the Third World and to provide mainly military aid to the United States' less developed military allies. Although he did not renounce the more ambitious and progressive objectives set out by Truman, he did little to implement them either. Second, his administration significantly expanded the use of covert action to achieve U.S. foreign policy goals in the Third World. Third, Eisenhower announced that the Middle East was (in addition to Latin America) a region of high priority in U.S. foreign policy.

Alarmed by the communist revolution in China and the Korean War in the Far East, the Eisenhower administration concluded several military alliances pledging the assistance of U.S. troops if less developed countries were attacked. A bilateral pact was signed with South Korea at the end of the Korean War. In 1954 the United States, along with Britain, France, Australia, New Zealand, the Philippines, and Thailand, agreed to form the Southeast Asia Treaty Organization (SEATO). The organization was bound by the weak pact that, in the event of outside aggression or internal subversion designed to overthrow any Southeast Asian government, the members of the organization would "consult immediately" to determine appropriate countermeasures in compliance with each member nation's "constitutional processes." A similar pact designed to shore up the defense against communism in the Middle East was also formed in 1959. It was called the Central Treaty Organization (CENTO) and included Turkey, Iran, Iraq, Pakistan, and Britain as members. The United States did not formally participate, but Eisenhower quickly concluded executive agreements with each of these nations, binding the United States to defend them in certain situations.[21]

The Eisenhower administration soon learned the advantages of covert action over direct military intervention to protect the Third World from advancing communism. In the short run, U.S. covert operations worked in Iran and in Guatemala. In Iran, Nationalist sentiments ran strong in the post-World War II period. Britain had long dominated the oil industry and, through the oil industry, had interfered in Iranian political affairs. After the war a movement developed in Iran for expropriating the oil industry and expelling the British, and in 1947 Mohammed Mossadeq, prime minister of Iran, headed a government committed to that end. The Truman administration had been friendly to the new regime, but by 1953 the Eisenhower administration was convinced that Mossadeq was a communist.[22]

Mossadeq repeatedly asked the Eisenhower administration to increase U.S. aid to Iran and to buy more Iranian oil, but Eisenhower refused. In response, Mossadeq turned to the Soviet Union for similar assistance,[23] and at this point Eisenhower authorized agents of the Central Intelligence Agency (CIA) to remove him from power. They secretly contacted the shah, Mohammed Reza Pahlavi, and convinced him to dismiss the prime minister by royal decree, setting off a chain of events leading to Mossadeq's removal. Within three days after his removal from power, the United States promised increased foreign aid to Iran.[24]

The Guatemalan story has a similar ring to it. In 1954 a leftist, allegedly communist movement won control of Guatemala, and the new government quickly seized the holdings of the U.S.-based United Fruit Company, providing very little compensation to the corporation. Jacobo Arbenz, the leader of the Guatemalan government, claimed that the United Fruit Company had been seized because it was a barrier to necessary reform. In his view, the company exercised so much power over the country that it threatened the integrity of his nation.[25] The initial U.S. response was only moral castigation and diplomatic isolation, but relations with the United States worsened when the Guatemalan government allegedly received a large shipment of arms from Poland. The U.S. government countered with the provision of arms to Guatemala's neighbors.

John Foster Dulles, secretary of state under Eisenhower, explained the depth of the U.S. concern over the situation in Guatemala:

Guatemala is a small country. But its power, standing alone, is not a measure of the threat. The master plan of international communism is to gain a solid political base in this hemisphere, a base that can be used to extend Communist penetration to other peoples of the other American governments. It was not the power of the Arbenz government that concerned us but the power behind it.[26]

This view of the steady advance of Soviet-backed communism from state to neighboring state became known as the "domino theory," a theory that motivated U.S. foreign policy for many years.

President Eisenhower explained his administration's "domino theory" to the American public in a press conference on April 7, 1954. He had been asked why communist movements in faraway places like Southeast Asia were important to the United States. He responded by describing what he called the falling domino principle: "You have a row of dominoes set up, you knock over the first one, and what will happen to the last one is the certainty that it will go over very quickly. So you could have a beginning of a disintegration that would have the most profound influences." As examples of those profound influences, he predicted that millions of people and the resources their governments controlled would be lost to the free world, perhaps forever. This argument was used to justify the Eisenhower administration's early involvement in Vietnam and the even deeper involvement by the administrations of Presidents John F. Kennedy, Lyndon Baines Johnson, and Richard M. Nixon. Although the end of the Cold War makes the domino theory less useful as a guide for foreign policy, some Nationalist thinkers still find it compelling.

In contrast to Dulles's threatening portrayal of the events in Guatemala, the historian Richard Immerman has argued that the leftist movement in Guatemala between 1944 and 1954 had little to do with the Soviet Union, the Cold War, or even communism. In his view, Guatemala had endured a long period of underdevelopment, economic exploitation, and both cultural and political repression. A redistribution of wealth and political power from the few to the many was necessary and long overdue. Immerman portrays the actions of the Arbenz government as the natural progression of an indigenous movement to achieve those ends.[27]

In 1954 the Arbenz government was challenged by an army of Guatemalan exiles aided by the U.S. government. The leader of the exiles, Carlos Castillo Armas, was handpicked by the U.S. government and the United Fruit Company. The CIA provided $3 million to finance the effort, and the United Fruit Company smuggled arms into Guatemala through its port facilities. The rebels operated out of bases in Nicaragua, with the active cooperation of the U.S.-backed Somoza government. Within a few months, all the main elements of the plan, including the role of the United States, the United Fruit Company, and Somoza, were public. Still, the State Department characterized allegations of U.S. involvement as preposterous. Intimidated, Arbenz resigned his position. Armas was selected as provisional president, with elections scheduled a few months later, in October 1954. The elections were a farce. They were not secret, and government officials were stationed at the polling places. Out of about a half a million votes cast, Armas received all but four hundred.[28]

There is some evidence that Eisenhower was not entirely comfortable with the almost exclusive mutual defense emphasis of U.S.–Third World relations during his presidency. Shortly after Joseph Stalin's death in 1953, he promised that if East-West tensions declined and there was a "peace dividend" resulting from lower military expenditures, he would advocate more humanitarian assistance to Third World countries. In his speech of April 1953, he said:

> This Government is ready to ask its people to join with all nations in devoting a substantial percentage of any savings achieved by real disarmament to a fund for world aid and reconstruction. The purposes of this great work would be: To help other peoples to develop the underdeveloped areas of the world, to stimulate profitable and fair world trade, to assist all peoples to know the blessings of productive freedom.[29]

Unfortunately, Stalin's death did not lessen Cold War tensions at all. As a result, the foreign aid program emerging from Congress in 1953 consisted of appropriations of $4.5 billion, of which 70 percent was direct military aid and another 20 percent "defense support," referring to economic assistance to less developed military allies.

In the absence of a "peace dividend," Eisenhower took a position on development policy that was similar to that of his Republican predecessors. In a March 1954 message to Congress, he listed the major elements of his assistance plan for the Third World nations:

> Aid — which we wish to curtail;
> Investment — which we wish to encourage;
> Convertibility [of currencies] — which we wish to facilitate;
> Trade — which we wish to expand.[30]

Clearly, then, the focus was not on forceful U.S. government action in the Third World using aid and technical assistance to bring about economic development, and social and political reform, but on the use of transnational corporations and trade agreements to promote capitalism. In turn, capitalism would stimulate economic development. The rationale was that economic development would facilitate the LDCs' efforts to enact social and political reforms. Moreover, increased North-South trade would lead to improved North-South diplomatic relations.[31]

On the question of whether tax resources should be set aside to support less developed countries that were not explicitly allied with the United States, Eisenhower consistently said "no." There were some arguable "exceptions" to this policy during his administration. He did support the passage of PL-480 in 1954, allowing the sale of U.S. grain surpluses to less developed countries at reduced prices and in return for local, frequently unconvertible currencies. But most analyses of the passage of this "food aid" bill suggest that it was designed mainly to cultivate the farmers' support for Eisenhower's administration and to develop foreign markets for U.S. products.[32]

Also, late in his second term of office, Eisenhower's administration helped establish two loan funds to finance economic development in the Third World — the Development Loan Fund (DLF) and the Inter-American Development Bank (IADB). The DLF, established in 1957 only after several more ambitious alternatives were rejected, was a small pilot project designed to stimulate long-term economic development efforts in the Third World.[33] As Dulles explained to Congress, a loan fund had at least two advantages over conventional foreign aid. First, a loan fund, once established, was potentially renewable. Loans could be made, and, when repaid, the same funds could be loaned again. Second, a loan fund could be used to finance long-term projects because the loan administrators could commit funds for several years. Conventional foreign aid, on the other hand, was subject to the vicissitudes of the annual budget cycle.[34] Eisenhower requested only $500 million for the Development Loan Fund in the first year, and he did not ask for any increase in the total amount of foreign aid the United States would provide Third World countries that year. Instead, he proposed that the DLF be created by reallocating funds already requested for foreign aid.[35] Congress only reallocated $300 million to be spent on the DLF.

Most members of the Organization of American States had long favored the establishment of a Latin American regional development bank based on principles similar to those of the DLF. This public, regional bank would provide concessionary loans to assist the long-term economic development efforts of member states. For several years, the Eisenhower administration remained opposed. In 1959, however, the administration dropped its opposition, and the Inter-American Development Bank (IADB) was established. The IADB provides technical assistance and participates in cofinancing with other multilateral agencies. By charter provision, loans cannot exceed 50 percent of project cost.

Unlike the DLF, which is a bilateral loan program, the IADB is a multilateral lending organization. Like the World Bank, voting on loans is on a weighted basis according to each country's contribution to the bank's loan fund, so the United States has always had a strong voice in bank policies. As of mid-1988, the voting weights of the leading bank contributors were the United States (34.7 percent), Argentina (11.6 percent), Brazil (11.6 percent), Mexico (7.5 percent), and Venezuela (6.2 percent).[36]

The establishment of the DLF and IADB represented movements away from the Eisenhower administration's staunch opposition to providing U.S. tax funds to any nation that was not allied militarily with the United States. But both were small steps. In the case of the DLF, the fund was small and did not even require an increase in total U.S. foreign aid provided the Third World. Moreover, in general, loan funds are not very helpful to the poorest countries in the world, because impoverished countries are not good credit risks. Indeed, the IADB's lending policies during the first two decades were quite conservative, generating much criticism that the IADB had neglected the region's neediest nations and had not had much positive impact on the region's destitute people.[37]

During the Eisenhower administration, U.S. tax dollars were also occasionally used to purchase anti-communist commitments from the leaders of certain Third World countries. Some less developed countries in the Eastern Hemisphere — most notably Egypt and India — developed a strategy of playing the two superpowers against one another in order to maximize benefits. The United States and the Soviet Union bid against one another for the privilege of helping Egypt build the Aswan Dam; the United States finally withdrew its bid after Cairo decided to purchase arms from Czechoslovakia in 1955. A week after the United States withdrew its offer, Egypt seized the Suez Canal, which was owned mainly by French and British stockholders. When inadequate compensation was produced, Britain, France, and Israel, apparently without consultation with the United States, launched a military attack designed to recapture the Canal in 1956. The United States joined in a United Nations Security Council resolution demanding withdrawal of the offensive forces and U.N. mediation of the dispute. The attacking forces did withdraw under protest, returning control of the Canal to Egypt.

Following the Suez crisis, Eisenhower, in formal recognition of the importance of the oil-rich Middle East to U.S. military security and economic prosperity, asked a joint session of Congress in January 1957 to endorse a new strategy for U.S. foreign policy. His new approach had three elements. First, he requested the authority to provide increased foreign aid to noncommunist Middle Eastern states. Second, he proposed extending military aid and cooperation to any Middle Eastern state requesting it. Third, as the most controversial element of his new strategy, he suggested that Congress authorize "employment of the armed forces of the United States to secure and protect the territorial integrity and political independence of such [Middle Eastern] nations, requesting such aid, against overt armed aggression from any nation controlled by International Communism."[38] There was nothing particularly humanitarian about Eisenhower's proposal to provide more foreign aid to noncommunist Middle Eastern states. His strategy was firmly and, for all practical purposes, exclusively rooted in the pursuit of the United States' interest in maintaining access to oil. After two months of inconclusive debate concentrating mainly on what conditions would justify U.S. military intervention into the Middle East, Congress authorized the president to spend $200 million on foreign aid in the region.

The military intervention component of the Eisenhower Doctrine was tested in 1958 when the president of Lebanon, fearing the overthrow of his regime, asked Eisenhower for help. Since the perceived external threat came from Gamal Abdel Nasser's Egypt, which was not a nation controlled by international communism, the situation did not fall within the qualifications established by the Eisenhower Doctrine. Furthermore, some have argued that the real threat to the Lebanese president was internal subversion, not external threat. Eisenhower, undeterred by these fine points, quickly sent 14,000 marines, who, unopposed, occupied Lebanon. On the day of the intervention, Eisenhower, in a television address to the nation, stated that U.S. military forces had entered Lebanon to safeguard U.S. lives and property and to defend the political integrity of the country.[39] At the request of the United States, the United Nations mediated the conflict, and the marines were withdrawn about two months after landing. Other than the Korean War, this was the only open use of military force by the United States anywhere in the world between 1946 and 1961.

The last major test of American anti-communism during the 1950s came when a revolution in Cuba led by Fidel Castro overthrew the Batista regime in 1959. Like Marcos after him, Fulgencio Batista fled the scene with much money, all the while criticizing U.S. leaders for not providing him with more support against the revolution. The United States was not immediately hostile to Castro, since his reform agenda did not preclude a friendly relationship; the United States even accorded his regime formal recognition in the surprisingly short time of one week. But Castro did not trust the Eisenhower administration, which had quietly supported Batista and opposed his revolution.

In 1960, just days after Batista left Cuba, Eisenhower restated the U.S. policy on Cuba. He noted that the United States remained committed to a policy of nonintervention in the domestic affairs of other countries in accordance with international law. He also reassured the new regime that the United States recognized the right of the Cuban government to undertake social, economic, and political reforms which, "with due regard for their obligations under international law," they judged desirable.[40] But the interests of Castro's revolutionary regime conflicted with the Eisenhower administration on this last point. Castro had come to power on a program of agrarian reform, requiring a redistribution of land and wealth from those who had much to those who had little. Americans owned a significant amount of the land and wealth in Cuba. International law allows a nation to expropriate private property within its jurisdiction for public purposes, but coupled with that right is an obligation to provide "prompt, adequate, and effective compensation."[41] Castro, like the leaders of many LDCs, either could not afford or did not want to pay compensation. He quickly made it clear that his regime would be militantly anti-Yankee and would actively aid revolutionary Marxist movements in the Caribbean and, eventually, he hoped, throughout Latin America.

In reprisal, the United States cut off sugar imports, dealing a severe blow to the Cuban economy, and imposed an embargo on the export of virtually everything from the United States except food and medicine. The Soviet Union quickly stepped in to provide Cuba with much needed economic and military assistance. Castro demanded that the United States vacate its naval base at Guantanamo (despite the existence of a 1934 treaty granting the United States base rights there basically in perpetuity) and reduce its diplomatic staff from an alleged 300 to 11. In response, President Eisenhower severed diplomatic relations on January 3, 1961. Seventeen days later his successor, John F. Kennedy, inherited the problem. The most severe challenge to the Monroe Doctrine thus had been delivered.

THE ENDS JUSTIFY THE MEANS

An "ends justify the means" approach to foreign policy attained greater currency during the early years of the Cold War. After the Second World War, the United States demonstrated a greater willingness to interfere in the internal affairs of weaker states outside Central America than ever before. In the name of anti-communism, the United States also openly supported many repressive regimes in the developing world and opposed virtually all regimes that were formally allied with communist countries. Critics of this foreign policy stance derisively pointed out that it was based on two principles: the enemies of our enemy are our friends, and the friends of our enemies are our enemies.

A number of vigorous reform-oriented, left-wing movements in most Latin American nations developed in the years following the end of the

Second World War. The leaders of those movements invariably portrayed
them as popular and as designed to achieve social, economic, and political
justice. In the United States, however, they were viewed with some alarm
as Soviet inspired. Following the second foreign policy principle noted
above—"the friends of our enemies are our enemies"—the United States
almost always opposed them.

Anti-communism became so important in U.S. foreign policy that
covert action came to be regarded as a more acceptable means to achieve
U.S. foreign policy ends. Covert action was employed often during this
period, most successfully in Iran in 1953 and in Guatemala in 1954. Of
course, the United States and most other nations of the world had long
engaged in intelligence activities, collecting information and interpreting
its significance. Most such information comes from public sources, and
some from espionage. In the United States, the main responsibility for
conducting intelligence activities is vested in the Central Intelligence
Agency (CIA).

The CIA's Directorate of Operations plans and conducts all secret
activities, including covert actions—secret activities in foreign nations
designed to affect their domestic affairs in ways that advance U.S.
interests. The success of secret paramilitary operations against the Ger-
mans and Japanese during World War II led Truman to propose and
Congress to pass legislation establishing the CIA in December 1947.
George Kennan, a member of the Truman administration, believing
conflict with the Soviet Union would be prolonged, was an outspoken
advocate of covert action, which he described as:

> propaganda, economic warfare; preventive direct action, including sabo-
> tage, anti-sabotage, demolition and evacuation measures; subversion
> against hostile states, including assistance to underground resistance
> movements, guerrillas and refugee liberation groups, and support of
> indigenous anti-communist elements.[42]

He believed that such activities should be conducted so that "any U.S.
Government responsibility for them is not evident to unauthorized persons
and that if uncovered the U.S. Government can plausibly disclaim any
responsibility for them."[43]

Gregory Treverton describes many kinds of covert operations, including propaganda, paramilitary operations, and political actions designed to support preferred regimes and undermine "bad" ones.[44] Political
action operations probably have been the most common. Included in this
category are relatively innocuous activities such as providing support to
the press and to labor unions, activities often justified as support for the

infrastructure of democracy. Also included in this category are some much less savory activities such as buying particular stories in the press, supporting favored political parties, influencing the outcomes of elections, and, if all else fails, even assassinating foreign leaders.

Although it is unlikely that Kennan ever expected covert actions to become a frequently used weapon in the U.S. arsenal, they have been commonly employed against relatively weaker states in the Third World. Covert action represented an extension of other, less controversial forms of U.S. interference in the internal affairs of weaker states. One well-known case of relatively minor interference occurred in Argentina shortly after World War II. The leader of Argentina, Colonel Juan Peron, was openly opposed by the U.S. ambassador. In 1946, with elections approaching, the Department of State published a document detailing the cooperation of the Peron regime with the Nazis. The document was designed to discredit Peron and cause him to lose the elections. Peron's followers denounced the act as "Yankee Imperialism," and he won by a comfortable margin.[45] American meddling may have actually helped his campaign.

This kind of intrusion into the internal political affairs of other governments is now accepted as routine in the United States. In recent elections in both Nicaragua and El Salvador, the United States contributed generously to the campaigns of favored candidates. But this kind of interference in the domestic affairs of other nations violates international norms of diplomatic practice and, prior to World War II, was not a conventional part of U.S. foreign policy toward the Third World. Most Americans find nonviolent intervention, whether overt or covert, to be more ethical than any kind of violent interference. The lessons drawn by U.S. policymakers from more violent, "successful" covert operations during the Eisenhower administration in Iran and in Guatemala were crucial in justifying ever increasing frequency of use of this approach.

THE GOALS: 1946–1960

Halting the advance of communism was the major new concern of U.S. foreign policy after the Second World War. Since direct confrontation between the superpowers was unthinkable in the nuclear age, the war against communism was to be fought mainly over the hearts and minds of people in the developing countries. Marxist critics of U.S.–Third World relations during this period contend that the real reason why the United States emphasized the importance of anti-communism in foreign policy was the growing fear that the communist movement would present a significant challenge to capitalism as the dominant system for organizing economic relations within and among nations. Even Henry Wallace, formerly Truman's secretary of commerce, waged an unsuccessful third-party campaign against Truman in 1948, denouncing the Truman Doctrine as inspired by Wall Street and by the forces of military imperialism.[46]

Critics also condemn the status quo, counterrevolutionary tendencies in U.S. foreign policy toward the Third World that took firm root during this period. Truman's declaration that the United States was willing to use its power to help free people maintain their free institutions and their national integrity against aggressive movements was seen by skeptics as a declaration against popular revolutions. Even if Truman did not mean that the United States would help all friendly governments repel all threats, even internal ones, there were practical problems in differentiating between popular rebellions against unjust regimes and externally inspired revolutions.

Truman, Eisenhower, and later administrations wrestled with this problem, and, in retrospect, we can see the inadvisability of many of the particular decisions they made in support of existing regimes against what now appear to have been genuine, popularly supported leftist revolutions. Even mainstream critics believe that the United States' increased interference into the internal affairs of Third World countries during this period for short-term political gains was regrettable. Like most of their successors, both Truman and Eisenhower had difficulty distinguishing between indigenous, leftist movements in the Third World (whether or not encouraged by the Soviet Union), on the one hand, and the advance of Soviet influence and power around the world, on the other. When the circumstances were ambiguous, they took no chances. Truman sponsored the legislation that established the CIA, and Eisenhower presided over a period of increasingly frequent use of covert methods, an expansion of the purposes to which they were employed, and other ethically suspect means to achieve U.S. goals vis-à-vis Third World states.

Even during this period of hysterical anti-communism, however, some movement was made toward a more Progressive U.S. foreign policy. Both Truman and Eisenhower continued to support democratization in the Third World rhetorically, although stopping the spread of communism was clearly more important when the two objectives came into conflict. We have firm evidence that supporting democracy was an important U.S. foreign policy objective in the Third World: the largest recipients of U.S. foreign aid among less developed countries during this period were either democratic (India and Israel) or were perceived by U.S. policymakers as directly threatened by external communist threat — South Korea, Greece, and Turkey. Both Greece and Turkey are democratic states today, and South Korea is slowly moving in that direction.

To this longstanding single-item Progressive agenda, Truman added his support for advancing the economic well-being of the poorest people in the Third World. In doing so, he acknowledged the United States' role in helping the poorest people of the Third World gain access to adequate food, shelter, health, and education. The United States assumed this responsibility in some small part because it was the morally right thing to do, and in larger part because abject poverty was likely to provide fertile ground for genuine communist revolutions. As usual, altruism was mixed with national self-interest; nonetheless, most Third World regimes welcomed Truman's "Point Four" initiative. Truman, the Democrat, advocated the bold new U.S. initiatives of foreign aid and technical assistance to help underdeveloped countries allied with the United States ward off internal communist movements and potential external threats from the Soviet Union. Eisenhower, the Republican, embraced the same objectives, but, like many of his Republican predecessors, he preferred to rely more on private trade and investment to shore up less developed allies.

Both presidents managed to avoid the use of military force in the Third World except in the cases of Lebanon and Korea. The contrast between their policies on military intervention in the Third World and those of most of their predecessors is striking. The movement away from the use of force toward the use of aid, technical assistance, trade, investment, and loans represented a small step away from sanctions toward incentives as a means of influencing the political, social, and economic development of Third World states. Providing or withholding foreign aid has become the principal instrument of U.S. foreign policy toward the Third World mainly because under Cold War conditions using force or threats of force was impracticable.

Both presidents also showed more respect for international law and the sovereignty of weaker states than had many of their predecessors. Though tempted to respond unilaterally, the Truman administration worked closely with the United Nations to develop a multinational response to the attack on South Korea by North Korea. The United States led the multilateral effort by prodding the United Nations to take firm action, by being the first nation to send military forces, and by sending more military force than any other state. But the Korean War was, in a very real sense, a United Nations response to state aggression. Significantly, even after the unilateral U.S. invasion of Lebanon, Eisenhower requested the United Nations' mediation, which helped permit an early evacuation of U.S. troops. The United States also voted with the majority of other nations to allow the partition of Palestine, even though doing so risked the United States' national self-interest in maintaining access to Arab oil.

Moreover, the United States was a prime mover behind the Bretton

Woods Agreement and the consequent establishment of numerous multilateral lending agencies, including the World Bank and the IMF. Today these agencies are the main public sources of desperately needed external capital to less developed countries. Food aid (PL-480), established during the Eisenhower administration, has some shortcomings, but it remains an important source of humanitarian aid to some of the neediest countries in the world.

Truman's rhetoric and actions demonstrate that he was the United States' first Progressive president. Not only did he inaugurate the U.S. foreign aid and technical assistance programs, but he also risked U.S. economic interests in the Middle East to support the creation of the state of Israel, and he worked within the framework of the United Nations in responding to the invasion of South Korea. Of course, Truman and Eisenhower shared many Nationalist principles. When push came to shove, promoting the macroeconomic prosperity of the United States and defending the United States from external threat were their first priorities. Truman simply gave a little more weight to advancing the economic rights of Third World people, to advancing the human rights of Jews, and to acting multilaterally than most of his predecessors or successors would have.

Both presidents resisted spending scarce U.S. tax dollars on facilitating political, social, and economic reform in less developed countries unless those countries were either allied militarily with the United States, formally or informally; or noncommunist and explicitly threatened by the Soviet Union, directly or indirectly. However, John F. Kennedy was among the strongest advocates in the Senate of loosening these criteria; his election to the presidency in 1960 heralded another milestone in U.S.-Third World relations.

NOTES

1. Charles W. Kegley, Jr., and Eugene R. Wittkopf, *American Foreign Policy: Pattern and Process,* 3rd ed. (New York: St. Martin's Press, 1987), p. 151.

2. See W. W. Rostow, *Eisenhower, Kennedy, and Foreign Aid* (Austin: University of Texas Press, 1985) for an in-depth discussion of the debate over U.S. policy in the Third World during the Truman and Eisenhower presidencies.

3. *Congressional Record,* 80th Congress, 1st session, p. 1981 (March 12, 1947).

4. Cecil V. Crabb, *The Doctrines of American Foreign Policy* (Baton Rouge: Louisiana State University Press, 1982), p. 115.

5. Barbara Ward, J. D. Runnalls, and Lenore d'Anjou, eds., *The Widening Gap: Development in the 1970s* (New York: Columbia University Press, 1971).

6. For an example of this type of argument, see James R. Schlesinger, *The Political Economy of National Security* (New York: Praeger, 1960), pp. 227-232; and

James R. Schlesinger, "Strategic Leverage from Aid and Trade," in Walter Laqueur and Brad Roberts, eds., *America in the World 1962-1987* (New York: St. Martin's Press, 1987), pp. 429-444.

7. Rostow, *Eisenhower, Kennedy,* p. 75.

8. Arthur S. Banks, *Political Handbook of the World 1989* (Binghamton, N.Y.: C.S.A. Publications, 1989), p. 841.

9. See Richard Goode, *Economic Assistance to Developing Countries Through the IMF* (Washington, D.C.: Brookings Institution, 1985) for an account of the history of the IMF and its current mission.

10. Banks, *Political Handbook 1989,* p. 853.

11. Edward C. Banfield, *American Foreign Aid Doctrines* (Washington, D.C.: American Enterprise Institute, 1963).

12. Seymour Martin Lipset, *Political Man* (Garden City, N.Y.: Anchor Books, 1963).

13. Banfield, *American Foreign Aid Doctrines,* p. 65.

14. Thomas A. Bailey, *A Diplomatic History of the American People,* 8th ed. (New York: Appleton-Century-Crofts, 1969), p. 805.

15. James Edward Miller, *The United States and Italy, 1940-1950* (Chapel Hill: University of North Carolina Press, 1986), especially pp. 237-249.

16. Bailey, *A Diplomatic History,* p. 793.

17. Ibid., p. 794.

18. James Irving Matray, *The Reluctant Crusade* (Honolulu: University of Hawaii Press, 1985). See also Dean Acheson, *The Korean War* (New York: W. W. Norton, 1971).

19. *Public Papers of the Presidents of the United States: Harry S Truman, 1950* (Washington, D.C.: U.S. Government Printing Office, 1965), p. 532.

20. Rostow, *Eisenhower, Kennedy,* p. 81.

21. CENTO superseded the so-called Baghdad pact of 1955, which had a similar purpose. The United States did not formally participate in the earlier pact either, but it became a full member of the pact's military planning committee. See William Stivers, "Eisenhower and the Middle East," in Richard Melanson and David Mayers, eds., *Reevaluating Eisenhower* (Urbana: University of Illinois Press, 1987), pp. 192-219.

22. Richard Cottam, *Nationalism in Iran* (Pittsburgh, Pa.: University of Pittsburgh Press, 1979).

23. Kermit Roosevelt, *Countercoup: The Struggle for the Control of Iran* (New York: McGraw-Hill, 1979).

24. Gregory F. Treverton, *The Limits of Intervention in the Postwar World* (New York: Basic Books, 1987), p. 68.

25. Speech by Guillermo Toriello Garido, leader of Guatemala, on March 5, 1954. Reprinted in Thomas G. Paterson, ed., *Major Problems in American Foreign Policy. Volume II: Since 1914* (Lexington, Mass.: D. C. Heath and Co., 1989), pp. 449-451.

26. Speech by Dulles on March 5, 1954, reprinted in Paterson, ed., *Major Problems . . . Volume II,* pp. 451-453.

27. Richard H. Immerman, *The CIA in Guatemala* (Austin: University of Texas Press, 1982).

28. Treverton, *Limits of Intervention,* p. 73.

29. Ibid., p. 91.

30. Ibid., p. 92.

31. See Thomas Zourmaras, "Eisenhower's Foreign Economic Policy: The Case of Latin America," in Melanson and Mayers, eds., *Reevaluating Eisenhower,* pp. 155-191. For a very different view of Eisenhower's foreign policy toward the Third

World, see Burton I. Kaufman, *Trade and Aid: Eisenhower's Foreign Economic Policy, 1953-1961* (Baltimore: Johns Hopkins University Press, 1982), pp. 7, 58-73.

32. See, for example, Jacob J. Kaplan, *The Challenge of Foreign Aid* (New York: Frederick A. Praeger, 1967), pp. 50-52.

33. Russell Edgerton, *Sub-Cabinet Politics and Policy Commitment: The Birth of the Development Loan Fund* (Syracuse, N.Y.: Inter-University Case Program, 1970).

34. Rostow, *Eisenhower, Kennedy,* pp. 129-130.

35. Ibid., p. 133.

36. Banks, *Political Handbook 1989,* pp. 801-802.

37. Ibid., p. 801.

38. Crabb, *The Doctrines of American Foreign Policy,* p. 154.

39. Ibid., p. 184.

40. Richard E. Welch, Jr., *Response to Revolution* (Chapel Hill: University of North Carolina Press, 1985), p. 43.

41. Ibid., p. 37.

42. Cable reprinted in William M. Leary, ed., *The Central Intelligence Agency: History and Documents* (University of Alabama Press, 1984), pp. 131-133.

43. Ibid.

44. Treverton, *Limits of Intervention.*

45. Bailey, *A Diplomatic History,* p. 806.

46. Ibid., p. 804.

CHAPTER 8

Fostering Social Justice

Between 1961 and 1980 the Progressive foreign policy agenda grew in size and importance. This era began with the election of a Democrat, John F. Kennedy, to the presidency (1961-1963). As noted earlier, as a U.S. senator, Kennedy had been a strong advocate of a Progressive foreign policy toward developing countries. Like Truman and Eisenhower, Kennedy acknowledged that the United States should have a role in the economic development of the Third World. At the same time, he recognized that economic development would not necessarily bring about a fairer distribution of economic wealth and political power in developing countries. Thus, his contribution to the Progressive agenda was to establish a new U.S. foreign policy goal—improving the well-being of the poorest people in Third World societies.

This period of expansion of the Progressive agenda ended with the presidency of another Democrat, Jimmy Carter (1977-1981). More than any other president in the postwar era, Carter emphasized North-South relations in his foreign policy. He made the goal of improving the human rights practices of governments around the world the centerpiece of that policy. Carter's contribution to the Progressive agenda of U.S. foreign policy toward the Third World was so significant that it is discussed separately in the next chapter.

The legacies of the three presidents between Kennedy and Carter— Johnson (Democrat, 1963-1969), Nixon (Republican, 1969-1975), and Ford (Republican, 1975-1977)—are more mixed. All three conducted foreign policies in which Nationalist principles dominated most of the rhetoric, policy efforts, and impacts. Johnson presided over the massive expansion of U.S. involvement in the Vietnam War, and the Nixon administration negotiated the peace treaty ending it.

The most significant action-forcing events affecting U.S. foreign policy toward the Third World during this period were the Cuban Missile Crisis of 1962 and growing communist-led activity against the government of South Vietnam in the 1950s and 1960s, the fall of the shah of Iran in

1979, and the Iranian hostage crisis of 1980. The lessons of history that Americans drew from the consequences of the U.S. response to these events have had a lasting effect on U.S. foreign policy toward the Third World.

KENNEDY

Kennedy viewed America as a powerful and potentially positive force in international affairs, and he wanted world opinion to judge that force as being clearly on the side of social justice for the poorest people in the Third World. He advocated a Progressive foreign policy agenda, at least in part, as he said in his inaugural address in January 1961, because it was the morally right thing to do. In addition, if the United States was successful in stimulating reforms in the Third World, much of the impetus for revolutionary movements in LDCs would be removed. This, too, was an important element in Kennedy's thinking.

The Kennedy administration was the first to propose a policy toward developing countries that fairly directly advanced the interests of the neediest people in the Third World. Prior to 1961, U.S. foreign policy toward the Third World emphasized an interest in stopping the spread of communism. As discussed earlier, the vast majority of aid was in the form of military assistance to those countries that were willing to help the United States in the struggle against militant communism. The needs of the developing countries themselves, if considered at all, were relatively unimportant. During the Kennedy administration, the amount of funds available to aid economic development in the Third World was dramatically expanded, and its distribution was not as closely tied to formal or informal military alliances.

Unlike his predecessors, Kennedy was willing to work toward regional solutions to conflicts in the Third World, predisposed to work closely with the United Nations and other international organizations on international problems, and willing to make greater use of positive incentives and less use of sanctions in order to achieve U.S. objectives. He realized that the conflicts between the superpowers would be ideological and would be fought to win over the hearts and minds of underprivileged people. Overwhelming coercive force would be less useful than good words and deeds.

In his inaugural address, Kennedy announced his expanded vision of the rationale for U.S. foreign policy toward the Third World:

> To those peoples in the huts and villages of half the globe struggling to break the bonds of mass misery, we pledge our best efforts to help them

help themselves, for whatever period is required—not because the communists may be doing it, not because we seek their votes, but because it is right. If a free society cannot help the many who are poor, it cannot save the few who are rich.[1]

Interestingly, in his address Kennedy references the poor people of the Third World directly, not their governments. This concern with the neediest in the Third World and with distributive justice is characteristic of those who adhere to Progressive foreign policy principles.

Declaring an Alliance for Progress between the United States and Latin American republics, he continued:

To our sister republics south of our border, we offer a special pledge to convert our good words into good deeds, in a new alliance for progress, to assist free men and free governments in casting off the chains of poverty.

He concluded this part of his address with a stern restatement of the Monroe Doctrine:

But this peaceful revolution of hope cannot become the prey of hostile powers. Let all our neighbors know that we shall join with them to oppose aggression or subversion anywhere in the Americas. And let every other power know that this hemisphere intends to remain the master of its own house.

What is distinct about this speech is that the mutuality of interests between the United States and the people of developing nations of the Third World was for the first time emphasized as a cornerstone of U.S. policy. At least in terms of Kennedy's rhetoric, developing nations became less objects or instruments of U.S. interests and more partners in a noble cause. The effect was to deemphasize the U.S. role as peacekeeper and to move toward a role as facilitator of needed reforms in the Third World.

The United States' commitment to the cause of improving the lot of poor people in developing countries where most people are not of white, European descent, was somewhat ironic, given the outburst of racism in the United States during the height of the civil rights movement in the late 1950s and early 1960s. Eisenhower and Kennedy's use of armed forces to desegregate the schools did not go unnoticed by the leaders of the developing countries. And, later, neither did the assassinations of key supporters of the civil rights movement such as John Kennedy, Robert Kennedy, and Martin Luther King.

The three goals of the new Alliance for Progress in the Western

Hemisphere were to accelerate the rate of economic development; to encourage more progressive taxation and a more equitable distribution of landownership; and to support democratic movements and democratic systems against dictatorships of all kinds. The Progressive goals of supporting economic development and democratization were by now familiar. But the emphasis on social justice—the insistence on a fair distribution of the burdens (taxes) and benefits (landownership and government expenditures) of the policies pursued by Latin American countries—was new.

Significantly, the United States did not unilaterally impose these objectives on its Latin American neighbors. In August 1961, at the Conference of the Inter-American Economic and Social Council of the Organization of American States held in Uruguay, leaders of the democratic Latin American republics agreed to strengthen democratic institutions, speed up economic development, work to provide decent housing for the poor, encourage landownership reforms, improve working conditions, eliminate illiteracy, promote better health, reform the tax system, and take other measures necessary to help those at the bottom of the social class structure. The United States, for its part, agreed to provide substantial economic assistance.

In the effort to convert good words into deeds, the Kennedy administration

1. Established the Agency for International Development (AID) to reorganize and consolidate a myriad of ongoing overseas economic assistance programs and to bolster flagging public support for U.S. foreign aid to developing countries.

2. Supported legislation modifying the existing Public Law-480 food assistance program. The program was designed by the Eisenhower administration to allow U.S. farmers to sell government produce, which was then shipped as a gift to developing countries. The PL-480 program received a higher budgetary priority under the Kennedy administration and was renamed the Food for Peace Program.

3. Established a Peace Corps of U.S. technical advisers in the Third World. Consisting mainly of recent college graduates, the Peace Corps provided a way for idealistic, dedicated, altruistic Americans to carry their knowledge about education, sanitation, basic medicine, nursing, agronomy, and carpentry to developing countries willing to accept their assistance.

4. Scrapped the old Mutual Security Act of 1953 and replaced it with the Foreign Assistance Act of 1961. This piece of legislation, with amendments, still provides the ground rules for granting U.S. foreign

aid. Changing the name of this program dramatized what many hoped would be the beginning of a new age in U.S.–Third World relations.

By and large, the United States followed through on the Alliance for Progress commitments during the period Kennedy served as president. Critics noted that the resources provided were inadequate to produce great changes quickly, and some were unhappy that the effort was not more massive. A more serious criticism was that, under the auspices of the Alliance, U.S. aid was provided to the oppressive, dictatorial regimes of General Alfredo Stroessner of Paraguay and "Papa Doc" Duvalier of Haiti.

One interpretation of this seemingly inconsistent behavior is that the pro-democracy and social justice themes of Kennedy's rhetoric were simply a smokescreen for other motives. Another is that the United States was willing to work with independent dictatorships in the effort to wean them away from oppression and to win them over to more open and democratic practices.[2] What is clear is that Kennedy's main concern in Latin America, like Monroe's before him, was that the republics of that region remain independent and not fall under the domination of foreign regimes. He promoted Progressive objectives in Latin America only when they did not seriously conflict with U.S. military and economic interests in the region.

At a key moment, however, Kennedy proved his willingness to both wield the big stick in Latin America and use it on the side of a democratic, not just an anti-communist, movement. That moment came in 1961, when Rafael Trujillo was assassinated in the Dominican Republic after more than 30 years of dictatorial and despotic rule. There was strong popular sentiment for elections and democracy, but Trujillo's son controlled the military. When, in November 1961, it appeared that the son was preparing to reestablish the dictatorship, Kennedy sent eight ships and 1,800 marines to take up a station off the coast of Santo Domingo. The elections took place, and the younger Trujillo ultimately left the country.

That same year Kennedy suffered his greatest foreign policy defeat. Before leaving office, Eisenhower had authorized the CIA to train about 1,500 Cuban exiles for a possible invasion of Cuba. In April 1961 Kennedy allowed the invasion to take place, but it was badly bungled and failed miserably. The controversy was heightened when Kennedy agreed to a ransom of $53 million worth of food and medical supplies in return for the release of 1,100 prisoners from Cuban jails. Criticized by many, this payment was even termed international blackmail by Republican Senator Goldwater. The failed Bay of Pigs invasion strengthened Castro's image at home and throughout Latin America. U.S. prestige in the region tumbled.

Not surprisingly, the Monroe Doctrine was again challenged soon afterward when, in October 1962, U.S. intelligence agencies discovered that Soviet technicians were assembling nuclear missiles in Cuba capable of reaching U.S. cities. Kennedy ordered the missiles dismantled and removed and announced a quarantine on all ships carrying offensive weapons to Cuba. In an unusual show of support, the Latin American members of the Organization of American States voted unanimously to back the U.S. position.[3] The Soviet Union, not wishing to risk a nuclear holocaust, complied with Kennedy's request, and U.S. prestige in the region received a major boost. The U.S. policy toward Cuba since then has been designed to produce political isolation and economic hardship, thereby undermining the Castro regime. In 1964 all members of the Organization of American States except Mexico voted to support the United States' economic reprisals against Cuba. On one level, most Americans judged the U.S. response to the Cuban missile crisis as a success, for the United States had demonstrated its military superiority relative to the Soviet Union, at least in its own backyard. The more lasting lesson, however, was that direct confrontation between the superpowers in a nuclear age was too dangerous.

When Kennedy took office in 1961, he encountered a Congo policy that, like the prevailing policy toward Cuba, was already in motion. However, unlike Eisenhower, whose administration generally neglected African affairs, Kennedy viewed the formerly colonized societies in Africa as deserving of more serious policy consideration.[4] The rhetorical support of the U.S. government for anticolonial movements had been remarkably consistent during the twentieth century, even though it had often caused conflict with the colonial powers of Europe. During the 1800s, when the anticolonial movement was centered in Latin America, an anticolonial position also had been consistent with U.S. interests in military defense, because the U.S. mainland was easier to defend against external threats if foreign powers did not have bases in the Western Hemisphere. In the twentieth century, when the anticolonial movement was centered in Africa, U.S. military interests were either not at stake or were weakened by the independence movements in the region. Thus, speaking up for anticolonial movements there gained little and risked provoking the ire of Western European economic and military allies.

Still, Kennedy, both as senator and as president, was outspoken against colonialism. While in the Senate, he had been chairman of the African Subcommittee of the Committee on Foreign Relations. There he developed a reputation as a champion of African nationalist, anticolonial movements. As president, he worked hard to convince the leaders of African nations that he was more on their side than on the side of European ex-colonial powers. In 1960 the U.S. commitment to anticolonialism was severely tested when Belgium, confronted by internal riots and external pressures, granted independence to the once-Belgian Republic of the Congo. Europeans there were soon subjected to rioting, looting, and other forms of extreme harassment. The Belgians responded by halting their withdrawal and sending a larger military force to maintain order. Despite the apparent justification for Belgian intervention, the United States joined the other members of the United Nations Security Council in condemning Belgian "imperialism." The United States also contributed military support to the U.N. peacekeeping force sent to the Congo to keep the Belgians out.

This was an important test because the Congo is a mineral-rich country. Thus, more than symbols were at stake. Even once the triumph of African nationalism was assured, the United States could have supported Moise Tshombe as that country's leader, but Tshombe was widely regarded as a neocolonial agent. Patrice Lumumba, his rival, was expected to steer a more independent course. The United States supported Lumumba despite the risk that the independent course he would steer would be detrimental to immediate U.S. interests. When Lumumba was murdered, the U.S. government actively supported another independent-minded African nationalist, Cyrille Adoula, who, in 1961, became head of state.

Similarly, in a 1961 U.N. vote, the United States advocated an end to Portuguese rule in Angola, even though this move sparked anti-American protests in Lisbon and threatened U.S. access to its air base in the Portuguese-controlled Azores. Later, the U.S. anticolonial position on Angola softened, but Kennedy worked hard to explain the U.S. dilemma to moderate African leaders. Because of his generally pro-African posture, these efforts met with some success.[5]

During his 1990 visit to the United States, Nelson Mandela reminded Americans that Kennedy also was the first American president to impose sanctions on South Africa to force an end to that nation's policy of apartheid. In August 1963 the United Nations Security Council, with U.S. support, adopted Resolution 181 calling on all states to cease shipments of arms to South Africa.[6] This was a departure from the previous U.S. position at the United Nations opposing the imposition of specific sanctions as likely to be ineffective.[7] While in the South African case, Kennedy was willing to use sanctions to achieve Progressive foreign policy objectives, he was less likely than many other presidents to use sanctions to accomplish short-range, narrowly conceived political objectives in the Third World. When he failed to convert Ghana's Kwame Nkrumah from a pro-Soviet to a pro-American foreign policy, for example, the United States gave Ghana a large share of its African economic development funds anyway.

Kennedy's emphasis on Progressive goals for U.S. foreign policy in the Third World did not mean that he had lost sight of the nation's national economic self-interest in the Third World. Although the U.S. government had consistently used its influence to prevent foreign governments from expropriating the property of U.S.-based multinational corporations, the ground rules got tougher and more explicit during the Kennedy administration. The policy initiative came from the Senate, perhaps because Kennedy's idealism raised doubts about his commitment to protecting U.S. foreign investment. In the end, however, Kennedy gave the measure his support.

The initiative came in the form of an amendment to the foreign aid bill of 1962, proposed by Senator Bourke Hickenlooper. The Hickenlooper Amendment created a statutory link between the disbursement of foreign aid and the prompt compensation for property expropriated by a foreign government. Unless a foreign government made prompt compensation or initiated "appropriate steps" to do so, U.S. foreign aid of all kinds—including food shipments under the Food for Peace Program—would be stopped.[8] Senator Henry Gonzalez used the same provision to place similar constraints on U.S. approval of multilateral loans such as those made by the World Bank.

Although the provisions of the amendment were invoked only once (against Ceylon in 1963), invocation was considered against several countries including Brazil (1962), Honduras (1962), Argentina (1964), and Peru, Ecuador, and Bolivia in the late 1960s. Charles Lipson, supporting the critical theory perspective, argues that the punitive provisions of the legislation were seldom invoked and eventually were repealed in 1973, not because they were wrong, but because they were ineffective. Although the legislation made the suspension of aid mandatory, the president was permitted to determine whether an expropriation had occurred and whether compensation was adequate. As the record shows, most presidents had chosen not to invoke the punitive provisions of the act.

As evidence of the interest of big business in getting the punitive provisions off the books, Lipson notes that the repeal in 1973 was supported by the multinational corporations themselves.[9] However, there is room to doubt this interpretation. If the legislation was ineffective, why would MNCs care one way or another about its repeal? After all, it was not replaced by more effective legislation. On the other hand, no administration, including Kennedy's, ever argued that the anti-expropriation legislation was morally inappropriate, only that it was ineffective. This is a significant point, since the principle of full compensation for expropriated property was a substantial barrier to agrarian reform within many developing countries. So insisting on it for U.S.-based multinational corporations made such reform more difficult.

JOHNSON

Lyndon Baines Johnson became president in 1963 after John F. Kennedy's assassination. His handling of the Vietnam conflict and the consequences of those policies as perceived by the American public constitute his main lasting contribution to the character of U.S.–Third World relations. Some view the Vietnam War as an internal revolution against the government of South Vietnam. Others regard it as a war against the external aggression of North Vietnam. The war was supported and directed by Communist North Vietnam. It resulted in the unification of North and South Vietnam. But it is still unclear which side the people of South Vietnam supported.

U.S. involvement in Vietnam was deep even before Johnson came to office in 1963. During the Eisenhower administration, the United States had begun helping the South Vietnamese government in its struggle for survival by sending foreign aid and military advisers. Kennedy escalated the U.S. involvement by sending more aid and more advisers. By the end of each successive year, the contingent of U.S. advisers grew larger: 1960 – 875; 1961 – 3,164; 1962 – 11,326; 1963 – 16,263; 1964 – 23,210.[10] The 1964 Gulf of Tonkin Resolution gave President Johnson congressional approval "to take all necessary steps including the use of armed force, to assist any member or protocol state of the Southeast Asia Collective Defense Treaty requesting assistance in defense of its freedom." It stated that the United States should commit military force to the protection of South Vietnam from the communist North, not because of any military or territorial motives of the United States, but because the South Vietnamese "peoples should be left in peace to work out their own destinies in their own way." When he signed the Gulf of Tonkin Resolution into law, Johnson interpreted the resolution broadly to mean: "To any armed attack upon our forces, we shall reply. To any in Southeast Asia who ask our help in defending our freedom, we shall give it."[11]

Johnson took U.S. involvement to a new and higher level when he chose to escalate U.S. involvement to over a half million troops, making it the third largest war in U.S. history. It seemed that victory was always just around the corner, but the war dragged on and on. In 1965, shortly after Johnson had decided to send a massive military force to Vietnam, he explained his decision in a speech at Johns Hopkins University:

> We fight because we must fight if we are to live in a world where every country can shape its own destiny, and only in such a world will our own freedom be secure. . . . We are there because we have a promise to keep. Since 1954 every American President has offered support to the people of

South Viet-Nam. We have helped to build, and we have helped to defend. Thus, over many years, we have made a national pledge to help South Viet-Nam defend its independence.[12]

Beseeching the leaders of North Vietnam to stop the aggression, Johnson continued in that same speech to describe U.S. desires to improve the conditions of life for all Vietnamese, North and South:

> For our part, I will ask Congress to join in a billion dollar American investment in this (economic development) effort as soon as it is under-way. . . . The vast Mekong River can provide food and water and power on a scale to dwarf even our own T.V.A. . . . The wonders of modern medicine can be spread through villages where thousands die every year from lack of care. Schools can be established to train people in the skills needed to manage the process of development. And these objectives, and more, are within the reach of a cooperative and determined effort.

Given these humanitarian sentiments and the antipoverty emphasis of his domestic Great Society programs, we cannot help but wonder what legacy Johnson would have left in foreign policy toward the Third World had the energies of his presidency not been so consumed by the Vietnam War.

Throughout his presidency, Johnson was beleaguered by attacks from all sides over his handling of the Vietnam War. To most Americans, the war was a great defeat for the United States and a great victory for the forces of communism. The victory was magnified because the winner was David and the loser was Goliath. The North Vietnamese had won against a much stronger foe and, for most of the war's duration, through the use of a masterful hit-and-run military strategy. The legacy of the Vietnam War was a lasting reluctance to commit U.S. troops to potentially long-lasting, low-intensity conflicts in the Third World. The U.S. response to the Iraqi invasion of Kuwait in 1990 and the generally supportive reaction of the American public to the commitment of troops there indicate that this "Vietnam syndrome" may be passing. However, even in that instance, the public supported a swift victory, with little probability of heavy U.S. ca-sualties, not a prolonged, low-technology ground war like the one fought in Vietnam. The outcome of the Vietnam War also damaged the image of the United States in the Third World. The military defeat resulted in lower prestige, and the sheer scale of U.S. involvement reinforced the Third World notion that the United States was an aggressive, imperialist nation.

To make matters worse, Johnson confronted serious problems in Central America and in the Caribbean. Because of his reaction to them and because of his general neglect of the Progressive foreign policy agenda in Latin America, Robert Kennedy, then a U.S. senator, accused him of backsliding on the Alliance for Progress goals of economic development, and social and political reform. The Johnson administration's reaction to difficult situations in Panama and the Dominican Republic provides some support for Kennedy's charges. The problem in Panama arose in 1964 when that government demanded that the 1906 treaty that gave the United States control over the Panama Canal "in perpetuity" should be renegotiated. The Johnson administration stalled. Although he did not actually promise to renegotiate the treaty, Johnson did agree to review and negotiate any issue the country of Panama wished to raise and he did not rule out the possibility of renegotiating the treaty. After his landslide reelection in 1964, he did finally promise to negotiate an entirely new treaty with Panama on the Canal. These negotiations were completed during the Carter administration in 1977. The Senate, after a long fight, finally ratified the treaty in 1978 despite the active opposition of soon-to-be president Ronald Reagan.

Johnson also was faced with continuing instability in the Dominican Republic. Problems with the Dominican Republic had come to a head in 1963 when the popularly elected, reform-minded government headed by Juan Bosch was overthrown in a military coup. The U.S. government had long been suspicious of Bosch's leftist orientation, but when he proved in a free and fair election that his people were behind him, Kennedy decided to support him. Kennedy saw U.S. government support for Bosch as the only way to demonstrate that the United States really intended to back constitutional democracy and social reform in Latin America. Just before his assassination, Kennedy, apparently disappointed by the military overthrow of the Bosch government, cut off all foreign aid to the Dominican Republic.[13] The Johnson administration, however, did little to help restore Bosch to power. Instead, it quickly recognized the new military government and stepped up U.S. foreign aid to the Dominican Republic.

Another coup occurred in 1965, and this time law and order broke down. Johnson ordered the navy and the marines to help evacuate U.S. citizens. Within a short time there was a U.S. military force of about twenty-one thousand in the Dominican Republic. In a television address, Johnson told the public that U.S. forces had intervened to protect the lives of U.S. citizens and to prevent a communist government from coming to power. Theodore Draper, a critic of the U.S. intervention, argues that a large-scale military intervention was not necessary to protect the lives of U.S. citizens, but was really designed to prevent the leftist, reform-minded Bosch government from returning to power.[14] There is no evidence, however, that the U.S. government instigated the revolution in the Dominican Republic.[15] In his own speeches to the American people in the wake of the Dominican intervention, Johnson gave some credence to the

Draper thesis. In what has become known as the Johnson Doctrine on Latin America, he said: "The American nations cannot, must not, and will not permit the establishment of another Communist government in the Western Hemisphere."[16] This statement coupled with the Dominican intervention just the month before made it clear that Washington was willing to act unilaterally to prevent the spread of communism into Latin America, no matter how strong the opposition of the leaders of other American republics.

Most observers agreed that Johnson's strong anti-communist position, especially in Latin America, was largely dictated by the historical and political conditions affecting the foreign policy decision-making process in the immediate aftermath of the successful communist revolution in Cuba.[17] The Dominican action was generally applauded by the American public, as most U.S. military interventions into the Third World other than Vietnam have been. But Senator William Fulbright, chairman of the Senate Foreign Relations Committee, was publicly critical of the administration's action. He argued that the conditions in the Dominican Republic did not warrant military intervention, that the intervention had alienated Latin America, that the action was not motivated by a desire to promote human welfare in the Third World, and that it reflected an official bias against revolutionary change there.[18]

The Organization of American States (OAS) also vehemently protested the military intervention as unwarranted and as an unwelcome return to "gunboat diplomacy." The Johnson administration justified its action by citing the OAS agreement in 1962 which declared communism to be "incompatible with the principles of the inter-American system," and it urged OAS members "to take those steps that they may consider appropriate for their individual and collective self-defense."[19] Another major development during the Johnson administration that had a substantial effect on relations between the United States and the Third World was the Six-Day War between Israel and the United Arab Republic, Algeria, Syria, Iraq, Sudan, and Yemen in 1967. The United States did not intervene militarily, but provided intelligence and other support to Israel. As a result, the six Arab states broke off diplomatic relations with the United States.

NIXON

Richard M. Nixon came to power in 1969 amidst strong public demands to end the terribly costly Vietnam War one way or the other. His administration promised "peace with honor." Whether that objective was achieved remains a matter of some debate, but the Paris peace accord was signed in January 1973, and all U.S. troops were withdrawn soon after. The war experience forced the American public and its leaders to reexamine the unilateral, international police role of the United States. There were many indirect and limited confrontations between the superpowers after World War II, but the Vietnam War was special: large numbers of U.S. troops were committed for a prolonged period to fight against revolutionaries equipped by the Soviet Union and China, and, despite that massive U.S. effort, the revolutionaries won.

The loss of the war in Vietnam marked the first time U.S. troops had been committed to the losing side of a war. In this instance the "forces of freedom" had lost to an opponent generally recognized as having greater will but less military or economic power. Thus, both the United States and the French had learned that there were limits to military force as a means toward the ends of major powers in the developing world. And, since military might had not prevailed, the use of other sometimes covert methods, previously avoided as immoral or unethical, became even more credible.

Distancing himself from the ambitious Truman Doctrine, Nixon made it clear that in Asia, at least, in the future the United States would come to the assistance of only those nations with which it had treaty commitments. In 1969 he said:

> I believe the time has come when the United States, in our relations with our Asian friends, [must] be quite emphatic on two points: One, that we will keep our treaty commitments, for example, with Thailand under SEATO; but, two, that as far as the problems of internal security are concerned, as far as the problems of military defense, except for the threat of a major power involving nuclear weapons, that the problem will be increasingly handled by, and the responsibility for it taken by the Asian nations themselves.[20]

That same year, while on a round-the-world trip, Nixon elucidated his own view of future military involvements in Asia. Whereas in the past the United States had been willing to provide both personnel and weapons, in the future, he explained, it would provide weapons only to those governments willing to provide the soldiers to defend themselves. In Nixon's mind, this was "not a formula for getting America out of Asia, but one that provided the only sound basis for America's staying in and continuing to play a responsible role in helping the non-Communist nations and neutrals as well as our Asian allies to defend their independence."[21] Still, most observers concluded that, chastised by the Vietnam experience, the United States would in the future be very reluctant to use military force to achieve its ends in the Third World, especially outside of Latin America and the Middle East.

This policy of nonintervention in Asia was put to the test indirectly in 1971 when India attacked Pakistan. Both countries had a history of relatively cordial relations with the United States, but India had just signed the Soviet-Indian Friendship Treaty, bringing India more firmly into the Soviet camp. The military government of Pakistan had been preparing for an imminent change to civilian rule, but also had been engaged in the oppression of many citizens in East Pakistan, who were pressing for the formation of an independent state (later to be known as Bangladesh). In reaction to the severe oppression in East Pakistan, the United States had cut off economic aid to Pakistan.

The war was caused in part by the movement of large numbers of refugees from East Pakistan to India and, according to Henry Kissinger, a Nixon adviser, by the desire of India's leader, Indira Gandhi, to conquer and rule all of Pakistan. Before the partition of 1947, Pakistan had been part of the Indian nation. Kissinger argues that the creation of the independent state of Bangladesh was all but assured, without the necessity of war, and that the establishment of the new state would have stopped the refugee problem and the oppression which, together, provided the immediate justification for India's invasion.[22]

The situation presented a severe and complicated test of U.S. foreign policy. The weight of public and congressional opinion was on India's side. The Soviet Union also supported India by supplying arms and diplomatic support. China, with a long history of tensions along its border with India, supported Pakistan. The Nixon administration desired a strong China as a counterbalance for Soviet strength, and a victory for India would have undermined this objective.

Furthermore, the United States had signed a bilateral military agreement with Pakistan in 1959, similar to agreements it had signed with several less developed countries in Asia. The 1959 agreement stipulated that, in the event of foreign aggression, the U.S. government would take "appropriate action" subject to its constitutional processes. Although the language was weak, when considered in the context of a history of communication between Pakistan and several U.S. presidents and secretaries of state, the United States wanted to reassure Pakistan in no uncertain terms that it would receive U.S. assistance in the event of an attack by India. Other less developed countries in the region with whom the United States had similar agreements undoubtedly were watching.

But India also had a long-term close relationship with the United States and was viewed as strategically important in the existing balance of power. Strong actions against India could have driven that country to an even closer relationship with the Soviet Union. Nonetheless, Washington requested that India stop its military advance against the much weaker Pakistani army. When the request did not bring quick results, Nixon ordered naval units into the Indian Ocean in a show of military force. He assured the Soviet Union that the United States would not allow West Pakistan to be conquered, and he cut off economic aid to India. Soon afterward, Gandhi offered an unconditional cease-fire, and tensions dissipated. We will never know whether the United States would have committed military personnel to the area if Gandhi had not complied, whether Nationalist power objectives in the region would have outweighed the moral commitment represented by the treaty with Pakistan.

Perhaps Nixon's greatest foreign policy accomplishment was the reestablishment of diplomatic relations with Communist China which had been broken after the Maoist takeover in 1949. The improvement in relations between China and the United States was underscored by Nixon's visit there in 1972. Improving relations with China has been a high priority of all Republican presidents since.

With regard to the Middle East, the 1967 Six-Day War and the humiliating defeat suffered by the Arab participants in it had caused lingering anti-American bitterness in this region. With another war inevitable, much of the diplomatic effort of the Nixon administration was directed toward cooling off tensions in that region. Despite those efforts, in October 1973, during the Jewish holy days, Egypt and Syria attacked Israel. The Soviet Union supplied arms to Egypt and Syria; the United States did the same for Israel. The outcome was another defeat of the Arab states.

Partly as a result of this second disgrace, the Organization of Petroleum Exporting Countries (OPEC) announced an oil embargo against the United States. This was the first time in history that lesser powers had publicly banded together to apply an economic sanction against a superpower. The embargo was short-lived, but OPEC was successful in raising the price of oil substantially. The raising of energy costs began an inflationary spiral that led to an economic recession in the oil-importing states, including the United States, Japan, and Western Europe. Inflation in the 1970s also was a major contributor to the debt crisis in many Third World states which had been forced to borrow while rates were high.

The leaders of many developing nations were angered when in 1968 the United States and the Soviet Union signed the Nuclear Nonproliferation Treaty designed to limit the use of nuclear weapons to the five nations—the United States, the Soviet Union, Great Britain, China, and France—that already had such capability. The treaty allowed all states to use nuclear power for civilian purposes, but required the periodic international inspection of nuclear power plants in those states without nuclear weapons to make sure that the plants did not produce weapons. The five nuclear weapons states would not be subject to the same inspection provision. The agreement was obviously in the self-interest of those five nations and of all others that were a long way from having the technical capacity and economic base to take the nuclear path. But several other nations, including the developing nations of Argentina, Belgium, Brazil, India, and South Africa, were on the verge of having nuclear weapon capacity and refused to sign the treaty.

India led the opposition, arguing that the treaty represented "an attempt by the armed to disarm the unarmed." The representatives of India and similarly situated governments wondered whether the nuclear powers were willing to extend credible security guarantees to states foreswearing nuclear weapons, but no such reassurances were forthcoming. Most nations that were not then in the nuclear weapons club resented being relegated to second-class citizenship in the international system. In the end, even France and China, two of the five members of the nuclear club, refused to sign the treaty.

Although the focus of U.S. foreign policy was on the Middle East and on Vietnam through most of the Nixon presidency, these were situations his administration inherited, not situations it created. More significant for the Third World, in general, were the United States' new reluctance to commit military personnel to battle in developing countries and the First World governments' reemphasis on the private sector to assist the economic development efforts of less developed countries.

This reemphasis on the private sector began in 1969 with the inauguration of President Nixon and, except for the brief interlude of the Carter administration between 1976 and 1980, continues to the present. Nixon explained this return to an old theme in U.S. foreign policy toward the Third World in a 1973 report to Congress on U.S. economic policy in Africa:

> In the economic sphere, while the United States was able to maintain the level of its governmental assistance, the most promising source of capital to finance African development were now trade and private investment. The means of African support for African development would thus necessarily be more diverse, and the first responsibility for mobilizing energies and resources would clearly rest on the Africans themselves.[23]

The close working relationship between multinational corporations and government agencies in American foreign policy toward developing countries was illustrated when government guarantees of private investment against risks stemming from war and expropriation were vastly expanded. A small pilot program had been established in 1948, but the Overseas Private Enterprise Development Corporation (OPIC) was created in 1969 to manage a newer and much larger government insurance program.[24] The larger program reflected the Nixon administration's emphasis on aiding Third World development through private initiatives rather than through government expenditures.

Conventional analysis suggests that the expansion of OPIC was needed to help encourage the flow of funds from private sources to Latin American countries, because there had been a substantial slowing of private investment in Latin America following the Cuban revolution and the massive expropriation there. Critics suggest that the expansion of government insurance for foreign investment came as a result of growing pressures from large U.S. corporations for government actions that would increase profits.[25] The Nixon administration's response to the establishment of a socialist-leaning regime in Chile provides some evidence for this point of view.

EXPANDED USE OF COVERT METHODS

In the early 1960s Salvador Allende emerged as a powerful leader of the Communist party in Chile. Running in the presidential election campaign in 1964, he announced his intention, if elected, to nationalize basic industries, many of which were multinational corporations based in the United States or Western Europe. Representatives of ITT and other multinational corporations made their concerns known to the U.S. government and asked for assistance in preventing Allende from implementing these policies.

Nixon had a long and well-earned reputation as an anti-communist, so his administration was especially angry when Chile threatened to become the second government in Latin America to come under the rule of a communist regime. According to a 1975 report by the Senate Select Committee to Study Government Operations with Respect to Intelligence Activities (the Church Committee), the CIA had been "directed to undertake an effort to prevent the accession to power of Salvadore Allende."

The most common covert activity in Chile was propaganda. For example, the CIA paid to have editorials and articles favorable to U.S. interests printed by a Santiago daily. The effort also involved producing materials falsely labeled as the product of a particular individual or group in an attempt to sow discord among such Chilean groups as the communists and the socialists. By far the largest expenditures by the CIA during the period were in support of Chilean political parties opposing Allende.

The aim of these and other activities was to influence the direction of political events in Chile. In particular, they were designed to prevent Allende, an avowed Marxist and leader of the Chilean Communist party, from defeating the Christian Democratic candidate in 1964. Allende did lose, but covert activities continued, with the aim of undermining support for the Allende candidacy in the 1970 campaign. This time, however, Allende won. According to Kissinger, Nixon's closest adviser on foreign policy, these efforts were directed mainly toward maintaining the survival of opposition groups that U.S. leaders believed to be threatened. Kissinger has argued that taking such measures in support of internal forces seeking to maintain a democratic counterweight to radical dominance is morally justifiable.[26]

After Allende's election, despite the CIA-inspired efforts against him, he moved quickly to nationalize basic industries and some foreign companies and defaulted on most foreign debts, including those to the United States. Compensation was paid to the owners of the foreign companies, but at a level that the Nixon administration judged to be well below full value.[27] Nixon then ordered CIA activities to be undertaken to remove Allende from power. The Church Committee report describes the subsequent development of a close working relationship between CIA personnel and multinational corporations in Chile. The corporations provided cover for CIA operatives, financing for the plot, and information.

In September 1973 a successful coup occurred. The plot was executed by the Chilean military and no American personnel were present, but most believe that the behind-the-scenes role of the U.S. government was substantial. During the coup, Allende either committed suicide or was killed. The boldness of the covert actions in Chile angered the leaders of many other Latin American countries. Members of Congress and the press also severely criticized U.S. involvement in Chile. The Church Committee report describes U.S. efforts in Chile as "striking but not unique" and as on a scale that was "unusual but by no means unprecedented."

In one sense, American foreign policy toward Chile during this period is puzzling. The United States worked hard to bring Allende's leftist regime down, and then, when it was replaced by the right-wing Augusto Pinochet regime, which was not stridently anti-American but which placed a moratorium on elections and other civil rights and liberties, Congress stopped all foreign aid to Chile. This apparent inconsistency in U.S. foreign policy behavior is a manifestation of the rising tide of reform in U.S. government which occurred in the aftermath of the Watergate scandal in the United States. This reform movement led to Nixon's resignation in August 1974 and tarnished most of the policies he championed, including his foreign policy in Chile. An integral part of the reform movement was a new, more idealistic view of the means and ends of U.S. foreign policy toward the Third World, a view that reached its high point during the Carter presidency.

Kissinger, in his memoirs, noted that during the earlier Cold War period, CIA activities had observed certain limits. They were used to counter military threats to the United States, few of which emanated from Third World states. The new emphasis on changing the domestic affairs of other states, on the other hand, "justifies unlimited intervention to promote internal change in countries that are both friend and foe; it has been directed against countries that do not threaten our national security and that may indeed be allies of the United States."[28]

When the Kennedy administration announced that the economic, social, and political development of less developed nations was to be a foreign policy goal of the U.S. government, Kennedy stated boldly for the first time that U.S. foreign policy should seek to affect not just the foreign policies of other nations but their domestic affairs as well. Ironically, this new emphasis on helping the masses in the Third World was sometimes used to justify increased covert activities to influence domestic outcomes in weaker nations. For example, according to press reports in the late 1960s, the CIA made several attempts between 1960 and 1965 to assassinate Fidel Castro. These allegations were substantiated in the 1975 Church Committee report, which describes at least eight plots involving the CIA. Although some of the plots did not advance beyond the planning stage, others were executed, though without success. None involved the use of U.S. personnel, but all were instigated by the U.S. government.

Noting the embarrassing examples of the U.S. government's abortive attempts to assassinate Castro and the successful effort to remove Allende, some observers now advocate that the United States virtually abandon the use of covert action as a means of achieving foreign policy objectives except under extraordinary circumstances. Few suggest taking covert action out of the U.S. arsenal completely, since such methods might have to be used to counter a clear and present danger to the military security of the United States. But proponents of this view suggest that there should be a presumption against the use of such methods, so that each use would have to be justified as an exception.

In 1976 a U.S. law was passed prohibiting the assassination of foreign leaders through covert operations. But even this presumption was removed in the recent effort to bring down the Noriega regime in Panama. In November 1989 the Bush administration, with the approval of congressional oversight panels, ordered the CIA to conduct covert operations that might lead to violence against Noriega or even to his death. "This is obviously not a plan to assassinate Noriega," a government official said. "But if there is loss of life, that's not constrained." According to anonymous sources, the operation was given a $3 million budget and was designed to instigate a military coup. A month earlier, U.S. military forces in Panama had assisted an unsuccessful coup attempt by blocking a road that rescuers could have used to reach Noriega at his headquarters.[29] The Bush administration initiated similarly well-publicized measures in 1992 to remove Saddam Hussein from power in Iraq.

THE GOALS: 1961–1976

Beginning with the Kennedy administration, new Progressive goals for U.S. foreign policy toward the Third World were put forward. Kennedy argued for social, economic, and political reforms that would help the poorest people in Third World countries. Undoubtedly, Kennedy had a theory that linked progress in these areas to the U.S. national interest, but what that theory was, or whether it was accurate, is not clear. Perhaps he thought reform would bring greater political stability to developing countries, but it could also cause rapidly rising expectations and ultimately even greater instability. These are important empirical questions, but the most important point is that Kennedy said that the United States should lend its resources to promote reform in the Third World and that we should do it, most of all, because it was the right thing to do.

Some historians would not accept the generally positive account of the Kennedy administration given in this chapter. They might emphasize Kennedy's escalation of U.S. involvement in the Vietnam War, his handling of the Bay of Pigs invasion, his use of the CIA in Southeast Asia and Cuba as detailed by the Church Committee, his support for anti-expropriation legislation, and the seamy side of his private life.[30] These are not minor points, but, in my mind, they are outweighed by an amazing list of achievements during his very short tenure as president. Many of those accomplishments entailed the creation of programs and organizations that have had a lasting impact on U.S. foreign policy. His administration's programmatic or institutional innovations included the development of the Alliance for Progress with Latin America, the establishment of the Agency for International Development, the redesign and reemphasis of the Food for Peace Program, the establishment of the Peace Corps, and the reshaping of the U.S. foreign aid program. Evidence of Kennedy's Progressivism was also apparent in his reaction to specific problems in U.S.–Third World relations which cropped up while he was president.

Most notably, at crucial moments he stood for democracy in the Dominican Republic, against colonialism in the Congo, and against apartheid in South Africa. Like Truman, Kennedy had not abandoned Nationalist objectives; he was simply more willing to risk them to achieve objectives on the Progressive agenda.

Kennedy's successors — Johnson, Nixon, and Ford — did not emphasize the Progressive foreign policy agenda toward less developed countries. However, all but Ford were preoccupied with the Vietnam War during their presidencies. The Progressive foreign policy agenda again took center stage in the rhetoric and actions of the Carter administration. By the end of Carter's term, the advancement of human rights had become an important goal of foreign policy, one that his successors have been able to redefine but unable to ignore.

NOTES

1. On January 6, 1961, about two weeks before the Kennedy address, Soviet Premier Nikita Khrushchev, in a speech at the world meeting of Communist parties, noted that "national liberation wars" in the Third World were inevitable. He defined these as wars in which insurgent people fight for the right of self-determination, for their social and independent national development, and against corrupt reactionary regimes. He pledged the help of the Soviet Union, so Kennedy knew what the Soviet Union intended to do in the Third World when he gave his inaugural address.

2. The more generous interpretation of U.S. motives is discussed by James E. Dougherty and Robert L. Pfaltzgraff, Jr., in *American Foreign Policy: From FDR to Reagan* (New York: Harper and Row, 1986), pp. 151–153.

3. Thomas A. Bailey, *A Diplomatic History of the American People,* 8th ed. (New York: Appleton-Century-Crofts, 1969), p. 883.

4. Henry F. Jackson, *From the Congo to Soweto* (New York: William Morrow, 1982).

5. Dougherty and Pfaltzgraff, *American Foreign Policy,* p. 165.

6. Margaret P. Doxey, *Economic Sanctions and International Enforcement,* 2nd ed. (New York: Oxford University Press, 1980), p. 62.

7. Mark David, "United States-South African Relations," in Sidney Weintraub, ed., *Economic Coercion and U.S. Foreign Policy: Implications of Case Studies from the Johnson Administration* (Boulder, Colo.: Westview Press, 1982).

8. For a detailed description of the debate over the Hickenlooper Amendment and its eventual repeal in 1972, see Charles Lipson, *Standing Guard: Protecting Foreign Capital in the Nineteenth and Twentieth Centuries* (Berkeley: University of California Press, 1985), Chapter 6, pp. 200–226.

9. Ibid., p. 202.

10. Timothy J. Lomperis, *The War Everyone Lost — and Won* (Washington, D.C.: Congressional Quarterly Press, 1984).

11. See Johnson's statement on August 10, 1964, as quoted in Eugene G. Winchy, *Tonkin Gulf* (Garden City, N.Y.: Doubleday, 1971), p. 25.

12. This speech is reprinted in Thomas G. Paterson, ed., *Major Problems in American Foreign Policy Volume II: Since 1914,* 3rd ed. (Lexington, Mass.: D. C. Heath and Co., 1989), pp. 572–575.

13. See Theodore Draper, *The Dominican Revolt: A Case Study in American Policy* (New York: A Commentary Report, 1968), pp. 7–8. Draper's account of the developments in the Dominican Republic and the U.S. response charges that the military coup was quietly encouraged by the Pentagon, undercutting Kennedy's Dominican policy.

14. See Draper, *The Dominican Revolt,* pp. 58–63. For a defense of the U.S. intervention, see Bruce Palmer, Jr., *Intervention in the Caribbean* (Lexington: University Press of Kentucky, 1989).

15. On this point, see Charles Roberts, *LBJ's Inner Circle* (New York: Delacorte Press, 1965), p. 206; Abraham F. Lowenthal, *The Dominican Intervention* (Cambridge, Mass.: Harvard University Press, 1972), p. 64; and Cecil V. Crabb, Jr., *The Doctrines of American Foreign Policy* (Baton Rouge: Louisiana State University Press, 1982), pp. 247–248.

16. *Public Papers of the Presidents of the United States, Lyndon B. Johnson, 1965* (Washington, D.C.: U.S. Government Printing Office, 1966), II, 461–474.

17. See Gar Alperowitz, *Cold War Essays* (Garden City, N.Y.: Doubleday Press, 1970), pp. 76–77; and Crabb, *Doctrines of Foreign Policy,* pp. 253–254.

18. Speech by Senator J. William Fulbright, *Congressional Record,* 89th Congress, 1st session, III, pp. 23855–23865.

19. Dougherty and Pfaltzgraff, *American Foreign Policy,* p. 199.

20. Paterson, ed., *Major Problems in American Foreign Policy Volume II,* p. 623.

21. Richard Nixon, *The Memoirs of Richard Nixon* (New York: Grosset and Dunlap, 1968), p. 395.

22. Henry Kissinger, *White House Years* (Boston: Little, Brown and Co., 1979), pp. 873–913.

23. Richard M. Nixon, *U.S. Foreign Policy for the 1970's: Shaping a Durable Peace.* A Report to the Congress, May 3, 1973, p. 153.

24. Alan C. Brennglass, *The Overseas Private Investment Corporation* (New York: Praeger Publishers, 1983), p. 120.

25. Lipson, *Standing Guard,* Chapter 7, pp. 227–257.

26. Kissinger, *The White House Years,* p. 659.

27. Ibid., p. 657.

28. Ibid., p. 658.

29. Michael Wines, "U.S. Plans New Effort to Oust Noriega," *New York Times,* A3, November 17, 1989.

30. For example, see Thomas C. Reeves, *A Question of Character* (New York: Free Press, 1991).

CHAPTER 9

Advancing Human Rights

Making the advancement of human rights an important concern in U.S. foreign policy was the focus of a congressional initiative beginning in the mid-1970s, even before Jimmy Carter assumed the presidency. It was part of a growing assertiveness by Congress about many aspects of foreign policy in the wake of the Vietnam War and the Watergate scandal. The distinguishing characteristics of Carter's foreign policy, however, were his emphasis on North-South relations, his own concern for the advancement of human rights around the world, and, more generally, his faith in the value of the Progressive foreign policy agenda. Besides its well-known initiatives to advance human rights, the Carter administration also cooperated with Third World leaders to meet many of their demands for a new international economic order. Moreover, Carter generally turned away from both unilateral military intervention and covert action as appropriate methods for achieving U.S. foreign policy objectives vis-à-vis weaker states.

Carter's Nationalist detractors criticized his foreign policy because, in their view, it paid too little attention to East-West relations and gave too little weight to the pursuit of national military and economic interests. For example Jeane Kirkpatrick contended that Carter's foreign policy was fatally flawed, because it disregarded the "centrality" of the East-West conflict and evidenced a "predilection for policies that violated the strategic and economic interests of the United States."[1] Instability in Iran, an ally of the United States, brought national security and human rights goals into direct conflict. And most Americans interpreted the fall of the shah as the result of Carter's new foreign policy priorities. The Carter administration's steady drumbeat on behalf of human rights also caused strained relations with several other Third World regimes that had poor human rights records but a history of friendly relations with the United States, such as South Korea, the Philippines, South Africa, and El Salvador.

HUMAN RIGHTS

Carter believed that all people, no matter where they lived, had certain basic rights simply because of their status as human beings. These rights included the right to be free from some types of government interference and the right to receive some types of benefits from government. Rights in the first category are sometimes called "negative rights," whereas those in the second category are often referred to as "positive rights," because the availability of positive rights is more dependent on the expenditure of government resources.[2] The Carter administration sought to advance both types of human rights, but emphasized protection of the right to be free from government violations of the person's integrity such as torture; cruel, inhuman, or degrading treatment or punishment; arbitrary arrest or imprisonment; denial of a fair public trial; and the invasion of the home. Although Carter's human rights views affected all of U.S. foreign policies, it had the most profound impact on policies toward the Third World where violations of these types of human rights were most prevalent.

Cyrus Vance, for a time secretary of state in the Carter administration, in a 1977 speech at the University of Georgia Law School, discussed the two other categories of human rights which the United States sought to advance: economic rights, and civil and political rights. After first describing the right to be free from governmental violation of the integrity of the person, he said:

> Second, there is the right to the fulfillment of such vital needs as food, shelter, health care and education. We recognize that the fulfillment of this right will depend, in part, upon the stage of a nation's development. But we also know that this right can be violated by a government's action or inaction — for example through corrupt official processes which divert resources to an elite at the expense of the needy, or through indifference to the plight of the poor.
> Third, there is the right to enjoy civil and political liberties — freedom of thought; of religion; of assembly; freedom of speech; freedom of the press; freedom of movement both within and outside of one's country; and freedom to take part in government.[3]

Whether one compiles a list of human rights from congressional formulations, the speech by Secretary Vance, or the series of human rights identified in the Universal Declaration of Human Rights, all the lists contain basically the same items. But various actors in the world system would place different priorities on the different categories of rights. For the Carter administration, the priorities were probably reflected by the order in which Secretary Vance listed them: (1) rights of the integrity of the person, (2) economic rights, and (3) civil and political rights and liberties. The Reagan-Bush priorities have been different and are discussed in the next chapter.

Several things happened during the mid-1970s that made consideration of human rights a permanent part of U.S. foreign policy-making. Many new laws were passed mandating that human rights practices be considered when various types of foreign policy decisions are made. Congress also required that the Department of State prepare an annual report card evaluating the human rights practices of virtually every nation of the world. Congressional committees dealing with foreign policy were reorganized to consider human rights practices more explicitly in congressional foreign policy deliberations. And the United Nations along with other international organizations, to some extent following the lead of U.S. policymakers, placed greater emphasis on promoting international human rights. Most of the significant legislation on human rights and U.S. foreign policy was enacted between 1973 and 1980.[4] These laws generally mandate that the U.S. government take punitive action against "the government of any country which engages in a consistent pattern of gross violations of internationally recognized human rights." David Forsythe, in his excellent review of these laws on human rights, noted the following kinds of stipulations as of 1984:[5]

1. No security assistance should be provided to governments with poor human rights practices unless the president certifies that extraordinary circumstances exist or that there have been significant recent improvements in human rights practices (Foreign Assistance Act of 1961, as amended in 1974, Section 502B).

2. No economic assistance should be provided to regimes with poor human rights records unless the assistance will directly benefit needy people. This stricture also applies to O.P.I.C. insurance and to PL-480 food aid (Foreign Assistance Act of 1961, as amended in 1974, Section 116, Harkin Amendment).

3. Regimes with nonmarket economies are to be denied most-favored-nation trade status and trade credits if they unduly restrict emigration (Jackson-Vanik amendment to the Trade Act, 1974).

4. United States Representatives on the decision-making boards of international financial institutions are required to use their voices and votes to advance the cause of human rights (International Financial Assistance Act of 1977).

5. The Export-Import Bank should deny applications for credit which would encourage trade with countries with poor human rights practices (Export-Import Bank Act of 1945, as amended).

In a related development, during Carter's last year in office, his administration supported legislation changing national policy on the admission of refugees. Before 1980, U.S. law, obviously shaped by the Cold War, allowed the admission of refugees mainly from communist countries or from the Middle East, giving the U.S. attorney general discretion to admit some from other countries as well. The Refugee Act of 1980, supported by the Carter administration, incorporated the United Nations' definition of "refugee" into U.S. law, bringing the United States into greater conformity with international principles and precepts about refugees. The 1967 U.N. Protocol Relating to the Status of Refugees and, since 1980, U.S. law, define a refugee as a person who

> owing to a well-founded fear of being persecuted for reasons of race, religion, nationality, membership of a particular social group or political opinion, is outside the country of his nationality and is unable or, owing to such a fear, is unwilling to avail himself of the protection of that country; or who, not having a nationality and being outside the country of his former habitual residence, is unable, or owing to such fear, is unwilling to return to it.

Persons judged to fall under this definition are said to be "political refugees" as opposed to "economic refugees" or ordinary migrants. The law requires that officials of the U.S. government grant refugee status to all applicants who fall under this definition. Moreover, the act clarified the legal status of refugees and provided a path to the rights and prerogatives of legal permanent residents after a year in the United States. Most important, the act gave voice to a humanitarian ideal — to offer liberty and safety to persons from other lands who are persecuted.[6]

In 1977 Congress, with the endorsement of the Carter administration, also created new organizations within the Department of State, including an assistant secretary of state for human rights and humanitarian affairs to monitor human rights developments in other countries. Some members of the Department of State opposed this idea, preferring that human rights concerns be integrated throughout U.S. diplomacy rather than be isolated in a particular bureau. Congress and the Carter appointees preferred that the new human rights thrust in U.S. foreign policy be given a distinct administrative base. As the first president to have the opportunity to fill this new position, Carter chose Patricia Derian. Under Derian, the bureau was aggressive, sometimes confrontational in interactions with other government agencies, and moralistic.[7] Few question the sincerity of her efforts, but some maintain that Derian's singleminded views conflicted with the pursuit of other national interests, thereby undermining the effectiveness of the bureau.[8]

Recognizing that it is impossible to change any condition unless it can be measured, Congress also required that the secretary of state prepare and transmit to Congress, each fiscal year, a full and complete report on the human rights practices of other countries. The report, titled *Country Reports on Human Rights Practices,* now includes information about almost all countries in the world except the United States. The first two reports produced under the supervision of Secretary of State Kissinger were thin in substance and delayed in publication, but subsequent reports have evidenced considerably more compliance with congressional intent.[9] Published in February of each year, it is a consequential and controversial document that over time has become more detailed and, by most accounts, more accurate.[10] To ensure that the information gathered in this report along with other information about human rights practices around the world would inform U.S. foreign policy-making, the Committee on Foreign Affairs in the House of Representatives was reorganized to include a new Subcommittee on Human Rights and International Organizations. This subcommittee gives special attention to human rights reporting, implementation of human rights policy, and important human rights developments in other countries.

Although some of these actions were initiated before Carter assumed office, his administration encouraged a fuller elaboration and more consistent application of a then skeletal human rights policy. Secretary of State Kissinger and other members of the Nixon and Ford administrations had been critical of congressional initiatives on human rights, and, later, of Carter's endorsement of them. Summing up the substantive concerns of many, Jeane Kirkpatrick, former U.S. ambassador to the United Nations, argued that totalitarian regimes engaged in far worse abuses of human rights than authoritarian ones did, because they did not recognize the supremacy of individual rights over the rights of the state. So the best way the U.S. government could advance human rights around the world, she said, was to advance the cause of democracy and to prevent the spread of communism.[11] This view later became the centerpiece of the Reagan and Bush human rights strategies.

The Carter administration took actions to implement human rights policies on several occasions. His administration cut off military assistance to several LDCs on the basis of their poor human rights records.[12] It also redirected some economic assistance away from human rights violators and from Third World regimes that were not using it to meet the basic human needs of their people.[13] Finally, it opposed multilateral bank loans to some human rights violators.[14] Progressive thinkers have criticized Carter for not doing enough, but almost everyone agrees that his administration took more actions to advance the cause of human rights than any of his predecessors or successors.[15]

Carter's detractors also note that his administration's emphasis on human rights was too selective. He was most forceful in pushing for the advancement of human rights in those areas where U.S. economic interests were not substantially at stake and where no communist threat existed.[16] There is also little evidence that human rights concerns materially affected the behavior of U.S. representatives on the boards of financial institutions or the policies of the Export-Import Bank. And there is some debate over whether the distribution of foreign aid among LDCs really reflected the rhetoric Carter used to proclaim his new human rights priorities.

ECONOMIC RELATIONS

In the area of trade, the Carter administration accepted the principle that LDCs should receive preferential treatment. The United States joined with Japan, the European Economic Community (EEC), and other wealthy countries to establish a Generalized System of Preferences (GSP), eliminating or severely reducing tariffs on certain manufactured exports from LDCs while maintaining the full rate on exports from other industrialized countries. In 1977 the Carter administration granted preferences to Third World countries on goods valued at about $4 billion imported by the United States.[17]

Similarly, the Carter administration moved closer to the Third World position on international agreements on commodity prices. In 1976 the United States had joined the International Tin Agreement and signed a new version of the International Coffee Agreement, which had more favorable terms than the old one. In 1977 the Carter administration took another step toward the Third World position by agreeing to establish a common fund to support higher and more stable prices for commodities exported from the Third World.[18]

Foreign economic aid also was increased substantially during the Carter years—from about $4 billion in 1976 to about $7 billion in 1980, or an increase of about 15 percent per year. Two factors prevented a larger increase, one practical and the other philosophical. The practical problem was that the U.S. economy performed badly during the late 1970s, falling into a condition many economists called stagflation. This condition was characterized by high unemployment, a low level of economic growth, and a high rate of inflation. Carter had a philosophical problem with a massive increase in the foreign aid program; namely, in his view, the distribution of benefits and burdens of the financing and expenditure sides of the program were unjust. As he explained in an interview, traditional forms of foreign aid represented little more than a "tax (on) the poor people of a rich nation to give aid to the rich people in the poor countries."[19]

LESS COVERT ACTION

With widespread public awareness of the U.S. government's role in the overthrow of the Allende regime in Chile, in the failed Bay of Pigs invasion, and in the plots to assassinate Castro, Congress began to assert greater control over the use of covert action to accomplish the United States' foreign policy goals. In 1974 it passed the Hughes-Ryan Act, the operative paragraph of which reads, in part:

> No funds appropriated under the authority of this or any other Act may be expended by or on behalf of the [CIA] for operations in foreign countries, other than activities intended solely for obtaining necessary intelligence, unless and until the President finds that each such operation is important to the national security of the United States and reports, in a timely fashion, a description and scope of such operation to the appropriate committees in Congress.[20]

The presidential judgment required by this provision came to be known as a "finding"—a written document submitted to Congress bearing the president's signature. Forcing the president to put his signature and reputation on the line, it marked the end of "plausible denial" as a desired goal in the conduct of covert actions.[21] Some members of Congress had wanted the amendment to require that the president give Congress prior notification of all proposed covert activities, and a few even wanted to assert the right to exercise a legislative veto over them. However, the language in the Hughes-Ryan Act gave Congress a much smaller role, stipulating only that Congress be informed of covert actions "in a timely fashion."

The Nixon and Ford administrations had been grudging partners in allowing Congress to play a greater role in choosing the means by which foreign policy would be conducted. Both felt that congressional consideration of proposed covert operations would damage the national interest. President Carter, however, promised even more reforms, expanding the role of Congress in the oversight of covert activities. First, he issued Executive Order No. 12036 in January 1978, changing the way covert actions would be considered by the executive branch, and, in the process, building in a presumption against the use of covert activities except as a last resort.[22]

The administration then cooperated with Congress in passing the groundbreaking Intelligence Oversight Act of 1980, the most important law passed by Congress in the realm of covert action.[23] Although the new act tightened up the "timely fashion" provision of the Hughes-Ryan Act, it still skirted the issue of prior notification. The "timely fashion" provision of Hughes-Ryan, by understanding, had come to mean "within 24 hours." The language in the new act indicated that Congress was to be kept "fully and currently informed" of all covert actions, including "any significant anticipated intelligence activity." Thus, prior notification was not absolutely required but was encouraged. In another provision, the president was given another escape clause in emergencies, allowing him to give prior notice to eight members of Congress—the chairmen and ranking minority members of the House and Senate intelligence committees, the speaker and minority leader of the House, and the majority and minority leaders of the Senate.[24] The Carter administration's interactions with Congress over covert activities were amicable, because he chose to use that measure very sparingly.

RESPONSES TO ACTION-FORCING EVENTS

Like Kennedy before him, Carter based his foreign policy on his own perception of needs and aspirations in the Third World. He was convinced that U.S.-Third World relations carried potential for mutual gains.[25] His emphasis on human rights was truly revolutionary, because it highlighted the plight of Third World peoples rather than the concerns of Third World regimes, which in many cases oppressed their citizens. Because it was so revolutionary, Carter's rhetoric on human rights was met with a great deal of skepticism and cynicism in the Third World and in the United States as well. The words sounded good, but many felt that there would be little change in real foreign policy actions. Several action-forcing events in less developed countries put this new policy to the test.

In 1978 the simmering border dispute between Somalia and Ethiopia erupted into a major armed conflict as Somalia occupied the strategically located Ogaden territory of Ethiopia. Since both nations had enjoyed friendly relations with the Soviet Union, the Soviets were forced to choose sides. They finally decided to side with Ethiopia and had cut off arms supplies to Somalia in 1977. At this point the United States became Somalia's arms supplier. Because of its role as arms supplier, the Carter administration found itself in the uncomfortable position of de facto ally of the aggressor in this border war. The United States' stakes got higher when, shortly after the Somalian invasion, about 10,000 Cuban soldiers arrived to help Ethiopia drive out the Somalian invaders. Many people regarded these troops as "surrogates" for the Soviet Union, and so the concern was raised that the Soviet Union was attempting to strengthen its presence in the Red Sea region through which much oil flowed from the Middle East. It already had a strong ally on the north side of the sea in South Yemen. Was it trying to create another strong outpost on the south side in Ethiopia?

Another administration in Washington might have stationed a naval fleet offshore or might even have ordered U.S. troops to intervene, but Carter took a low-key approach. He cut the level of military aid to Somalia, ordered the withdrawal of all foreign military personnel, and called for the mediation of the dispute by neutral African states. As a result, the Ethiopian army aided by the Cuban troops drove the Somalian invaders out. A U.S. ally had suffered a defeat, and, from a Nationalist perspective, U.S. interests had been damaged as well. To make matters worse, in 1979 Ethiopia concluded a 20-year Treaty of Friendship and Cooperation with the Soviet Union pledging mutual collaboration in military, political, and economic matters. Substantial numbers of Cuban troops are still stationed in Ethiopia.

In 1977 opponents of the Seko regime of mineral-rich Zaire attacked from neighboring Angola, another nation that both Cuba and the Soviet Union actively supported. The United States, which had been the arms supplier of Zaire, supplied just enough arms for defense and provided Morocco with the aircraft necessary for that country to send troops to help Zaire. The invasion was soon repelled without direct intervention by the United States and with the minimum force possible.

In southern Africa, the Carter administration set ambitious goals in accord with the new emphasis on human rights. Deciding to change the perception of the U.S. government as a force on the side of counterrevolution, Carter actively encouraged the development of black nationalism and black majority rule. Specifically, his administration worked toward black majority rule in Rhodesia and in South Africa; the elimination of foreign troops and arms sales on the African continent; and the independence of Namibia from South Africa. Black majority rule was achieved in Rhodesia, now Zimbabwe, in 1980, but little progress was made toward the other objectives.

In 1977 a leftist revolutionary movement in Nicaragua sought to remove the repressive military regime of Anastasio Somoza, an anticommunist government that had maintained friendly relations with the United States. The Carter administration was sympathetic to the cause of the Sandinista rebels, encouraging Somoza to step down or at least to allow an election that was sure to remove him from office. Somoza finally consented to allowing the United States to mediate the conflict between the Nicaraguan government and the radical opposition, but the mediation was not successful. In frustration, the United States terminated all economic and military assistance. Partly as a result, the Somoza regime was overthrown and replaced by the Sandinistas in 1979. Fearing the expansion of the leftist revolution into neighboring Honduras and El Salvador, the Carter administration increased military aid to both countries. Opposition to the new leftist regime, including former supporters of Somoza, along with disillusioned veterans of the revolution, formed a new revolutionary movement called the Contras. This group, based in neighboring countries including Honduras and El Salvador, began guerrilla attacks on the new government. The Carter administration, hoping to reconcile with the Sandinista government, stayed out of this new conflict.

The year 1979 also witnessed the buildup of Soviet military strength in Cuba. When U.S. intelligence activities discovered the presence of a Soviet combat brigade there, Carter asked that the brigade be withdrawn, but the Soviets refused. This refusal strained East-West relations and probably slowed progress on the nuclear arms limitation talks between the Soviet Union and the United States, but no other effects were apparent.

One key objective of Carter's foreign policy in Latin America was the renegotiation of the Panama Canal Treaty on terms that would be more palatable to Panama. This treaty, negotiated in 1903, had given the United States rights "in perpetuity"; these rights had become a symbol of Washington's dominance over Latin America and its neocolonial role there. Presidents Johnson, Nixon, and Ford had all worked to various degrees on the renegotiation effort, but none had made it a high-priority objective of their foreign policy, partly because renegotiation was a very controversial issue in domestic politics. Just as the canal and the treaty had become symbols of dominance and oppression in Latin America, they had become symbols of U.S. superiority, nationalism, and empire at home. A new treaty was drawn up that was acceptable to the Panamanian government and to the Carter administration, and it was ratified by the U.S. Senate in 1978.

Given the Third World focus of Carter's foreign policy and the importance of the Middle East to the future economic prosperity of the United States, it is not surprising that the Camp David Accords in 1978, providing for normalization of relations between Egypt and Israel after decades of hostility and three wars, are regarded as his administration's greatest foreign policy triumph. Consistent with Carter's general approach of working with the leaders of developing nations as equal partners to achieve goals of mutual interest, the peace negotiations began with the historic and dramatic trip to Israel by President Anwar Sadat of Egypt in 1977. This visit, which was interpreted as the extension of the olive branch of peace, stunned governments around the world and caused a split among the leaders of the Arab nations, most of whom did not favor reconciliation with Israel. The visit set the precedent for face-to-face negotiations between Arabs and Israelis. But the negotiations soon bogged down over fundamental questions about Israeli security and the return of Arab lands. After several months of bilateral negotiations with negligible progress, President Carter took a bold gamble by inviting President Sadat and Prime Minister Menachem Begin of Israel to Camp David, Maryland, for 13 days of intensive talks mediated by President Carter himself. The accords between Egypt, Israel, and the United States did not settle all the contentious issues between Israel and its Arab neighbors, but they did lay the groundwork for good relations among the three parties to the agreement for many years.

Unfortunately, things were not so peaceful elsewhere in the Middle East. Like no other action-forcing event during this period, the popular rebellion against the regime of the shah of Iran brought the U.S. foreign policy goals of military security and promotion of human rights into direct conflict. Some members of the Carter administration wanted the United States to actively support the shah's regime by assisting in the suppression of his internal, domestic opposition. Doing so would have required a severe stretch in the meaning of the Eisenhower Doctrine, since opposition to the shah was not communist and was not externally supported. Instead of a military intervention, Carter urged reconciliation and negotiation between the shah and his opponents. He tried to save the regime and improve human rights in Iran at the same time, but instead the shah was overthrown and his regime was replaced by an equally, if not more, repressive one led by the Ayatollah Khomeini. The military security interest of the United States suffered a substantial defeat, with no corresponding immediate gain in Carter's human rights goals.

The administration's critics howled their displeasure. The clamor against Carter's "failed" foreign policy reached a crescendo with the Iranian occupation of the U.S. Embassy there in 1979 and the taking of 51 American diplomatic representatives as hostages. Carter's attempts to free the hostages included moral condemnation, economic sanctions, and an unsuccessful rescue mission by a small military force. All these responses only served to further whip up anti-American sentiments within Iran, strengthening the position of the Khomeini regime.

Within the United States, many urged a military intervention to teach Iran a lesson. There were large demonstrations throughout the country.

The image of the Ayatollah being burned in effigy appeared on the front pages of many U.S. newspapers. Even many young people urged war. In the 1980 presidential election campaign, Carter's challenger, Ronald Reagan, promised swift action to free the hostages once elected.

Carter stoutly resisted the temptation to order a major military intervention into Iran. Instead, his administration imposed economic and diplomatic sanctions, and, when those failed, it authorized a small commando raid designed only to free the hostages. As if to rub salt in Carter's wounds, Khomeini ordered the hostages released only days after Carter relinquished the presidency to his successor. Never before had a leader of a less developed country had such a profound effect on the outcome of a U.S. presidential election. There is some evidence that Khomeini's decision not to free the hostages until after the 1980 elections was a deliberate attempt to punish Carter for the United States' previous policy toward Iran.

Criticism of the human rights practices of the shah of Iran almost certainly contributed to the successful revolution against his regime, though rapidly growing Islamic fundamentalism and resentment toward Western-style economic development were other important causes. No matter what the most important and proximate cause, the overthrow of the shah and his replacement by the regime of Ayatollah Khomeini represented the most serious foreign policy setback of the Carter administration. The setback was especially grave because Iran was a strategically located, oil-rich country that had been a steadfast military ally of the United States. Nationalists and Progressives drew different lessons from the fall of the shah and the ensuing hostage crisis. For Nationalists, the episode illustrated how placing a high priority on human rights could damage the short-run economic and military interests of the United States. The hostage-taking had also shown the potential power of state-sponsored terrorism and the need for the United States to act forcefully against it. Some Nationalists used these developments to argue that improving human rights practices around the world should be a low-priority foreign policy goal, should be pursued only through quiet diplomacy, and should be sacrificed whenever they came in conflict with short-run U.S. military, economic, or political objectives.

Progressives were much less critical of the outcome. Since they viewed the shah's regime as doomed because of oppressive policies at home, continued U.S. support of his regime was not in the long-term national interest anyway. Moreover, the fall of the shah did not present an immediate threat to the military security or economic prosperity of the United States. Thus, Carter's strategy was viewed as appropriate, and the outcome, while lamentable, was still acceptable because a truly Progressive foreign policy takes risks. Sometimes it is necessary to risk sacrificing some amount of military security or economic prosperity in order to advance democracy, social justice, and human rights elsewhere. And some risks, like this one, will not pay off.

Although to some it seemed a bit late, Carter issued his own doctrine in 1980 expressing the resolve of the United States to support its national interests in the Middle East:

> Let our position be absolutely clear: Any attempt by any outside force to gain control of the Persian Gulf region will be regarded as an assault on the vital interests of the United States of America, and such an assault will be repelled by any means necessary, including military force.[26]

This was the strongest statement by far of U.S. commitment to anti-communism in any region other than Latin America. It reaffirmed the basic continuity of U.S. foreign policy by endorsing the main principles of the Eisenhower Doctrine. In doing so, it acknowledged the growing importance of the Middle East to U.S. military and economic interests. After the Six-Day War in 1967, the United States had become increasingly dependent on oil shipments through the Persian Gulf. The United States obtains about 25 percent of its oil from the Persian Gulf area and U.S. allies in Europe obtain about 70 percent.[27] Although the Carter Doctrine had little immediate significance, it laid the groundwork for the U.S. response to the Iraqi invasion of Kuwait in 1990.

With an election approaching, Carter probably hoped that his strong statement on U.S. policy toward the Middle East would improve his public image at home, but his popularity continued to sag. His record regarding the containment of communism was not good. Indeed, many thought that his administration was the opposite of Theodore Roosevelt's; he had talked too much and had carried too small a stick. Therefore, many doubted that he would follow through with the implied threat embedded in his Middle East doctrine.

Nationalist thinkers within the United States argued that a foreign policy stressing human rights and peace would only encourage Soviet expansionism. They had their opportunity to gloat when, in 1979, the Soviet Union invaded neighboring Afghanistan. During the decade prior to the invasion, Afghanistan had been moving from a position of nonalignment in the East-West balance of power to a position closer to the Soviet sphere of influence. In 1978 the elected, civilian government was overthrown by a coup led by radical leftist elements of the military. Widespread opposition to the new military government developed quickly, leading to the assassination of its leader in 1979 and a Soviet invasion that same year.

The U.S. response to the Soviet invasion was moral condemnation, the suspension of nuclear arms negotiations with the Soviet Union, an embargo on grain sales to the Soviet Union, and a boycott on the 1980 Olympic games held in the Soviet Union. The embargo on grain sales hurt the target, but it also damaged the domestic farm industry, especially in the Midwest. As a result, this action cost Carter votes. Moreover, these painful measures were not effective. The Soviet Union did not withdraw its troops until 1988, long after Carter had left office.

THE GOALS: 1977–1981

Many people have sharply criticized the Carter administration's foreign policy. Specifically, it is charged that the gap between the administration's human rights rhetoric and actions was too large; that the administration failed to provide a strategy linking ethical concerns about human rights to national security; and that the policy was ineffective in achieving either the new or the longstanding foreign policy goals of the United States.

The argument about the gap between symbolic statements and actions rests on examples of human rights violators who continued to maintain good relations with the United States during the Carter administration. David Forsythe has noted, for example, that the United States focused little diplomatic attention on Chinese transgressions of human rights, even though the human rights record of that country was no better than the records we criticized more consistently, vehemently, and publicly.

Carter, however, never claimed that the protection and advancement of human rights was the only goal of his foreign policy; he only said that it was an important one. Indeed, in a speech before the United Nations, he admitted that preserving national security, achieving arms control, and building a better economic order were all more important to the United States than advancing human rights around the world.[28] Under his leadership, U.S. foreign policy was designed to champion human rights everywhere, but only when doing so did not threaten the attainment of other important U.S. foreign policy objectives.

The second criticism, focusing on the lack of a clear and public strategy for making tradeoffs among these objectives when they conflicted in concrete cases, came mainly from advocates of Carter's Progressive foreign policy ideas. How much achievement in other areas would the United States be willing to risk in order to make gains in human rights? Under what circumstances? These critics contended that a plan was needed for implementing the human rights policy along with a method for evaluating the costs of implementation.[29] No such plan or methodology was forthcoming, however, because even during the Carter administration, the State Department insisted that general guidelines were not useful. Instead, the U.S. policy toward different countries had to be made on a case-by-case basis, weighing the circumstances against the full range of U.S. policy objectives.

Reagan the challenger, hitting on the ineffectiveness theme during the 1980 presidential election campaign, asked the American people to decide whether they were better or worse off after four years of the Carter administration. If they were worse off, he argued, then they should vote for him. Along with being blamed for severe domestic economic problems, Carter was portrayed by his opponents as having presided over a misguided foreign policy toward the Soviet Union and toward the Third World. The invasion of Afghanistan and the Iranian government's taking of U.S. diplomats as hostages were identified as noteworthy fruits of that failed policy. Carter's foreign policy was bad in Reagan's view, not because it pursued immoral ends or because it used unethical methods, but because some of its consequences damaged U.S. economic and military interests.

In the short run, this is a fair and accurate criticism. But, through his rhetoric, his support for human rights legislation, his other initiatives designed to institutionalize the consideration of human rights and other Progressive values in foreign policy decision making, and his responses to action-forcing events, Carter had a lasting impact on U.S. foreign policy toward the Third World. His legacy was to add human rights, including economic and social rights, to the Progressive foreign policy agenda and to bring U.S. foreign policy actions more in line with Progressive principles.

NOTES

1. Jeane Kirkpatrick, "Dictatorships and Double Standards," *Commentary,* November 1977, pp. 34–45. There are many other Nationalist critiques along these lines. See, for example, Donald S. Spencer, *The Carter Implosion: Jimmy Carter and the Amateur Style of Diplomacy* (New York: Praeger Publishers, 1988) and the works cited therein.

2. Shue argues that the distinction between positive and negative rights is largely a false one. See Henry Shue, *Basic Rights: Subsistence, Affluence, and U.S. Foreign Policy* (Princeton, N.J.: Princeton University Press, 1980). For a slightly different treatment reaching the same conclusion, see Jack Donnelly, *Universal Human Rights in Theory and Practice* (Ithaca, N.Y.: Cornell University Press, 1989).

3. Quoted in *Human Rights Conditions in Selected Countries and the U.S. Response.* Prepared for the Subcommittee on International Organizations of the Committee on International Relations, U.S. House of Representatives by the Congressional Research Service of the Library of Congress (Washington, D.C.: U.S. Government Printing Office, July 24, 1978), p. 9.

4. All U.S. laws on human rights as of 1983 are listed in House of Representatives, Committee on Foreign Affairs, *Human Rights Documents* (Washington, D.C.: U.S. Government Printing Office, 1983).

5. David P. Forsythe, *Human Rights and U.S. Foreign Policy* (Gainesville: University Presses of Florida, 1988), p. 6.

6. Doris M. Meissner, "The Refugee Act of 1980: What Have We Learned?" *Revue Européenne,* 6, No. 1 (1990): 129–140.

7. Ibid., Chapter 6.

8. Ibid., p. 121.

9. Ibid., p. 17.

10. See, for example, Judith Innes de Neufville, "Human Rights Reporting as a Policy Tool: An Examination of the State Department Country Reports," *Human Rights Quarterly* 8, No. 4 (November 1986): 681–699.

11. Jeane J. Kirkpatrick, "Dictatorships and Double Standards," *Commentary* 68 (November 1979): 34–45.

12. Forsythe, *Human Rights and U.S. Foreign Policy,* p. 54.

13. Ibid., p. 58.

14. Ibid., pp. 60–68. Although the U.S. representatives often voted against loans for human rights reasons, all the loans opposed in this way were eventually approved anyway, indicating that the United States did not use its influence to change the votes of others.

15. See Donnelly, *Universal Human Rights in Theory and Practice;* Stephen B. Cohen, "Conditioning U.S. Security Assistance on Human Rights Practices," *American Journal of International Law* 76 (April 1982): 246–279; and Lars Schoultz, *Human Rights and United States Policy Toward Latin America* (Princeton, N.J.: Princeton University Press, 1981).

16. Forsythe, *Human Rights and U.S. Foreign Policy,* p. 97.

17. Stephen D. Krasner, "North-South Economic Relations," in Kenneth A. Oye, Donald Rothchild, and Robert J. Lieber, eds., *Eagle Entangled* (New York: Longman, 1979), p. 136.

18. Ibid., p. 136.

19. Quoted in Spencer, *The Carter Implosion,* p. 130. In contrast to the view presented here, in Chapter 8, Spencer argues that Carter's foreign policy toward the Third World was all rhetoric and no substance, that he was well meaning but inept.

20. Officially, Section 622 of the Foreign Assistance Act of 1974.

21. Gregory F. Treverton, *Covert Action* (New York: Basic Books, 1987), p. 238.

22. Ibid., pp. 248–249.

23. Ibid., pp. 249–250.

24. Ibid., p. 250.

25. On this point, see C. Fred Bergsten, *The World Economy in the 1980s* (Lexington, Mass.: Lexington Books, 1981), pp. 115–126.

26. Carter's State of the Union Address, January 23, 1980.

27. Cecil V. Crabb, *The Doctrines of American Foreign Policy* (Baton Rouge: Louisiana State University Press, 1982), pp. 330–331.

28. Speech before the United Nations, March 1977. Described in David P. Forsythe, *Human Rights and World Politics* (Lincoln: University of Nebraska Press, 1983).

29. See, for example, Stanley Hoffman, *Duties Beyond Borders* (Syracuse, N.Y.: Syracuse University Press, 1981).

PART IV

Reagan, Bush, and the Future, 1981–

CHAPTER 10

A Shortened Progressive Agenda

As president, Ronald Reagan deemphasized North-South issues and lowered the priorities Jimmy Carter had placed on the Progressive agenda in U.S. foreign policy. Instead, his administration stressed the promotion of U.S. economic and military interests in relations with LDCs and was more willing to use both covert action and military force. The Reagan administration also advocated a recipe of private enterprise combined with democracy as the answer to economic development problems in the Third World. Several occurrences in the international environment aided this strategy. Perhaps most important was the global economic depression in the early 1980s which was deeper and longer lasting in the South than it was in the North. The depression created a debt crisis for most LDCs that continues to this day. It also diminished political solidarity within the Third World, because relatively successful LDCs such as Taiwan, South Korea, and Singapore (the so-called Newly Industrialized Countries, or NICs) broke ranks with other Third World countries, undermining efforts toward bloc politics. Most countries that did attract large amounts of bilateral and multilateral aid changed their policy priorities, seeking to attract direct foreign investments and promote exports, changes approved by the Reagan administration. The governing boards of public multilateral lending agencies and of private international banks also encouraged these shifts in the policy priorities of Third World countries.

President George Bush, as he promised during the 1988 election campaign, has maintained the broad outlines of the foreign policy strategy developed during the Reagan years, apparently with good reason. The rapid democratization of the former Soviet Union, Eastern Europe, and several Third World countries, especially in Latin America, beginning in 1989 and continuing in the 1990s was widely proclaimed domestically as a foreign policy triumph for the United States. The 1989 elections in Nicaragua, resulting in the defeat of the Soviet and Cuban-backed Sandinista regime, were heralded as a particularly significant vindication of a controversial U.S. policy openly committed to the removal of that government. Noting the recent lessening of East-West tensions, Secretary of Defense Richard Cheney suggested that a 30 percent decrease in Defense expenditures would soon be possible. This potential "peace dividend" was widely perceived as one of the fruits of a successful Reagan-Bush foreign policy.

There were other positive developments as well. The South African government, having been subjected to sanctions by the United States and other governments around the world for over a quarter of a century, announced its intention to abolish apartheid. The Philippines, South Korea, Haiti, and Panama all took small steps away from dictatorship. The Soviet Union pulled out of Afghanistan. Even in China, there were massive demonstrations for democracy. Although the Chinese government quashed these student-led demonstrations, most experts expect the popular pressure for more political, social, and economic freedom in that country to continue.

On the darker side, the situation in El Salvador became more violent. There was a bloody revolution against the U.S.-supported Doe regime in Liberia. And in a development that had the potential to start another world war, Iraq invaded neighboring Kuwait, upsetting an already unstable, fragile peace in the Middle East and driving the United States to the brink of large-scale war. Both Reagan and Bush were more willing to use military force to accomplish U.S. foreign policy goals in the Third World than any president since Woodrow Wilson and Lyndon Johnson. Both were also more willing than Carter to use covert action to accomplish foreign policy objectives. The goal of human rights promotion in U.S. foreign policy was not abandoned, but it diminished in importance and the meaning of human rights was redefined.

THE REAGAN DOCTRINE

In 1985 President Reagan produced his own statement regarding the use of American power in the developing world, reflecting the new priorities of his administration—the containment of communism, the pursuit of democracy, the expansion of the free enterprise system, and the maintenance of U.S. military security:

> We must stand by all our democratic allies. And we must not break faith with those who are risking their lives—on every continent, from Afghanistan to Nicaragua—to defy Soviet-supported aggression and secure rights which have been ours from birth.

The Sandinista dictatorship of Nicaragua, with full Cuban-Soviet bloc support, not only persecutes its people, the church, and denies a free press but arms and provides bases for communist terrorists attacking neighboring states. Support for freedom fighters is self-defense and totally consistent with the O.A.S. and U.N. Charters. It is essential that the Congress continue all facets of our assistance to Central America. I want to work with you to support the democratic forces whose struggle is tied to our own security.[1]

Perhaps the most extraordinary element of the Reagan Doctrine is the inclusion of an explicit rationale for U.S. sponsorship of revolutionary activity against internationally recognized governments in the Third World. The contention that providing support for a violent revolution thousands of miles away is justifiable as an act of national self-defense is seen by Progressive thinkers as a perversion of the spirit of the U.N. and OAS charters. Both the U.S. action in Nicaragua and the interpretation of international law that accompanied it are good examples of the almost absolute power of militarily strong states to do as they will in the anarchy of the international system.

THIRD WORLD ECONOMIC DEVELOPMENT

One big difference between Reagan and Bush, on the one hand, and Kennedy and Carter, on the other, was the respective view each camp had concerning the responsibility of the U.S. government to assist economic growth and to encourage social and political reforms in Third World nations. Reagan insisted that solutions to problems of development were to be sought mainly through private enterprise rather than through public policy. Issues of distribution need not be confronted, because a rising tide of economic prosperity would benefit even the poorest Third World citizen. He insisted that U.S. foreign policy toward developing countries should be designed to help those poorer countries which, for reasons beyond their control, had not been able to improve their standards of living.[2] Countries that had too much state involvement in the economy, had erected barriers against the investments of MNCs, and had resisted the "structural adjustment" policies of the World Bank and IMF had not done everything within their own control to solve their own problems and, therefore, did not deserve much assistance from other richer states.

I. G. Patel has called this view of a limited U.S. government role in advancing the plight of the poor in the Third World "the new fundamentalism."[3] To implement the new fundamentalism, Reagan and Bush decided to concentrate on the development of bilateral investment guarantee treaties, reviving the Overseas Private Investment Corporation (OPIC), creating a new Bureau for Private Enterprise within the Agency for International Development, and improving the tax treatment of U.S. exporters and of personal income earned in another country. The Reagan administration sought to expand OPIC's activities by authorizing that organization to take on a greater potential insurance liability and by relaxing the rules that placed restrictions on doing business in the wealthier developing countries. The volume of insurance written by OPIC expanded by one third in FY1981 and again expanded substantially in FY1982.[4]

Even the U.S. Agency for International Development (AID) was turned into an instrument to promote capitalism in the Third World. Reagan appointees at AID noted that many of the programs of the 1960s and 1970s designed to reach the neediest in the Third World "frankly, haven't worked."[5] They had been short-term consumption subsidies with no consequential positive long-term consequences. In the future, AID officials announced, the agency would concentrate not on income redistribution, but on wealth generation, not on coercive and inefficient public sector projects, but on private sector initiatives.[6] As noted earlier, a special Bureau of Private Enterprise was created within AID to support indigenous private sector projects in the Third World and to advise governments about how to create a favorable business climate. AID officials also made it clear that governments unwilling to cooperate with private sector development initiatives would receive less U.S. foreign aid.[7]

Anxious to promote free trade, the administration resisted domestic protectionist pressures to impose restrictions on imports from LDCs. However, the Reagan administration delivered a blow to Third World economic and political interests when it refused to ratify the Law of the Sea Treaty negotiated mainly by the Carter administration. It objected to the treaty provisions that gave Third World states a disproportionate voice on the governing board of the regulatory body created by the treaty, and that required the transfer of seabed mining technology from private firms to national government authorities.[8]

In 1982 Reagan proposed a package of trade concessions and investment incentives, generally referred to as the Caribbean Basin Initiative, that typified his preferred approach to supporting economic development in the Third World. First, the program would apply only to countries in the Caribbean, an area of strategic military and economic interest to the United States. Second, the program, as finally implemented, clearly placed the national self-interest far above any humanitarian concerns. The package as initially proposed by the administration called for some increase in foreign aid, but Congress saw that part of the proposal as a thinly disguised effort to provide more funds to El Salvador. The trade concessions portion of the proposal was weakened because opponents complained that the bill would take jobs away from Americans. As signed into law in 1983, the scaled-down benefits would apply to any Central American or Caribbean nation as long as it

1. Was not communist.
2. Had not expropriated U.S. property and had not violated the contracts or trademarks of U.S. citizens.
3. Did not have preferential trade practices with other countries to the detriment of U.S. commerce.
4. Had not broadcast U.S. copyrighted material without the permission of the owners.
5. Cooperated with the United States to prevent drug trafficking.
6. Had signed an extradition treaty with the United States.[9]

In the two decades between the early 1950s and early 1970s, the world economy achieved both a high rate of growth and a low rate of inflation. Less developed countries generally prospered in this environment, growing at an average annual rate of 5 percent per year.[10] However, the oil shortage in the mid-1970s, protective trade practices in the developed countries, declining terms of trade for many Third World exports, the 1980–1982 recession in the developed countries, and too much borrowing by some countries have created a significant debt problem for most Third World countries.

In 1981, for example, the net capital inflow to Latin America from all developed countries totaled $20 billion, but 85 percent of that amount came in the form of private loans which, at some point, will have to be repaid. The annual interest charge to Latin American countries in 1981 had risen to $22 billion, or $2 billion more than the inflow of capital that same year. The problem is so large that some less developed countries have threatened to default on their debts—in effect declaring bankruptcy. It has been exacerbated by continued pressure from the Reagan and Bush administrations to shift bilateral foreign aid to most countries from outright gifts or grants to loans with concessionary terms.

During the Reagan and Bush administrations, however, the United States did develop refinancing agreements with several countries to prevent default. The terms of the agreements are complicated, but the vast majority simply move the debt burden into the future. Rolling the debt over, or delaying most or all of the interest payments to a point late in the loan period, is only a slight concession to a debtor country. It buys time for the developing country to improve the performance of its economy by providing short-term cash flow relief. At the end of the loan period, however, balloon payments are required that could cause an even greater crisis for the debtor nation. The Reagan administration reached an agreement of this type in 1988 with Egypt, for example, refinancing debt accumulated under the U.S. Foreign Military Sales Program. Both Bush and Reagan have argued that the best way to lessen the Third World debt crisis is to hold interest rates down to lower the cost of future borrowing. But they have resisted more radical solutions to the debt crisis, such as placing a cap on the debts each Third World country can accumulate and then forgiving all debt beyond that ceiling.[11]

The foreign policy statement in the Republican party platform of 1980 also signaled a return to Nationalist objectives in the foreign aid program:

No longer should American foreign assistance programs seek to force acceptance of American governmental forms. The principal consideration should be whether or not extending assistance to a nation or group of nations will advance America's interests and objectives. The single-minded attempt to force acceptance of U.S. values and standards of democracy has undermined several friendly nations, and has made possible the advance of Soviet interests.[12]

Once in office, the Reagan administration shifted its bilateral aid program toward the promotion of military security interests by increasing military assistance relative to economic assistance. Initially, the Office of Management and Budget also proposed a massive shift of foreign aid from multilateral to bilateral programs, so that it could be controlled more directly, but this effort failed.

Early in the Reagan administration, U.S. conservative groups severely criticized the World Bank for fostering socialism in the Third World. Critics noted that recent changes in voting procedures had given LDCs greater voice in World Bank decisions than their contributions to bank funds justified. A study by the Treasury Department countered those charges by showing that multilateral development banks (MDBs) like the World Bank contributed to U.S. global economic objectives. They encouraged capitalism and provided expanded opportunities for U.S. exports and investments. The United States military and political objectives also were aided by MDB policies encouraging economic development, because economic development reduced the likelihood of political instability. Moreover, the geographic distribution of multilateral loans generally conformed with the distribution of U.S. foreign aid.[13]

Some members of Congress and the Reagan administration still wanted to decrease support to the multilateral banks, but the debt crisis that put additional demands on already stretched MDB funds convinced Reagan to abandon that strategy. In a September 1983 speech before members of the international finance community, he outlined the problem in stark terms. "If Congress does not approve our participation, the inevitable consequence would be withdrawal by other industrial countries from doing their share. At the end of this road would be a major disruption of the entire world trading and financial systems — an economic nightmare that could plague generations to come."[14] A few weeks later Congress approved an increase in the U.S. contribution to the IMF.

In turn, much of the increased funding to the IMF and the World Bank provided by the United States and other developing countries was used to roll over Third World debts. One cost of the rollovers was a series of commitments to austerity measures by the debtor countries that often threatened fragile social and political systems. We also have some evidence that increasing debt pressures on developing countries are causing them to exploit their natural resources to a degree that is harmful to the world environment. For example, recent research has shown that, among nations with tropical rain forests, those with the greatest international debt are destroying their forests more rapidly than the others.

At the October 1985 meeting of the World Bank and IMF in Seoul, South Korea, Secretary of the Treasury James Baker advocated what has become known as the Baker Plan. The United States and other wealthy countries, he said, should further increase their contributions to the public multilateral lending agencies, thus allowing them to work in concert with commercial banks to increase the level of lending to the poorest countries. In return, the debtor states would be required to agree to "comprehensive macroeconomic and structural reforms," including fiscal stringency, competitive exchange rates, higher domestic savings, freer trade, encouragement of foreign investment, and increased reliance on the private sector.[15]

Some types of foreign aid — namely, disaster assistance and food aid — continued to be distributed almost entirely on a humanitarian basis. Most U.S. policymakers view these two types of aid as assistance to Third World people, not their governments. Therefore, from the very beginning, they have been distributed mainly on the basis of need. When a devastating earthquake hit Iran in June 1990, the Bush administration quickly provided food, medical supplies, tents, and other materials to help the victims. Similarly, some U.S. food aid continues to be sent to help counter the effects of the Ethiopian drought, despite poor relations between governments.

During the Reagan administration, significant international pressure was applied to the United States by a broad-based coalition of both less and more industrialized countries to join the effort to protect the global environment. The Reagan administration steadfastly resisted all entreaties of this type, taking the position that the scientific evidence was not sufficient to support any particular national or international policy and that imposing the costs of greater environmental regulation on U.S. factories, trucks, and automobiles would damage the U.S. economy. Indeed, the Reagan administration denied that global warming was a real problem, a denial that has important implications since the United States is the world's largest industrial economy, its largest energy producer, and its most prolific polluter. It is also potentially the world's prime source of clean-up technology and money.

The Bush administration made a small concession in 1992, offering to enact policies curbing the increase in climate-warming gases released into the atmosphere from sources in the United States. But it still refused to make a firm commitment to stabilize the emission of these "greenhouse gases" at 1990 levels by the year 2000. The U.S. government's half-hearted position on protecting the global environment is sending an unfortunate message to the governments of less industrialized countries such as Brazil and Malaysia. The governments of these countries are caught in a crossfire between environmentalists who demand responsible, sustainable development strategies and their own citizens who demand rapid economic development, often without regard to environmental consequences.

HUMAN RIGHTS

Reagan was initially opposed to using U.S. foreign policy to promote human rights around the world. Although his attitude softened, Reagan (and then Bush) has insisted that human rights can be furthered best through "quiet diplomacy" and "constructive engagement." Reagan signaled his lack of concern about human rights when he waited a long time before filling the post of assistant secretary of state for human rights and humanitarian affairs and then nominated Ernest Lefever, who had publicly advocated repealing all human rights legislation and transforming all human rights policy into anti-communism.[16] Although his nomination was withdrawn after the Senate Foreign Relations Committee voted 13–4 against consent, the next nominee, Elliot Abrams, confirmed by the Senate, held similar views about the role of human rights promotion in U.S. foreign policy.[17]

Those who have examined the record of the Reagan administration on the advancement of human rights in the less developed world have given it mixed reviews. Most observers have concluded that his administration placed a lower priority on human rights than his predecessor had, proclaimed the symbolic goal of advancing human rights less frequently, and emphasized different kinds of human rights from the ones Carter did. For example, a recent study of the votes of U.S. representatives on the boards of multilateral development banks showed that during the Carter administration representatives often opposed loans on human rights grounds. Representatives of the Reagan administration seldom did.[18] Some have even argued that these differences between the Carter and Reagan administrations were so great that the Reagan administration was not really concerned about human rights at all. In contrast, Jack Donnelly contends that the Carter and Reagan policies on human rights, "despite their seemingly diametrically opposed starting points, can be seen largely as matters of degree or consistency."[19]

Indeed, those starting points were strikingly different. Secretary of State Alexander Haig announced at his first press conference that "international terrorism will take the place of human rights in our concern because it is the ultimate of abuses of human rights."[20] A few days later Ernest Lefever was nominated to the human rights post. Then, in its first months in office, the Reagan administration urged Congress to reinstate military aid to Argentina, Chile, Guatemala, and Uruguay—all of whom had been denied assistance by the Carter administration because of systematic violations of human rights. One reason for the difference of opinions over the Reagan-Bush record on human rights is that their administrations meant something different than Carter had when they invoked the cause of human rights. Reagan and Bush essentially coopted the human rights issue by equating the promotion of human rights with the promotion of democracy. Neither Reagan nor Bush acknowledged the existence of economic rights, and, unlike Carter, neither gave high priority to the protection of the rights of the integrity of the person.

The debate over which rights are the most basic human rights is an old one. Neither facetious nor cynical, it reflects real ethical differences concerning which types of human rights are most important to humankind. For the Reagan administration, respect for civil and political liberties such as freedom of speech, press, religion, and travel was the most important category of human rights. Once these rights were lost, all other rights were in jeopardy, because government tyranny over the people could no longer be checked. The administration also made a significant change in the terminology used in the *Country Reports on Human Rights Practices.* It provided evidence regarding its priorities among the other two categories of human rights: the right against violation of the integrity of the person and the right to a minimum standard of living. During the Carter administration, each report contained a section on "Government Policies

Relating to the Fulfillment of Such Vital Needs as Food, Shelter, Health Care and Education." This was the second category of rights discussed in each country's human rights report.

Beginning with the very first volume produced by the Reagan administration in February 1981 and continuing to the present, that section no longer appears. Instead, each report begins with an introduction, as before, followed by a description of conditions regarding respect for the integrity of the individual and for civil and political liberties. These sections are followed by a section on general economic and social "conditions" in the country. President Reagan explains the break with the past in his introduction to the 1981 *Country Reports:*

> The urgency and the moral seriousness of the need to eliminate starvation and poverty from the world are unquestionable, and continue to motivate large American foreign aid efforts. However, the idea of economic and social rights is easily abused by repressive governments which claim that they promote human rights even though they deny their citizens the basic rights to the integrity of the person, as well as civil and political rights. This justification for repression has in fact been extensively used. No category of rights should be allowed to become an excuse for the denial of other rights. For this reason, the term economic and social rights is, for the most part, not used in this year's Reports.

Thus, the Reagan and Bush administrations denied the very existence of economic rights. For both administrations, civil rights and liberties received highest priority, followed closely by rights of the integrity of the person, and, very distantly, if at all, by the obligation of government to provide for the economic and social welfare of its citizens. However, international human rights agreements do recognize the existence of economic rights. The 1966 international Covenant on Social and Economic Rights affirms that human rights include the right to work (Article 6), to enjoyment of just and favorable conditions of work, to equal remuneration for work of equal value, to a decent standard of living, to reasonable working hours (Article 7), to social security (Article 9), to adequate food, to clothing and housing (Article 11), to medical care (Article 12), to education (Articles 13 and 14), and to participation in cultural life (Article 15).

For many Third World leaders, economic rights are the most fundamental, since a minimum standard of living is a necessary condition for human dignity. Nearly as important are rights of the integrity of the person, but the leaders of many Third World nations do not consider civil and political liberties to be crucial if the exercise of those rights could interfere with the goal of improving economic and social conditions. Many of them would argue that government *for* the people is more important than government *by* the people.[21]

Although Reagan and Bush never formally acknowledged the existence of economic rights, Reagan did abandon his early strategy of open antagonism toward incorporating any human rights consideration into foreign policy decision making. (Nor has Bush taken up such a strategy.) Instead, by 1982 the Reagan administration pursued two tracks in the name of human rights. It made a positive effort to expound the advantages of democracy, and it pursued a negative policy of scolding friend and adversary alike for any abuse of their citizens' integrity of person and their rights to civil and political liberties. As Tamer Jacoby notes, this new strategy brought U.S. foreign policy more into line with the idealistic values of the American public.[22]

At the Reagan administration's urging, in 1983 Congress approved Project Democracy, a program designed to promote democratic institutions around the world. The program is administered by the National Endowment for Democracy (NED) and, according to the enabling legislation, it funds projects around the world to help build an infrastructure for democracy. Although it was not designed to support particular political parties or to affect the outcome of any particular election, many critics charge that funds have indeed been used for these prohibited purposes during the Reagan and Bush administrations, especially during the 1989 elections in Nicaragua.[23]

PROMOTING DEMOCRACY

Even when promotion of human rights is defined in terms of promoting democracy, the Reagan and Bush approach to achieving that goal has been essentially Nationalist rather than Progressive in character. Rather than use the influence of U.S. foreign policy to encourage freer, more open, and more democratic societies throughout the Third World, both administrations decided to respond only to targets of opportunity defined essentially in terms of the potential effectiveness of U.S. action. Thus, the Reagan and Bush administrations have generally not pressured dictatorships to move toward democracy unless there has been (1) a high probability of success; and (2) a low probability that such pressure would result in bringing to power a new regime hostile to U.S. interests. On at least three occasions during the Reagan presidency these conditions were met, and his administration acted forcefully to aid the emergence of democracy in Third World states ruled by friendly dictators. In all three cases—Haiti, the Philippines, and South Korea—the administration proclaimed that U.S. actions were taken in the name of advancing human rights. President Bush made a similar claim as part of his justification for the military intervention in Panama in 1989. In 1991 the Bush administration also took steps to oppose anti-democratic coups in Haiti and Peru.

The Duvalier family had occupied the presidency in Haiti since 1957 and had used that position to maintain a repressive and corrupt political organization. In 1985, succumbing to visible pressure from the United States and France, the Duvalier government released a number of political prisoners and announced a series of modest democratic reforms. After a series of intense antigovernment, pro-reform demonstrations later that year and extending into 1986, Duvalier, with the active encouragement of the Reagan administration, left the country on a U.S. plane to France. Although the Reagan administration portrayed this development as a positive step toward democracy and reform in Haiti, the country continues to be ruled by a repressive regime, and no significant social, economic, or political reforms have been instituted.

A similar scenario occurred in the Philippines, but with a slightly better outcome for the Filipinos than for the Haitians. When President Marcos assumed leadership of the Philippines in 1965, he promised significant economic and political reforms designed to empower the poor in his country. Dissatisfied with the pace of reform, a radical opposition formed and presented increasingly severe challenges to the Marcos government, including, by 1969, a revolutionary movement. The Marcos regime responded to this serious internal threat with even greater suppression of the legitimate opposition to his regime.

Amid widespread antigovernment demonstrations, Marcos announced that a special presidential election would be held in 1986 to "restore confidence" in his administration. When the election was held, both the opposition candidate, Corazon Aquino, and foreign observers charged the government with election fraud designed to rig the outcome. Aquino rallied the public in an expanded program of strikes, boycotts, and civil disobedience designed to force Marcos to step down from the presidency. The Reagan administration played a key role by quietly encouraging Marcos to leave the country and by supporting the new Aquino government. The United States hailed the outcome as another triumph of democracy. However, the revolution from the left against the government continued, and the apparent good faith efforts of the Aquino government to institute economic and political reforms met with considerable resistance from the military and large landholders. Progress was slow, and the government was lucky to repulse a series of attempted coups by military leaders. Thus, the Aquino government was squeezed from both ends of the ideological continuum. When reforms moved ahead too quickly, the military's opposition to her government increased. When she moved ahead slowly, the violent revolution against her government gained momentum. In 1992 she announced that she would not seek another term as president. Later that year, Fidel V. Ramos, a career military officer, was elected president.

The mid-1980s also witnessed great public dissatisfaction with the undemocratic and sometimes repressive policies of the South Korean government as indicated by the numerous violent clashes between police and campus demonstrators beginning in 1983 and occurring sporadically through 1987. In this instance, public unrest led to government reform rather than its collapse. Through quiet diplomacy, the United States is thought to have played an important role in preventing the South Korean police from using greater force against the demonstrators and for encouraging constitutional reforms making the South Korean government more open and democratic. The new constitution adopted in 1987 provides greater safeguards for basic rights, including freedom of press and assembly, the principle of habeas corpus, labor's right to organize and strike against employers, and the prohibition of detention without a court order.[24]

The United States' role in deposing the previously pro-U.S. dictator of Panama represents the Bush administration's most controversial action vis-à-vis the Third World. Since the Second World War, Panamanian political debate had increasingly centered on nationalistic sentiments arising from continuing U.S. control of the Canal Zone and the large U.S. presence in Panama. The provisional constitution adopted in 1972 provided the basis for regular presidential and legislative elections, but real power was exercised by the head of the National Guard, called the Panamanian Defense Force (PDF), which served as both an army and a police force.

In 1983 a series of constitutional amendments were approved in a national referendum, paving the way for a return to civilian rule. Although Panama conducted its first direct presidential balloting in 15 years in 1984, General Manuel Noriega, head of the PDF, refused to relinquish power to the newly elected government, claiming that the country's political situation was "out of control and anarchic."[25] This already troubled situation was complicated by a series of charges leveled by newspaper reporters in the United States and former Noriega associates that Noriega was involved in electoral fraud, money laundering, clandestine arms trading, the sale of high-level technology to Cuba, and drug trafficking. Reagan announced his support for General Noriega's opponents in 1987. A U.S. grand jury handed down indictments against Noriega in 1988, and American authorities demanded that he be extradited to the United States to stand trial.

Within a month of the grand jury indictment, the president of

Panama, Eric Arturo Delvalle, announced his intention to dismiss the general. But, on the following day, Delvalle was himself dismissed by the National Assembly on the grounds that he had exceeded his constitutional authority. He was placed under house arrest, but he escaped and fled the country. The Reagan administration at first worked quietly and then openly to have General Noriega step down and Delvalle reinstated as president, with constitutional authority superior to the military. As a first step, Reagan ordered economic sanctions against Panama to stir up opposition to Noriega. But the Noriega regime resisted both diplomatic and economic pressures from the United States and repulsed an attempted coup from within the PDF in 1988, promising to hold new elections in 1989.

This was the situation inherited by President Bush. In May 1989, Panama again held a national election. Although Noriega's candidate was clearly beaten by the anti-Noriega nominee, the Electoral Commission nullified the results because of alleged "obstruction by foreigners" and a "lack of . . . voting sheets [that] made it impossible to proclaim winners."[26] Bush continued the economic sanctions and diplomatic pressures and then issued an executive order allowing the CIA to become involved in covert activities designed to overthrow Noriega even if those activities resulted in Noriega's death. Another military coup, this time with some assistance from U.S. forces in Panama, failed in late 1989. Within a month after the failed coup attempt, Bush ordered a military intervention which was condemned by all of the leaders of Latin American nations. Noriega was apprehended and brought to trial in Miami, Florida, on drug trafficking charges. He was convicted in April 1992 and sent to prison.

The Bush administration was tested again when, in 1992, the government headed by President Alberto Fujimori of Peru instituted dictatorial rule. The justification of the coup was based on the inability of the democratic regime to fight the war against Maoist rebels (the Shining Path), to develop and implement a coherent and effective program of economic development, and to deal with corruption in the judiciary. President Fujimori also argued that the democratic regime had slowed the war against drug suppliers. While many inside observers viewed this last point as a cynical appeal for U.S. support, the reality of the other problems the Fujimori government faced was widely accepted.

The Shining Path guerrilla movement, which has been growing in strength, highlights a complex system of caste that exists in Peru and in many other South American countries that is based largely on color and cultural identification. A light-skinned criolle minority, descended from the Spanish colonizers, is pitted against a majority that stems mainly from

Indian stock. Most of the powerful positions in Peruvian society are held by the criolle minority. They dominate a four-step pecking order, followed by mestizos (mixed Indian and white), then darker or cholo mestizos, and, finally, Indians. The Shining Path is dedicated to mobilizing the majority and taking control of the nation's government. Unlike Fujimori, the Shining Path sides with the peasant coca producers and against the Peruvian government and its U.S. advisers in the U.S.-sponsored war against drugs.

Despite a friendly relationship with the Fujimori government, the Bush administration suspended new foreign aid to Peru in the wake of the coup and pledged cooperation with the Organization of American States in a strategy to restore democracy. The Japanese Foreign Ministry, in contrast, announced that it would not halt its foreign aid to Peru because Mr. Fujimori's actions and announced intention to restore democracy in one year were felt to be reasonable responses to the crisis. The U.S. position was complicated by widespread press reports that the Peruvian people backed their leader's actions and by an incident a few weeks after the coup when a Peruvian jet "accidentally" attacked a U.S. cargo plane, killing one U.S. crewman.

The outcomes of all these cases were mixed, but in all of them the United States supported pro-reform and pro-democracy forces against dictators who had previously conducted generally cooperative foreign policies toward the United States. In each case, other national interests were put at some risk to make an advance toward greater democracy in the Third World. For example, Aquino insisted on a renegotiation of the treaty providing for U.S. use of Clark Air Base and Subic Bay Naval Station, the two largest U.S. overseas military installations. After lengthy negotiations, the talks broke down in 1992, and the U.S. government announced that the U.S. military presence in the Philippines would end when the Subic Bay Naval Station lease expired. Marcos' terms would have been less demanding, had he still been in power, so the United States' military presence in the Philippines would have been prolonged.

Except in the case of Haiti in 1991, the Reagan and Bush administrations did not terminate military aid to any nation for human rights reasons,[27] but they reduced military assistance to some countries that had shown little respect for their citizens' rights and had resisted pressures for political reforms. For example, in 1990 Somalia's longtime ruler, Mohammed Siad Barre, promised that his country would move toward a multiparty political system after donors led by the United States slashed more than $100 million in annual economic and military aid in response to widespread human rights abuses.[28] In 1991, Barre departed for exile in Kenya.

RESPONSES TO ACTION-FORCING EVENTS

Neither Reagan nor Bush has been particularly concerned about the principle of nonintervention in the conduct of relations with Third World states. Instead, as a continuation of a long-term, disturbing trend in U.S.–Third World relations, both administrations have made frequent use of overt and covert intervention to achieve U.S. foreign policy objectives.[29]

It is difficult to accept the Reagan and Bush rationale that they opposed the Sandinista regime in Nicaragua to promote the forces of democracy. The United States had maintained friendly relations with the dictatorial, nondemocratic regime of Anastasio Somoza. For many Progressive thinkers, the U.S. policy in Nicaragua is best understood as following the maxim of befriending the enemies of our enemies (Somoza) and opposing the friends of our enemies (the Sandinistas). The Reagan administration began providing military assistance to the rebels fighting against the Sandinista government in December 1981. The CIA operations based in Honduras were well publicized, giving new meaning to the term *covert action*. In 1982 Congress passed the Boland Amendment which prohibited U.S. funding of groups whose purpose was the destruction of the Sandinista regime. Funding could only be provided to destroy staging areas in Nicaragua, from which supplies were being provided to the leftist rebels in El Salvador. Once military supplies were provided, however, Congress found that it could not control how they were used, so the Boland Amendment had little impact.

After several failed attempts in 1983 and 1984, Congress finally succeeded in limiting the level of aid to the Contras in 1984. The Senate Intelligence Committee, reacting in part to published reports in 1984 of CIA involvement in the mining of Nicaraguan harbors, laid down new restrictions on the use of covert aid to the Contras. Then, in 1985, Congress authorized only "humanitarian aid" to the Contras to be used for food, clothing, health care, and the like, and not for military purposes. The defeat of the Sandinista government in the 1989 elections has led to a more normalized relationship between the U.S. and Nicaraguan governments and to the dissolution of the Contra forces.

Unfortunately, the United States continues to be deeply involved in another violent conflict in Central America, this one supporting a rightist regime in El Salvador against a leftist revolution. For nearly half a century, the military on behalf of a group of 15 to 20 families has controlled the government of El Salvador; together these families owned nearly 60 percent of the country's economic assets.[30] A coup in 1979 led to the establishment of a civilian-military government that was ostensibly committed to a program of economic reform including substantial land redistribution.

President Carter had cut off military aid to El Salvador because of the government's record of oppression of opposition groups, but in his final months of office, he reluctantly restored aid out of fear that a Soviet- and Cuban-backed Sandinista-inspired revolution might erupt there. When the Reagan administration took power, it was anxious to step up foreign aid to the El Salvador government, but Congress was reluctant. Adopting a compromise position in 1981, Congress voted to require the president to certify at six-month intervals that El Salvador was making progress on human rights, moving toward the holding of free elections, bringing about agrarian reform, and seeking a peaceful solution to the civil war. Elections were held in 1982 and have been held regularly since then, but little progress has been made in agrarian reform or in other areas of human rights. Under these conditions, the patience of the American public for continued support is wearing thin and its outright opposition to aid has grown, fueled by reports of atrocities committed by the El Salvadoran military against Christian missionaries in 1989.

The instability in Central America was also profoundly disturbing to Nicaragua's and El Salvador's neighbors who feared its spread into their countries. The Contadora Group, consisting of Mexico, Venezuela, Colombia, and Panama, suggested the following framework for achieving a just peace in the region: the withdrawal of all foreign military forces; a pledge by all parties that their territory would not be used as a base for attacks on neighboring countries; a pledge by all parties that they would not provide arms to insurgent forces in other countries; and a pledge by the United States, the former Soviet Union, and Cuba that they would not provide military assistance to either Nicaragua or El Salvador. Whereas Nicaragua and the neighboring countries of Guatemala, Honduras, and El Salvador agreed to these conditions, Washington, fearing that the imposition of such conditions would soon lead to the crushing of the Contras and eventually to the fall of the government of El Salvador, did not. So the problems in El Salvador continued to fester.

In the early 1980s evidence was uncovered that the small Caribbean nation of Grenada was cooperating in the Soviet and Cuban effort to spread leftist revolution throughout Latin America. At that time construction had begun on a large airport, a project that was assisted by a contingent of several hundred Cuban workers, including some military personnel. The pro-Soviet and Cuban government of Grenada claimed that the airport would be used to promote tourism on the island. For its part the Reagan administration suspected that it would be used to export supplies and personnel to insurgent forces throughout Latin America. In 1983 a successful coup against the government of Grenada resulted in the installation of leaders who were believed to be even more pro-Soviet in their policies. The presence of about 1,000 American medical school students in the country raised fears that hostages would be taken to prevent U.S. intervention.

The Reagan administration acted quickly. Twelve days after the coup a U.S. military force invaded Grenada, secured the controversial airport, protected the students, freed imprisoned opposition leaders, and established them as the nation's new leaders. U.S. forces seized a large stockpile of weapons on the island, which the Reagan administration pointed to as evidence of the military objectives of the recently deposed regime. In less than two months all U.S. forces were withdrawn, and in December 1984 Grenada held its first elections in eight years.

In 1982 the Reagan administration was also presented with a crisis initiated by Argentina which forced it to choose between supporting Great Britain or Argentina. The action-forcing event was the seizure of the Falkland Islands by Argentina. These islands, located off the coast of Argentina, had been ruled by Britain since 1823. The United States provided intelligence and logistic support for Britain's successful military action to retake the Falklands but otherwise did not become involved. Since most Latin American nations sided with Argentina, the U.S. role probably served to fuel anti-U.S. feelings in the region.

During the 1980 election campaign against Carter, Reagan had chided his opponent for being too soft on less developed countries like Iran that dared to act in open opposition to U.S. interests. He hinted that if he was elected, his administration would teach the government of Iran a lesson. The Khomeini regime released the U.S. hostages days after the Reagan inauguration in 1981. But both Reagan and Bush have had their own problems in the Middle East, resulting in military confrontations against the governments of Libya and Iraq, as well as military involvement to restore political stability in Lebanon.

The Reagan administration believed that the regime of Colonel Qadhafi, the recipient of large-scale military aid from the Soviet Union, was a destabilizing force in North Africa and the sponsor of anti-American terrorism throughout the world. The United States engaged in hostilities with Libya three times in the 1980s, twice shooting down Libyan fighter planes and then bombing Tripoli in 1986. The 1986 attack was said to be in retaliation for recent instances of state-sponsored terrorism and was apparently designed to kill Qadhafi. The palace in Tripoli was damaged, Qadhafi's daughter was killed, and many civilians were killed or wounded, but he escaped unhurt. Like the Grenadan invasion before it, this intervention was widely praised in the press and in Congress.

In the aftermath of this intervention, Caspar Weinberger, secretary of defense, sought to formalize the criteria for the future use of military intervention to achieve foreign policy goals: the engagement should be clearly in the national interest; the commitment should be wholehearted, with a clear intention of achieving victory; political and military objectives should be precisely identified, with an appropriate strategy for using committed forces to attain them; the relationship between means and ends after forces have been sent into action must be continually reassessed; there must be a strong likelihood of support from both the American people and Congress; and U.S. military power in combat should be used as only a last resort.[31]

In the early 1980s the internal political situation in Lebanon became so unstable as to approach anarchy. The Reagan administration provided training and other assistance to the Lebanese army in the hopes of reestablishing order. Muslim and Christian forces within the country were engaged in a civil war, with other nations providing support to their favorites. Syria, with Soviet support, backed the Muslims. The United States supported the Christian-Phalangist forces. In 1983 Reagan ordered the navy to bombard and to launch carrier-based air strikes against Syrian military positions in Lebanon. Many innocent civilians were killed and wounded. He also ordered the marines to land and protect the U.S. embassy and the Beirut airport, but terrorists waged successful attacks against both locations, leading to the loss of over 250 American lives. The administration withdrew the remaining 1,200 marines in 1984.

Elsewhere in the Middle East, war had broken out between Iran and Iraq in 1980. Both countries were stridently anti-American. The Soviet Union supported Iraq, while the United States, Britain, and France deployed naval forces in the Persian Gulf to protect the movement of oil through the Strait of Hormuz. This narrow passage was within easy range of Iranian military strikes, and there were numerous minor military clashes between Iranian and U.S. naval forces, leading to some loss of lives on both sides. In a most unfortunate incident, a U.S. warship shot down an Iranian airliner, allegedly by mistake, killing about 300 innocent civilians. This incident fueled much anti-Americanism in the region. Most Nationalist observers argued that the main U.S. goals in the conflict were to keep the Gulf open and to see that neither side won an outright victory. If so, those goals were achieved when the adversaries agreed to a cease-fire in 1988 after a prolonged and mutually destructive stalemate.

In August 1990 Iraq, emerging from the war with Iran as a substantial military power in the world, invaded its neighbor, Kuwait. In an emergency session, the United Nations Security Council quickly condemned this act and ordered an economic boycott of Iraq by all member nations. The

United States and many other countries went even further, freezing all of Iraq's foreign economic assets and, for purposes of protection, Kuwait's assets as well. Despite early assurances that the invasion was temporary, within a few days Iraq's leaders announced that Kuwait no longer existed; it had been annexed and had become a part of Iraq. The United States Security Council quickly and unanimously condemned this act as well.

Some analysts felt that Saddem Hussein had ordered the invasion as a way of consolidating his position at home. Hussein himself defended the invasion on moral grounds. First, he claimed that the long war Iraq had fought against neighboring Iran benefited most other states in the Middle East, including Kuwait, but Iraq alone had borne the terrible costs of that war. Other states in the region had the resources to provide aid. Either by raising Iraq's OPEC production quota or by pumping less oil themselves, they could have made it easy for Iraq to make a rapid economic recovery, but they did not. Hussein also noted that Iraq had traditional claims to the territory of Kuwait, that the national borders of the Middle East had been imposed by former colonial powers, and, that in this case, they were designed to cripple Iraq. Finally, Hussein appealed to pan-Arabism by portraying himself as the champion of the Arab masses against the powers of the West. The Arab people, he said, had been denied the benefits of the tremendous wealth of the region so that a privileged few like the previous royal rulers of Kuwait could live in luxurious splendor and the West could receive plentiful supplies of oil at low cost.

The actions of the United Nations Security Council had little immediate effect on Iraq's policies. Evidence began to mount that Iraq was solidifying its hold on Kuwait and was even preparing to invade neighboring Saudi Arabia, an ally of the United States and a country containing the world's largest known oil reserves. U.S. leaders urged that a multinational peacekeeping force be sent to Saudi Arabia to defend it from this imminent threat and that a multinational naval force impose a naval quarantine on all Iraqi exports and imports. However, the United Nations was not yet ready to take stronger measures against Iraq.

President Bush ordered a massive military buildup of U.S. naval and air forces in the Persian Gulf, apparently in preparation for all contingencies. Upon invitation by the Saudi government, U.S. ground and air forces entered Saudi Arabia for the immediate purpose of defending an ally from hostile military threat. But Bush announced that the United States' other longer term objectives were to force Iraq to end its occupation of Iraq, to restore the previous government of Kuwait to power, and to safeguard U.S. lives and property in the region. Although he did not emphasize U.S. economic and military interests in the region, Iraq's actions began an escalation in the price of oil, which unchecked, could have sent the world's economy into long-term decline, significantly and negatively impacting on the quality of life in the United States.

Other nations soon joined the fray. On August 8, 1990, Mohammed Hosni Mubarak, the president of Egypt, called an Arab summit in the hopes of resolving the crisis peacefully. He proposed that the nations of the Middle East provide aid to assist Iraq's economy. In return, Hussein should agree to leave Kuwait. An all-Arab peacekeeping force would then patrol the Iraq-Kuwait border. The Iraqi delegation rebuffed his peace initiative as inadequate. Britain and some other NATO states sent naval warships and other equipment to the Gulf to assist the U.S. effort. The Soviet Union joined the condemnation of Iraq and announced that all Soviet military supplies would be cut off, but it took no military action of its own. Similarly, despite repeated requests by President Bush to the leaders of other Arab states, only Egypt and Syria joined what was quickly perceived by world opinion as a U.S.-led military venture. On August 26, the United Nations Security Council voted again, this time to allow the use of limited force to enforce the naval quarantine, with only Cuba and Yemen abstaining.

Nationalists noted that Bush's announced objective of returning the Emir of Kuwait to power was a mistake, because doing so had little to do with enduring U.S. strategic interests in the conflict. If those interests could be preserved by sacrificing the Kuwaiti government, so be it. Some Progressives favored U.S. military intervention, because they were more concerned that Iraq should not profit in any way from the aggression against Kuwait. Allowing Iraq to depose an internationally recognized, legitimate government was a form of profit. Others opposed intervention because it would benefit a nondemocratic state. Most Nationalists approved of unilateral military action by the United States, if necessary. Progressives urged that the United States comply with international laws against unilateral intervention, work in concert with the United Nations and other international organizations, and not unilaterally initiate military conflict with Iraq. Other than the leaders of Saudi Arabia, most Third World leaders either remained silent or condemned the U.S.-led military defense of Saudi Arabia as yet another example of U.S. economic imperialism. The war with Iraq also seemed to fuel existing widespread anti-American sentiments among the masses in the region.

On a more positive note, in the immediate aftermath of the war, Secretary of State Baker was able to convince representatives of several Arab states and of Israel to negotiate toward a settlement of their longstanding grievances. The Mideast Peace Talks which began in late 1991 thus marked the beginning of the first viable negotiating process between Arabs and Israelis since the Camp David talks in 1978. The central goal of the negotiations from the U.S. perspective was to effect a peaceful settlement of the differences between Israelis and Palestinians. If this goal is achieved and if the deep divisions between the Syrians and Israelis can be soothed, the nations of the Mideast will be able to work together to solve a variety of other common problems.

In Africa, Reagan's policies also differed significantly from those of his immediate predecessor. The Reagan administration continued support for black nationalism and for black majority rule, though more slowly and cautiously. In South Africa, the administration preferred a policy it called constructive engagement rather than confrontation with the white, apartheid regime. The administration supported the independence of Namibia from South Africa, but only if such independence was accompanied by withdrawal of all Cuban forces from nearby Angola. During the Reagan years little progress was made toward either goal. Some modest reforms were made in South African governance, giving nonwhites a somewhat larger voice in decisions, but not much larger. Namibia remained a territory of South Africa, and Cuban troops remained in Angola.

In the early years of the Reagan administration, the United States maintained quiet support for the white South African government by backing loans from the IMF and failing to oppose the formation of separate parliamentary chambers for Asians and people of mixed race, on the one hand, and for whites, on the other, even though this formula relegated the nonwhite chamber to a lower status and shut blacks out of government completely. However, public pressure mounted for the administration to take a more active role in promoting social justice in South Africa. As a congressional measure forcing such action was about to pass, in March 1985 Reagan finally gave in and issued an executive order imposing punitive measures.[32]

In late 1989 the moderate Botha government of South Africa announced a series of sweeping reforms intended to end apartheid there. As first steps, Pieter Botha reinstated previously banned African parties, and he ordered Nelson Mandela, a black leader of the anti-apartheid movement, released from jail. He also promised dialogue leading to a significant role for Africans in the government of South Africa. The Bush administration expressed a desire to ease sanctions against South Africa in recognition of these positive developments, but members of Congress and leaders of the anti-apartheid movement in South Africa restrained him from doing so before more significant progress occurred. Anti-apartheid forces within South Africa wanted a new constitution incorporating the one-person/one-vote principle, whereas the Botha government favored a constitution that would protect the minority cultural rights of white South Africans.

In 1990 U.S. troops were committed to battle in Africa when a rebellion against the regime of Samuel Doe of Liberia threatened the lives of Americans living there. Between 1980 and 1985, the United States had provided more aid per capita to Liberia than to any other country in Africa. But Doe's regime had become increasingly repressive, and, in the aftermath of a rigged election in 1985, human rights groups and some members of Congress pressed for reforms. Some contend that the 1985 elections were so unfair that the United States could have seized another target of opportunity to ease a dictator from power but did not.[33] Instead, when the tribal rebellion against his regime became extremely violent in 1990, Bush ordered a small contingent of troops to land and help to evacuate Americans from the area. Liberia's new leader, Charles Taylor, is no human rights champion either. He is a former Doe adviser, who has not yet mentioned a need for elections.

In 1991 the Bush administration did take strong action to support democracy in Haiti. On October 1, President Jean-Bertrand Aristide, the first popularly elected president in Haiti's history, was removed from power by a military coup. Aristide was a 38-year-old Catholic priest who had been elected in December 1990 by a landslide, on a platform pledging to give voice to Haiti's impoverished masses. The United Nations Security Council refused to discuss the coup. A Security Council spokesperson reportedly stated that a majority of the delegations felt that Haiti's problem should not be discussed because it was "an internal matter." In contrast to the inaction by the United Nations, the U.S. State Department refused to recognize the new government diplomatically and has used other diplomatic pressure to return Aristide to power. It stopped payment on that portion of the $84 million in economic aid to Haiti and $1.5 million in military aid that had been appropriated for the 1991 fiscal year but had not yet been spent. In addition, the State Department withdrew its request to Congress that Haiti be provided with $88.6 million in economic aid and $2.2 million in military aid for the 1992 fiscal year. France and Canada have also exerted similar pressure. Diplomats from the United States, Venezuela, and France negotiated to save Aristide's life, and the American ambassador to Haiti, Alvin Adams, was among those who escorted Aristide to the airport. Subsequently, the United States worked closely with the other members of the Organization of American States to develop other diplomatic and economic sanctions designed to pressure the coup leaders to step down. All these actions were courageous and consistent with the letter and spirit of U.S. legislation on human rights and with a Progressive approach to foreign policy toward the Third World.

THE GOALS: 1981–

By implication, the Bush administration is treated here as an extension of the Reagan foreign policy toward the Third World. However, the Bush response to action-forcing events such as the invasion of Kuwait by Iraq and the coup against the Aristide government in Haiti raises questions about that assumption. It is too soon to tell. Generally, the Reagan and Bush administrations have not repudiated the Progressive foreign policy goals enunciated most forcefully by Kennedy and Carter, but they have redefined them and relegated them to lower priority. In so doing, both administrations returned to a familiar pattern of largely Nationalist foreign policy priorities evident in the rhetoric of Republican presidents at least since Eisenhower. Their Democratic challengers in 1980, 1984, and 1988, Jimmy Carter, Walter Mondale, and Michael Dukakis, respectively, all promised a more Progressive foreign policy toward the Third World than what Reagan and Bush have delivered.

The human rights rhetoric remained, but U.S. foreign policy toward the Third World conducted on the basis of this rhetoric was aimed only at promoting democracy and opposing communism. This use of the term *human rights* for propaganda purposes had the effect of diluting the meaning of the term. By emphasizing so strongly the presence or absence of formal democratic institutions in places like El Salvador, Nicaragua, and even Haiti as almost the sole basis of U.S. foreign policy toward those countries, the Reagan and Bush administrations have appeared to be unconcerned about other kinds of human rights abuses by "democratic" regimes.[34] Moreover, in regions of the world where the prospects for democratization have been poor, there has been no real presidential human rights policy at all. If broader human rights concerns have affected U.S. foreign policy toward the Third World, the impetus has come mainly from Congress and it has been exercised using the legal framework established mainly in the 1970s.

During the 1980s excessive debt threatened to bankrupt many LDCs. The World Bank, the IMF, and other public and private international lending agencies quickly replaced multinational corporations as potentially the most significant sources of intrusive foreign influence on political, social, and economic affairs within debtor states. Thus far, the Reagan and Bush administrations have agreed with and probably are partly responsible for the conditions usually placed on new loans—for example, lower expenditures on social programs, freer trade, encouragement of foreign investment, and increased reliance on the private sector. The United States had found a powerful new tool for implementing its own policy priorities in the Third World.

The most recent cases of U.S. responses to action-forcing events in the Third World — the invasion of Kuwait, the rebellion in Liberia, and the coups in Haiti and Peru — are particularly interesting, because they all occurred after the Cold War ended, after perestroika had begun. The reactions to those cases give us clues about the future trajectory of U.S. foreign policy toward the Third World. But the cases are too few at this point and the confounding factors are too many for any clear trend to be detected. Future foreign policy toward the Third World is likely to adhere to one of three scenarios described in the next chapter.

NOTES

1. Ronald Reagan, State of the Union Address, February 6, 1985.

2. *Economic Report of the President Transmitted to Congress February 1982* (Washington, D.C.: U.S. Government Printing Office, 1982), p. 184.

3. I. G. Patel, *Current Crisis in International Cooperation* (New Delhi: Reserve Bank of India, March 15, 1982), p. 16.

4. Richard E. Feinberg, "Reaganomics and the Third World," in Kenneth A. Oye, Robert J. Lieber, and Donald Rothchild, eds., *Eagle Defiant* (Boston: Little, Brown and Co., 1983), p. 148.

5. As quoted in Christopher Madison, "Exporting Reaganomics — The President Wants to Do Things Differently at AID," *National Journal,* May 29, 1982, p. 962.

6. Feinberg, "Reaganomics and the Third World," p. 151.

7. Ibid., p. 152.

8. Ibid., pp. 156–157.

9. Quoted in *U.S. Foreign Policy: The Reagan Imprint* (Washington, D.C.: Congressional Quarterly, 1986), pp. 129–130.

10. The World Bank, *World Development Report 1987* (New York: Oxford University Press), p. 14.

11. Richard E. Feinberg, "American Power and Third World Economies," in Kenneth Oye, Robert J. Lieber, and Donald Rothchild, eds., *Eagle Resurgent?* (Boston: Little, Brown and Co., 1987), pp. 160–161.

12. Republican Party Platform, 26, 1980, *Congressional Quarterly Almanac,* p. 838.

13. U.S. Treasury Department, *Participation in the Multilateral Development Banks in the 1980s* (Washington, D.C.: U.S. Government Printing Office, 1982).

14. Quoted in *The Reagan Imprint,* p. 127.

15. Feinberg, "American Power," p. 154.

16. Ernest W. Lefever, "The Trivialization of Human Rights," in Tinsley E. Yarbrough, ed., *The Reagan Administration and Human Rights* (New York: Praeger Publishers, 1985).

17. See David P. Forsythe, *Human Rights and U.S. Foreign Policy: Congress Reconsidered* (Gainesville, Fl.: University of Florida Press, 1988), pp. 121–124.

18. Michael Stohl et al., "U.S. Foreign Policy, Human Rights and Multilateral Assistance," in Forsythe, ed., *Human Rights and Development,* pp. 196–212.

19. Jack Donnelly, *Universal Human Rights in Theory and Practice* (Ithaca, N.Y.: Cornell University Press, 1989), p. 247.

20. Quoted in Tamar Jacoby, "The Reagan Turnaround on Human Rights," *Foreign Affairs* (Summer 1986): 1967.

21. Rajni Kothari, "Human Rights as a North-South Issue," in Richard Pierre Claude and Burns H. Weston, *Human Rights in the World Community* (Philadelphia: University of Pennsylvania Press, 1989).

22. Ibid.

23. See Joshua Muravchik, *Exporting Democracy* (Washington, D.C.: AEI Press, 1991), Chapter 13, for a description of the organization and programs of the NED.

24. Arthur S. Banks, *Political Handbook of the World: 1989* (Binghamton, N.Y.: CSA Publications, 1989), pp. 337–342.

25. Ibid., p. 466.

26. Ibid., p. 467.

27. David P. Forsythe, *Human Rights and U.S. Foreign Policy* (Gainesville: University of Florida Press, 1988), p. 55.

28. Neil Henry, "A Continent's Leaders Hear Footsteps of Change," *Washington Post National Weekly Edition,* July 16–22, 1990, p. 17.

29. On the increased use of covert action, see Jay Peterzell, *Reagan's Secret Wars* (Washington, D.C.: Center for National Security Studies, 1984).

30. Banks, ed., *Political Handbook of the World, 1989,* p. 154.

31. James E. Dougherty and Robert L. Pfaltzgraff, Jr., *American Foreign Policy: FDR to Reagan* (New York: Harper and Row, 1986), pp. 389–390.

32. Jacoby, "The Reagan Turnaround," pp. 1080–1081.

33. Blaine Harden, "End of the Line for a Tyrant," *Washington Post National Weekly Edition,* June 11–17, 1990, p. 25.

34. Edward S. Herman and Frank Brodhead, *Demonstration Elections* (Boston: South End Press, 1984).

CHAPTER 11

The Past, Perestroika, and the Future

Over time and especially since World War II, U.S. policymakers have increasingly recognized the relative importance of universal values and of the duties to people living in other nations. This trend has not been linear, but it is visible in the changing rhetoric, actions, and consequences of U.S. foreign policy toward the Third World over the past two hundred years. As the history of U.S.–Third World relations reviewed in Chapters 5–10 illustrates, the Progressive evolution in U.S. foreign policy has been caused, in part, by the United States' changing place within the international power structure, by the longstanding rivalry with the former Soviet Union over alternative conceptions of the "good society," by the lessons learned from the Vietnam War, and, most importantly, by the institutional changes in foreign policy decision-making structures and processes wrought by Progressive administrations. The evolution toward a more Progressive foreign policy is likely being fueled by a shift in American values as well.

We sometimes lose sight of the trend toward Progressive foreign policy values and objectives because of a fixation on notable exceptions, cycles of party control that can obscure longer-term developments, an inability or unwillingness to step back from current events to see the larger historical picture, and an adherence to absolute rather than relative standards of performance. In this chapter, the main pieces of evidence supporting this thesis are reviewed along with some alternative standards that might be used to evaluate it. Then, three scenarios of future U.S.–Third World relations are developed, leading alternatively to greater isolation of the United States from North-South issues, a regression to previous patterns of gunboat diplomacy, or accelerated Progressivism.

PAST PATTERNS

Since World War II, the number of Progressive objectives expressed in relevant symbolic policy statements has increased. The record of U.S. actions in the Third World, whether unprovoked or in response to action-forcing events, demonstrates that the emphasis given to Progressive values and objectives in the making of U.S. foreign policy toward LDCs has also increased. The change in priorities guiding action has not been steady; it has been halting and cyclical, but over a long period of time, the overall direction of movement seems clear.

For the first 125 years of the United States' existence as a nation, there was little, if anything, that was Progressive about its foreign policy goals, objectives or methods in conducting relations with its weaker neighbors. In the last century, U.S. leaders have continued to place primary emphasis on Nationalist objectives in conducting those relations, but, at the margins, they have pursued others that are not solely connected with the national self-interest. Even since the beginning of the Cold War (and partly as a response to it), U.S. foreign policy has become increasingly affected by Progressive elements of the foreign policy agenda.

Progressive thinkers might argue over what set of values and objectives should guide U.S. foreign policy and, within that set, certainly would argue over which ones were most important. For almost all of them, the set would include support for human rights, self-determination and autonomy, economic development, and social justice. It would also include adherence to the strictures of international law, generally, and the principle of nonintervention, specifically. Over the years, at least some U.S. presidents have recognized all these elements as worth pursuing. Jimmy Carter was probably the only one who attempted to increase the priority of all of them in relation to other economic and military objectives in U.S. foreign policy. Still, with the possible exception of his administration, the overall record of adherence to the spirit of international law has been abysmal.

The order in which different values were introduced into the foreign policy debate is important, because a kind of primacy principle is at work. Nationalist goals of maintaining sovereignty, security from external threat, and national macroeconomic prosperity are fundamental. In the early years, when the United States was itself a developing country, they were the only mainsprings of foreign policy. These values were not replaced by later, more Progressive ideals. Instead, later objectives were added and generally have not been pursued vigorously except when prior goals have been satisfied or at least have not been seriously endangered. Similarly, the order in which Progressive values and objectives were interjected into U.S. foreign policy rhetoric is also significant — support for democracy, economic development, social justice, and human rights, in that sequence. The earliest ones accepted as part of the U.S. foreign policy debate continue to dominate over those introduced later.

Self-determination. Support for democratic movements or, at a minimum, for elections in LDCs has been a feature of foreign policy rhetoric at least since the Spanish-American War, when it was used as an important rationale for freeing Cuba from Spanish rule and then granting that state independence. This theme is so old and has been so persistent in U.S. foreign policy that it would be difficult to argue that a particular administration initiated it.

Economic Development. Although many U.S. leaders had expressed compassion for people living in poverty in the Third World, Truman, in the immediate aftermath of the Second World War, was the first to initiate a substantial public program to do something about it. The foreign aid and technical assistance programs his administration initiated and the international lending agencies it helped form provided the foundations for contemporary U.S. policies designed to foster Third World economic development.

Social Justice. By 1960 U.S. policymakers recognized that aggregate economic development, by itself, would not necessarily have a beneficial effect on the poorest people in Third World societies. The Kennedy administration, through both its rhetoric and its deeds, heightened U.S. concern for issues of social justice and political reform. During his brief tenure in office, Kennedy dramatically expanded the food aid program, established the Agency for International Development and the Peace Corps, and was the first U.S. president to sanction South Africa for its policies of apartheid.

Human Rights. In 1976 Jimmy Carter added promotion of human rights to the by now substantial Progressive foreign policy agenda. For Carter, protecting human rights primarily meant ensuring that individuals would not be abused by their governments. The Reagan and Bush administrations have chosen to emphasize the protection of the individual's civil and political human rights. Today the term *human rights* encompasses much of the Progressive foreign policy agenda. As a result, much of the current empirical research on ethical issues in U.S. foreign policy focuses on whether, to what extent, and in what way human rights considerations affect U.S. foreign policy toward the Third World. Recently, a few studies have also been conducted on whether U.S. foreign policy has any impact on the human rights practices of the Third World targets of those policies.

Progressive values and objectives have become more numerous in the rhetoric of U.S. foreign policy. They have also become more explicit in the legislation that guides the implementation of that policy and, arguably, more important in shaping the reality of that policy as well. However, the record on other important aspects of the Progressive agenda — general adherence to international law, reliance on a multilateral approach to international affairs, avoidance of the use of covert action except as a last resort, and observance of the principle of nonintervention, in particular — has not been impressive. Among U.S. presidents since World War II, only Carter worked hard to adhere to these Progressive goals and principles. And Carter's four short years in office were not enough to make much progress in these areas.

It is too soon to gauge President Bush's position in these previously neglected areas. Certainly, his handling of the Panama situation violated the spirit of international law, U.S. prohibitions against using covert action to assassinate foreign leaders, and the norm against unilateral military intervention. However, his administration's response to Iraq's invasion of Kuwait was quite different. At least during the early stages of that crisis, administration actions were consistent with (though at times they anticipated) pertinent resolutions of the United Nations Security Council. However, during those early stages the Security Council adopted, with minor modifications, every resolution advanced by the U.S. representative. The real test will come when the United States is forced to choose between its own foreign policy preferences and those expressed by the United Nations or by a conference of regional leaders.

There has been continuity in U.S. foreign policy since World War II in the sense that Nationalist objectives have maintained their preeminent places in the hierarchy. Progressive objectives, because they are newer and their positions less fixed, have received slightly different priorities by different administrations. The statements and actions of the Reagan and Bush administrations seem to reflect the following priorities among Progressive goals: (1) encourage the development of democratic institutions and civil and political liberties; (2) assist (free market) economic development efforts; (3) promote human rights of the integrity of the person; (4) promote social justice; (5) respect international law; and (6) avoid unilateral overt or covert intervention.

Various U.S. administrations have differed not only on the relative positions of different Progressive objectives of U.S. foreign policy toward the Third World, but also on the willingness to make tradeoffs between Nationalist and Progressive values. As noted at the outset, ethical choices rarely involve choosing between good and evil. Rather, one must usually choose between good and better or between bad or worse. Foreign policymakers must choose among inconsistent goals. As an example, anti-expropriation policies may promote the United States' short- and long-term economic self-interest, but such policies may also impede the ability of some underdeveloped nations to control assets such as natural resources within their own jurisdictions. This hurts the ability of Third World states to achieve either economic development or social justice. As another example, providing large amounts of military aid to a less developed country may allow it to cooperate more effectively in the United States' own military defense effort, but it may also increase the power of the military sector of a Third World society to the point where civilian leaders are unable to rule effectively. Under such circumstances, democracy will fail or will exist only as an empty form.

Since World War II, U.S. foreign policymakers have been increasingly willing to make tradeoffs that place Nationalist foreign policy values and objectives at significant risk. The Carter administration was criticized for taking too many risks of this type. But even the reactions of the Reagan administration to democratic movements in South Korea, the Philippines, and Haiti are all examples of risks taken by an otherwise risk-averse administration to promote democratic movements in the Third World.

The historical record since World War II also illustrates that Democrats have expanded the Progressive foreign policy agenda rhetorically and have made greater efforts to follow through on that rhetoric. Democratic presidents, presidential candidates, and members of Congress generally have advocated

1. Giving more foreign aid to developing countries.
2. Providing a higher proportion of economic (as opposed to military) aid.
3. Placing more emphasis on aiding self-determination and true democracy, not just on establishing regular elections.
4. Giving less emphasis to private investment as a foreign policy tool.
5. Using less military intervention and covert action.
6. Relying more heavily on need and human rights performance as criteria in the disbursement of economic aid.
7. Giving a higher proportion of foreign assistance in the form of multilateral (as opposed to bilateral) aid and in the form of grants (as opposed to loans).
8. Relying more heavily on regional and international (as opposed to unilateral) solutions to problems.

Republican administrations have tended to be more Nationalist in their approach to foreign policy. Hence, when Democrats have controlled the U.S. government, there has been a ratchet effect on the place of Progressive moral principles in U.S. foreign policy toward the Third World. If progress is measured as the addition of new foreign policy objectives related to improving the welfare of the poorest people in the Third World or as a willingness to take greater risks in the attainment of Nationalist objectives to achieve Progressive objectives, then Democrats have tended to ratchet the policy toward Progressivism during their tenures in terms of both rhetoric and actions. Republicans have tended to allow that upward progress to erode somewhat during their terms of office, but they have not turned the clock back completely. Thus, despite the current cycle away from the trajectory set by Carter, the trend over time since the end of World War II still is moving toward higher priority for Progressive foreign policy principles as guides for the conduct of U.S.-Third World relations.

STANDARDS OF EVALUATION

Evaluation of any policy requires establishing an implicit or explicit measurement standard. The presentation of historical material about U.S.-Third World relations in this work implies the use of past foreign policy behavior as a standard for evaluating present behavior. Most people who address the issue of ethics in international affairs do not use past behavior as their standard of evaluation. Instead, they have absolute standards of ethical behavior in mind. Nations like the United States either achieve or do not achieve them. U.S. foreign policy, as explained earlier, is not yet truly Progressive in any absolute sense. Thus, when absolute standards are used, the United States will fail. Instead, we should employ relative comparisons. Then, we should ask whether, in the United States, Progressive policies have been implemented (the efforts test) and whether Progressive goals have been achieved (the impact test). These tests are still demanding, but they are more realistic.

Relative Comparisons. One reasonable way to evaluate the extent to which U.S. foreign policy toward the Third World adheres to Progressive principles is to compare U.S. policies to those of other developed nations. With regard to promoting human rights around the world, Jack Donnelly, who is generally a critic of U.S. foreign policy, admits that "It is difficult to find countries that have done much more than the United States."[1] A brief examination of the foreign policies of the former state of the Soviet Union and present-day Canada will serve to illustrate his point.

No other nation except what was formerly the Soviet Union has been a military superpower in the international system since World War II. Superpower status places constraints on U.S. foreign policy options that other nations with fewer international responsibilities do not face; therefore, a comparison with Soviet policies from 1950 to 1989 is instructive. The former state of the Soviet Union viewed the international system as it presently exists as fundamentally unjust. In the view of its leadership, since capitalism and colonialism had caused underdevelopment in the Third World, fundamental revolutionary change was the best and perhaps the only way the Third World could receive justice. A nurturing foreign policy toward LDCs would only have supported the unjust structure of power and prolonged the inevitable.

Thus, the vast majority of the Soviet Union's foreign aid to Third World states was in the form of military assistance to communist or pro-communist allies, helping them to make the transition from capitalism to socialism in a politically and economically hostile international environment. Historically, the Soviet Union's main objective was to develop a network of Third World allies who would be willing to adopt the Soviet economic and political model. There is little evidence that the Soviets had humanitarian objectives or even that they generally embraced the goal of assisting the economic development efforts of less developed countries. Doing so would have forced them to prop up the world capitalist system. The Soviet position was that economic aid was compensation paid by former colonial powers for past exploitation. Never having been a colonial power itself, it owed no such compensation. Consistent with its philosophical position, the Soviet Union, unlike the United States, contributed little to international development agencies.[2] Instead, Soviet economic relations with LDCs were presumed to be mutually beneficial and were structured by what they called economic cooperation agreements.[3] Usually, the agreements presaged loans from the Soviet Union to Third World signatories at concessionary rates of interest. Such loans were often repayable in the form of local commodities.

The Soviet Union was more Progressive in its relations with Third World countries in its choices of methods to achieve its own foreign policy objectives. More than the United States, the Soviet Union showed respect for international law, for the sovereignty of other weaker states, and for the principle of nonintervention. With the notable exception of the invasion of Afghanistan, the Soviet Union generally did not use military force against Third World states. It is not clear whether this practice resulted from adherence to ethical principles or from fear of retaliation by the United States and its Western allies. Many accept the "fear of retaliation" explanation, because the Soviet Union, like the United States, was willing to use covert methods to achieve preferred policy outcomes in militarily weaker states.

Canadian foreign policy provides an opportunity for a different kind of comparison. Its policies, like those of the United States, are affected by a recent frontier experience and by Anglo-American values and traditions. Many of its people and leaders favor Progressive foreign policy principles. Consequently, Canadian leaders must face many of the same kinds of tradeoffs as those considered by U.S. policymakers. However, because of its geographic location and its place as a middle power within the international power hierarchy, its interests in the Third World are less intense and narrower in scope.

We would expect this combination of attributes to make Canada a leader in the application of Progressive thinking to foreign policy toward Third World states, but it has not. Canada has adopted Progressive principles regarding the methods, but not the goals and objectives, of foreign policy. Canada probably seldom uses covert actions and has never used direct unilateral military intervention to achieve its foreign policy objectives in the Third World. Neither has it assumed a leadership role in national or international forums to promote Progressive objectives in the Third World. Indeed, Canada has lagged well behind the United States in the use of foreign policy statements or actions to promote improved human rights practices by Third World regimes. In most other respects, Canada has shown about the same mix of Nationalism and Progressivism in its foreign policy objectives in the Third World as the United States. Canadian foreign policy toward the Third World has been designed mainly to further its own national economic objectives; to fulfill Canada's obligations stemming from its membership in various Western security, political, and economic alliances; and to avoid conflict with and maintain independence from the United States, the leading power in many of those alliances. Canadian foreign policy toward Central America has been independent of U.S. policy but not necessarily more Progressive. According to Rhoda Howard and Jack Donnelly, the three cornerstones of Canada's foreign policy toward Central America are a recognition that the instability in this part of the world is a product of: poverty, the unfair distribution of wealth, and social injustice; a preference for regional and multilateral solutions to unrest rather than unilateral intervention by the United States; and a focus on maintaining relations, especially trade relations, with all states, regardless of the practices of their governments.[4] On the basis of these criteria, over the past decade the Canadian government has maintained generally friendly relations with El Salvador, Honduras, Cuba, and Nicaragua.

One criticism of U.S. economic aid policies is that much of the aid provided is tied to the condition that it be used to purchase U.S. goods and services.[5] This proviso reduces the purchasing discretion of the recipient, and, therefore, the value of the monetary transfer, by as much as 20 percent. However, justifying foreign aid partly on the basis of developing markets for the donor country's goods and services is one way an executive administration in a democratic government maintains a winning legislative coalition in favor of its foreign aid program. The United States is not unique in this respect. More of Canada's economic aid is tied to the purchase of its own products and services than any other donor in the world except Australia.[6]

In absolute terms, the United States provided about six times as much official development assistance to Third World states in 1986 than did Canada, but Canada gave a higher amount as a percentage of GNP (0.44 percent to 0.22 percent).[7] Only since 1987 has Canada had a requirement linking economic aid to the human rights performance of potential recipients, and that requirement is much more ambiguous than the one stated in U.S. legislation. It appears as a statement in an obscure Canadian Development Agency report, and it states only that human rights protection is now one criterion of eligibility for foreign aid.[8] Implementation of the new policy will be impeded because, unlike the United States, Canada does not require any agency to measure the human rights practices of other nations and then to report periodically to policymakers. Indeed, only two other governments in the world compile reasonably comprehensive reports on the human rights practices of other countries—Norway, since 1985, and, even more recently, the Netherlands.

Apparently, as in the United States, there is some gap between human rights rhetoric and actual practices. A recent study concluded that Canada gives far more foreign aid in absolute terms to countries with poor human rights records than to countries with good ones.[9] And, perhaps because of a concern about disrupting trade relations, Canada has been even more reluctant than the United States to impose trade sanctions on South Africa.[10] As in the United States, promotion of Canadian arms sales to Third World countries has become an important objective of the Canadian government. Canadian law on military assistance is similar to U.S. law, prohibiting the export of arms to "countries whose governments have a persistent record of serious violations of the human rights of their citizens, unless it can be demonstrated that there is no reasonable risk that the goods might be used against the civilian population."[11] However, according to Project Ploughshares, in 1986 Canadian arms were sold to the repressive governments of Argentina, Chile, Guatemala, Indonesia, Pakistan, Paraguay, the Philippines, South Korea, and Syria.[12] Whereas U.S. law requires reasonably full disclosure of all arms sales, Canada has no such obligation.[13]

Unlike the situation in the United States, Canadian representatives on the boards of international financial institutions such as the World Bank are not instructed to consider the status of human rights observance in the applicant's country when making loan decisions. In this case, the Canadian government's policy against promotion of human rights is based on principle. In 1988 the minister of finance wrote: "I believe that the introduction of human rights criteria would politicize the World Bank's decision making with negative consequences for its activities."[14]

The Efforts Test. Yet another approach to assessing whether or not Progressive principles have motivated U.S. foreign policy behavior is to employ the efforts test. As described in this text, to see whether stated policies actually have been implemented, it is necessary to examine the patterns of actual foreign policy behavior. A total lack of effort or only minimal effort to implement a publicly stated policy would be evidence of official deception and immorality. Much research has been conducted on the extent to which the United States has a more favorable foreign policy toward states with better human rights records, as is required by existing U.S. legislation, but the evidence is not conclusive. There have been several statistical studies of the relationship between the human rights practices of LDCs and the amounts and kinds of U.S. foreign aid they have received. Studies of this type tend to measure human rights practices in a way that is consistent with Carter's emphasis on respect for rights of the integrity of the individual. The findings from Cingranelli and Pasquarello's research on the relationship between human rights practices and the distribution of economic and military assistance among Latin American countries in FY1982 indicated that no simple generalizations about the role of human rights in decisions regarding the distribution of U.S. foreign aid were possible.[15]

We found that decisions regarding the distribution of foreign aid to Latin America were made in two stages. During the gatekeeping stage of economic aid decisions, when certain countries may be excluded from the pool of potential aid recipients in a particular budget year, more developed nations often were eliminated, and human rights records were not a consideration in determining which nations received economic assistance. When U.S. policymakers decided on amounts of economic assistance, however, higher levels of economic assistance were provided to nations with relatively enlightened human rights practices. For military aid, nations with poor human rights records often were excluded at the gatekeeping stage, but once the decision had been made to provide military assistance, the human rights practices of the recipients could not explain the level of assistance.

In other words, we found that the human rights records of potential recipients played a role in some decisions but not in others. Pasquarello replicated this research, this time focusing on the distribution of foreign aid among African nations, and found that human rights considerations played a role, but a different one than was found for Latin America.[16] Steven Poe recently conducted research adopting our "gatekeeping-level" distinction, but examining a wider sample of countries. He also found statistical evidence suggesting that human rights concerns affected some aspects of foreign aid allocations, in ways prescribed by existing U.S. human rights legislation.[17]

Many other studies have reported no relationship between the human rights records of Third World states and the level of foreign assistance provided by the United States.[18] In doing so, some have criticized our Latin American study on methodological grounds.[19] But the debate contains some philosophical differences as well. Some analysts prefer to draw their conclusions from observing the human rights conditions that prevail within the boundaries of the largest recipients of U.S. economic assistance. In Latin America, for example, economic assistance to El Salvador accounts for approximately 25 percent of all U.S. aid supplied to the region. Human rights conditions in El Salvador are terrible, and some of the worst violations have allegedly been perpetrated by elements of that nation's military. The military itself is not under unified control and is not especially responsive to the civilian authorities. If we consider only or mainly U.S. foreign policy toward El Salvador, it is hard to argue that the U.S. government has more favorable economic assistance policies toward nations with good human rights practices. If, on the other hand, we admit the lesson of U.S. involvement in El Salvador, but then look at the distribution of U.S. economic assistance among the other Latin American nations, we find that in these less visible, more "routine" cases, nations with better human rights records receive higher levels of aid.

But which piece of evidence is more revealing of the efforts of U.S. policymakers to achieve Progressive outcomes in the Third World? U.S. policies toward El Salvador and Nicaragua since 1981 reflect the preferences of two Republican administrations with the reluctant cooperation of Congress. Foreign policy toward most of the other nations in Latin America, on the other hand, is less the subject of press reports and congressional debates. Instead, it is the product of longer standing decision rules, institutional arrangements, and policy processes.

Presidential administrations have great control over the making of foreign policy except in those areas where Congress, through legislation, has ensured a role for itself. Because of the existence of human rights legislation, during the Reagan administration Congress was able to use hearings and to enact numerous pieces of country-specific legislation to alter or at least to call into question U.S. foreign policy toward many countries including El Salvador, Nicaragua, Guatemala, Chile, Argentina, South Africa, and South Korea on human rights grounds. Congress can prohibit human rights violators from receiving any military assistance, but it exercises much less control over how much a country will receive if it does not implement that prohibition. Not surprisingly, therefore, no study has shown the *level* of military aid a country received to be proportionate to any measure of the human rights practices of the recipient country's government during any president's administration. The existence of a legislative platform does not guarantee close congressional oversight of administrative actions, but the absence of one makes such oversight almost impossible.

The Impact Test. Since morality is bound inextricably to consideration of consequences, the impact test is important too. Although we can find some anecdotal bright spots in the impacts of U.S. efforts to achieve Progressive foreign policy goals in the Third World, especially during the Carter administration, there has been very little systematic research on the impact of U.S. foreign policy on underdeveloped countries. And the limited work that has been conducted on this question shows very little evidence that Progressive objectives have had much impact. There are four possible reasons for these disappointing findings.

First, in order for foreign policy to be effective, it must provide resources or apply sanctions that are significant to the target.[20] The United States has lost some of its significance to many Third World countries because it has shifted much of its aid from bilateral to multilateral programs. Wealthier Third World nations like Brazil, Venezuela, and Singapore rely less on bilateral aid and more on loans from private international banks and public multilateral development banks (MDBs). Although the United States remains a strong voice in the lending policies of MDBs, its own priorities must be tempered by the need to persuade other voting members. Moreover, although the United States is still among the largest providers of official development assistance to the Third World, Japan has exceeded the United States in its absolute level of giving. The gap between the United States and the other contributors is shrinking as well. In some Third World countries, the U.S. aid program is so small that manipulating its size marginally is not likely to have any effect.

Second, to have any systematic impact, the U.S. policymakers' commitment to Progressive foreign policy objectives must be clear, sincere, and consistent.[21] The Reagan and Bush administrations gave anti-communist and other Nationalist objectives such high priority that Progressive objectives did not have a consistent impact on foreign policy rhetoric or actions. The Reagan and Bush pattern has been to provide foreign aid and other foreign policy benefits to noncommunist, market-oriented Third World regimes, pushing for Progressive reforms only when it was relatively safe and convenient to do so. Furthermore, their commitment to a domestic policy of trickle-down economics led them to subtly move away from aid programs directly benefiting the neediest in Third World countries to programs designed to stimulate macroeconomic growth instead. By pushing hard only when there were extraordinary targets of opportunities for democratization, the Reagan and Bush administrations have sent mixed messages to Third World leaders about their priorities.

Third, it is hard to measure the short-term impact of foreign policy. Most foreign policy is conducted through quiet, routine, low-intensity instruments. Its impacts are expected to be durable and long term. The symbolic emphasis of promotion of human rights through U.S. foreign policy is very new, so it is unrealistic to expect dramatic results. It would be difficult enough to identify the impacts of high-priority U.S. foreign policy goals on the behavior of Third World states. It is especially unrealistic to expect to find compelling evidence of the impacts of medium- and low-priority goals on policy outcomes, because much of the time they will be overshadowed by higher priority ones.

Finally, employing the impact test usually leads to disappointment because the instruments of U.S. foreign policy in the Third World are based too heavily on sanctions rather than on positive reinforcements. Congressional legislation designed to promote human rights around the world has no carrots in it, only sticks. The language of the legislation implies that human rights can be measured, so that the human rights practices of all nations can be at least ranked from best to worst. It also implies a threshold for the tolerance of human rights violations. When nations cross the implied threshold, the statutes require the U.S. government to react by voting against loans or by stopping bilateral foreign aid. The policy would have greater impact if nations received levels of rewards in proportion to the extent to which each exceeded the threshold. Nations with the best human rights practices, other things being equal, would receive higher levels of benefits from U.S. foreign policy than those just above the threshold. Those below the threshold would receive no benefits at all. Or the policy could reward improvements in practices regardless of the initial rank or starting point.

The few statistical studies of the impact of U.S. foreign policies on the targets of those policies have not found much evidence of achievement of Progressive goals. In a crude test of the effectiveness of U.S. human rights policy in improving the human rights conditions in LDCs, David Carleton and Michael Stohl selected a sample of 59 LDCs (from which the United States admits refugees) and found that political terror in 9 of the 59 countries lessened, but in 4 of the 59 it worsened. In the first five years of the Reagan administration, the number of cases where political terror worsened and where it improved was nearly equal. While the Carter record is a little better, the difference in impact between the two administrations could be due to chance rather than to the effects of different foreign policies.[22] On the basis of such slim evidence, it is hard to argue that the

Carter administration had much impact on improving human rights performance. But Carleton and Stohl note that the foreign policy rhetoric of the Carter administration had a profoundly positive effect on the oppressed and downtrodden in Third World states by providing them with hope. The authors noted that the Reagan and Bush "quiet diplomacy" approach, on the other hand, offers the victims much less hope.[23]

FUTURE TRENDS

The United States emerged from the Second World War as the richest and least damaged of the major world powers. Using these advantages, it helped finance the reconstruction of Europe, was the first nation to develop a substantial bilateral foreign aid program to assist development in the Third World, and was a leader in the establishment of several international development agencies. In recent years, however, things have changed dramatically. Today the United States has severe budget problems, and its economy is second to Japan and is losing ground to Germany. As recently as 1983, the United States was the world's largest creditor nation, but by the end of 1989, it was the world's number one debtor, falling $664 billion in the hole to foreigners, primarily the British and Japanese. In this environment of resource scarcity, new demands were made to cut back on the use of U.S. tax dollars to finance social, economic, and political improvements in the less developed countries. While budget resources were shrinking, potential demand on U.S. foreign aid skyrocketed.

Beginning in 1989, in the domestic arena, the Soviet Union, under the leadership of Mikhail Gorbachev, took a sharp turn away from political authoritarianism and economic central planning toward democracy and free market economics. In the area of foreign policy, Gorbachev proposed an end to the Cold War, advanced major new agreements limiting the development and deployment of nuclear and conventional weapons, pulled the Soviet military out of Afghanistan, and reduced its support for revolutionary movements in the Third World. At least some of these momentous changes will be long lasting. Indeed, the Soviet Union, the United States' principal ideological and military rival for more than half a century, no longer exists, having been replaced by a loose confederation of nations called the Commonwealth of Independent States. So a total reexamination and reorientation of East-West foreign policy is taking place.

Major changes in the former state of the Soviet Union touched off similar reforms in many Eastern European countries, including Poland,

Czechoslovakia, and East Germany, highlighted by the tearing down of the Berlin Wall in 1989. Most U.S. policymakers want the United States to be an active participant in these transformations. If current reforms succeed and become permanent, the result will be a safer world for the United States and its NATO allies. In the wake of these major changes in what used to be called the Soviet bloc, the United States confronts new demands to help finance democratization and free market reforms in Eastern Europe and the nations making up the Commonwealth of Independent States. A less hostile international environment may allow a decrease in the percentage of the annual U.S. budget allocated to national defense, from about one third during the early 1980s to as low as 20 percent. These "windfall" savings could be used to offset the large budget deficit, attack problems of poverty and environmental degradation domestically, or finance substantial new foreign assistance programs aimed at Eastern Europe and the Third World.

These dramatic developments in East-West relations are likely to alter the rules of the game for North-South relations as well. With respect to the world distribution of military power, the United States now holds a larger share. However, in the distribution of economic power, the United States is losing ground. The movement toward a single economy in Europe and the free market reforms in the former Soviet bloc are sure to produce even more economic competition in the near future. Because of these poor economic conditions, it is unlikely that transfers of tax dollars from the United States to Third World states will grow any faster than the rate of inflation for at least a decade.

Beyond that, three alternative models of U.S.-Third World relations in the twenty-first century seem possible and illustrate the range of choices. One possibility—the isolation model—predicts that the United States will lose interest in the Third World and drastically cut the level of bilateral and multilateral economic assistance it provides to developing countries. Another scenario—the regressive model—is that the United States, now unchecked by its previous superpower rival, will take even greater license in manipulating Third World nations to achieve its own self-interested ends. Yet another possibility—the Progressive model—is that U.S. leaders, now freed from viewing Third World nations as prizes in the balance of power among the superpowers, will give greater weight to items on the Progressive foreign policy agenda.

The Isolation Model. Now that the threat of Russian aggression has declined, U.S. leaders could begin to think about national defense beginning at the U.S. border. This would mean that the United States would be less interested in the internal political, social, and economic affairs of weaker states. Instead, U.S. resources would be used almost exclusively for domestic programs. Assuming the world is a relatively peaceful one, the United States will continue to provide foreign aid at about the same level as before, shifting the balance gradually away from military aid and toward economic aid. Of course, some of this aid will be siphoned off to help Russia and the members of the Commonwealth of Independent States and Eastern Europe, so the Third World's share will be diminished. Moreover, it is likely to be even more concentrated on allies whose cooperation is important for the continued macroeconomic prosperity and military security of the United States. Consistent with this model, Senator Robert Dole, majority leader in the Senate, suggested in early 1990 that the United States reduce its foreign aid to the top five recipients — India, Egypt, Pakistan, Israel, and the Philippines — and redistribute the "savings" to the less developed, newly democratizing nations of Eastern Europe.

Several pieces of historical evidence support this scenario. The U.S. foreign aid program was initiated when the U.S. economy was healthy, after the great depression and World War II had ended. In times of economic decline, the United States has not been particularly generous in providing tax dollars to poorer, less fortunate countries. Moreover, just as the Marshall Plan diverted foreign aid to Western Europe that might have been used for economic development in the Third World, U.S. participation in the reconstruction of Eastern Europe may have the same effect.

What is worse, aid levels to the Third World might even be reduced without a dramatic shift toward relative emphasis on economic aid. World peace would make it easier for the United States to make such a shift, but Iraq's invasion of Kuwait will make U.S. policymakers wonder whether there really will be much peace in the Third World. Just as the Korean War caused a shift from economic development aid to military aid, the confrontation with Iraq may stir fears of future wars with Third World dictators.

The Regressive Model. Confronted by a militarily weaker, less resolute superpower adversary, U.S. leaders might be emboldened to become more imperious in relations with Third World states. Some observers see evidence of this strategy in recent U.S. interventions into Lebanon, Libya, Grenada, and Panama, in the support of the Contra war against the government of Nicaragua, in the patrolling of the Persian Gulf during the Iran-Iraq War, and in the quick and militant U.S. response to the Iraqi invasion of Kuwait.

As further evidence, Secretary of Defense Richard Cheney has argued that in a world where nuclear weapons are less likely to be used, the United States must be more concerned about other threats from lesser powers including biological, chemical, and conventional warfare. The new buzzword at the Pentagon is LIC, for low-intensity conflict. Planners in the Department of Defense are advocating that the United States further develop its capability for the rapid deployment and projection of highly mobile military forces to fight limited wars. If they get their way, there may be no peace dividend after all.

In short, the United States may return to a model of foreign policy resembling the diplomacy of a century ago—the moralizing, big stick, make-the-world-safe-for-democracy variety.[24] The two military confrontations with Third World states in the post–Cold War era (with Panama and Iraq) have some characteristics in common and may be a preview of U.S.–Third World relations in the twenty-first century:

1. An obnoxious Third World dictator. More dictators will certainly emerge, and many like Saddam Hussein will have chemical, biological, or even nuclear weapons.

2. An absence of superpower stakes in the conflict. It is a one-superpower world. Balance of power concerns are no longer particularly important.

3. A lack of U.S. inhibitions. Note the lifting of the prohibition against assassinating foreign leaders prior to the invasion of Panama. Observing those events, Graham Fuller of the Rand Corporation observed that "The Soviets feel deeply unhappy about unilateral American power projection. Moscow's worry is that the United States will treat the current disarray in the East Bloc as an unfettered opportunity to use our power."[25]

4. A tendency toward overkill. If ten thousand troops could do the job, send fifty thousand to intimidate the opposition and minimize the risk of losing.

5. Little respect for Third World leaders. Just as Adolfo de la Huerta of Mexico had been a "plug ugly" to Woodrow Wilson, Manuel Noriega was presented to the American public as a "thug" and Saddam Hussein as "sick." The implication in both recent cases was obvious: there is no need to negotiate with uncivilized people like that.

The Progressive Model. Finally, the easing of tensions between East and West should lessen the concern about the expansion of Soviet-style communism, leading U.S. policymakers to be more tolerant of communist movements, socialist experiments, and instability in the Third World. Under these circumstances, foreign aid and other types of active U.S. assistance will be provided mainly to democratic governments that have an equitable distribution of political power and wealth within their societies, good human rights practices, and peaceful relations with their neighbors.

U.S. leaders will give more attention to North-South issues and will work to facilitate necessary reforms in the Third World. These actions will increase the security of the United States from external threat and lay the foundation for mutually beneficial economic relations between the United States and less economically developed countries. As a first step, U.S. leaders will convince the public that the foreign aid program is essential to world peace and, therefore, to national defense. Following the guidelines suggested by the New International Economic Order, the United States gradually will increase its foreign aid from a meager 0.22 percent of GNP to 1 percent or more. Congress will insist that covert action and unilateral military intervention not be used except under the most extraordinary circumstances and will insist on the right to veto proposed covert actions. It will censure any president who does not abide by the spirit as well as the letter of international law.

Each of these scenarios represents a different combination of choices with respect to many value dimensions. How much should the United States try to affect the internal affairs, including the domestic policies, of less developed countries? To what extent should scarce U.S. tax dollars be used to finance economic, social, and political reforms and economic development in Third World states? Under what conditions and to what degree should Nationalist objectives of expansion of U.S. military and economic power be risked in order to achieve Progressive objectives in the Third World? The three scenarios do not reflect all the possible permutations, but they do describe three distinctly different, yet possible, courses of action. A Progressive tradition in U.S. foreign policy toward the Third World is emerging, but there is no guarantee that it will continue.

NOTES

1. Jack Donnelly, *Universal Human Rights in Theory and Practice* (Ithaca, N.Y.: Cornell University Press, 1989), p. 245.

2. Karel Holbik, *The United States, the Soviet Union and the Third World* (Hamburg: Verlag Weltarchiv, 1968), pp. 27–28.

3. Quintin V.S. Bach, *Soviet Economic Assistance to the Less Developed Countries* (Oxford: Clarendon Press, 1987), p. x.

4. Rhoda E. Howard and Jack Donnelly, "Confronting Revolution in Nicaragua: U.S. and Canadian Responses," Case Study No. 7, Carnegie Council on Ethics and International Affairs, 1990.

5. See Judith Tendler, *Inside Foreign Aid* (Baltimore: Johns Hopkins University Press, 1975).

6. Peyton V. Lyon, "Introduction," in Peyton V. Lyon and Tareq Y. Ismael, *Canada and the Third World* (Toronto: Macmillan, 1976), p. xvi. See also Real P. Lavergne, "Determinants of Canadian Aid Policy" in *Western Middle Powers and Global Poverty* (Uppsala: Scandinavian Institute of African Studies, 1989), pp. 68–73.

7. World Bank, *World Development Report 1988* (New York: Oxford University Press, 1988), p. 262.

8. Rhoda E. Howard, "Monitoring Human Rights: Problems of Consistency," *Ethics and International Affairs* 4 (1990): 33.

9. T. A. Keenleyside and Nola Serkasevich, "Canadian Aid and Human Rights Observance: Measuring the Relationship," forthcoming in *International Journal.*

10. Rhoda E. Howard, "Black Africa and South Africa," in Robert O. Matthews and Cranford Pratt, eds., *Human Rights in Canadian Foreign Policy* (Kingston, Ont.: McGill-Queen's University Press, 1988), pp. 265-284.

11. Earnie Regehr, "Military Sales," in Matthews and Pratt, eds., *Human Rights in Canadian Foreign Policy,* p. 215.

12. T. A. Keenleyside, "Development Assistance," in Matthews and Pratt, eds., *Human Rights in Canadian Foreign Policy,* p. 218.

13. Ibid., p. 214.

14. Quoted in Renate Pratt, "International Financial Institutions," in Matthews and Pratt, eds., *Human Rights in Canadian Foreign Policy,* p. 184.

15. David L. Cingranelli and Thomas E. Pasquarello, "Human Rights Practices and the Distribution of American Foreign Aid to Latin American Countries," *American Journal of Political Science* 25, No. 3 (August 1985): 539-563.

16. Thomas E. Pasquarello, "Human Rights and US Bilateral Aid Allocations to Africa," in David L. Cingranelli, ed., *Human Rights: Theory and Practice* (London: Macmillan, 1988), pp. 236-254.

17. Steven C. Poe, "Bilateral Foreign Assistance Allocation by the U.S. Government: A Quantitative Study." Ph.D. dissertation, University of Iowa, 1989.

18. See, for example, Lars Schoultz, "U.S. Foreign Policy and Human Rights," *Comparative Politics* 13 (January 1980): 149-170; Michael Stohl and David Carleton, "The Foreign Policy of Human Rights: Rhetoric and Reality from Jimmy Carter to Ronald Reagan," *Human Rights Quarterly* 7 (May 1985): 205-229; and James M. McCormick and Neil J. Mitchell, "Human Rights and Foreign Assistance: An Update," *Social Science Quarterly* 70, No. 1 (December 1989): 969-979.

19. For the methodological debate, see David Carleton and Michael Stohl, "The Role of Human Rights in U.S. Foreign Assistance Policy: A Critique and Reappraisal," *American Journal of Political Science* 31, No. 4 (August 1987): 1002-1018; James M. McCormick and Neil Mitchell, "Is U.S. Aid Really Linked to Human Rights in Latin America?" *American Journal of Political Science* 32, No. 1 (February 1988); 231-239; and Poe, "Bilateral Foreign Assistance Allocation by the U.S. Government."

20. On this point, see David P. Forsythe, "US Economic Assistance and Human Rights: Why the Emperor Has (Almost) No Clothes," in David P. Forsythe, ed., *Human Rights and Development* (London: Macmillan, 1989), pp. 171-195.

21. On this point, see David A. Baldwin, *Economic Statecraft* (Princeton, N.J.: Princeton University Press, 1985), especially Chapter 6.

22. David Carleton and Michael Stohl, "The Foreign Policy of Human Rights: Rhetoric and Reality from Jimmy Carter to Ronald Reagan," *Human Rights Quarterly* 7, No. 2 (May 1985): 205-229.

23. Michael Stohl, David Carleton, Mark Gibney, and Geoffrey Martin, "US Foreign Policy, Human Rights and Multilateral Assistance," in Forsythe, ed., *Human Rights and Development,* pp. 208-209.

24. See David Ignatius, "Speak Softly and Carry a Big Agenda," *Washington Post National Weekly Edition* (January 1-7, 1990), pp. 16-17.

25. Quoted in ibid., p. 17.

Timeline of American Military Interventions in the Third World and Stated U.S. Policy Priorities, 1898–1992

Year	Country	U.S. Priorities
1898–1902	Cuba	(1) Liberate Cuba from Spanish rule. (2) Secure the right to build military bases. (3) Prevent default on foreign debts. (4) Promote democracy.
1903–1914	Panama	(1) Secure an agreement to build the Panama Canal. (2) Protect U.S. lives and property during the war of independence from Colombia and the construction of the Panama Canal.
1906–1909	Cuba	(1) Support the constitutionally elected government against a revolution.
1912–1925	Nicaragua	(1) Prevent default on foreign debts. (2) Prevent an attempted revolution. (3) Remain to assure stability.
1914–1919	Mexico	(1) Destabilize the Huerta regime. (2) Retaliate against terrorism and attempt to apprehend the terrorist, Villa.
1915–1934	Haiti	(1) Prevent default on foreign debts. (2) Maintain access to a seaport. (3) Promote the establishment of democracy.
1916–1924	Dominican Republic	(1) Support the constitutionally elected government against a revolution. (2) Maintain democracy. (3) Prevent default on foreign debts.
1917–1922	Cuba	(1) Support the constitutionally elected government against a revolution. (2) Maintain democracy. (3) Protect U.S. lives and the investments of U.S.-based MNCs.
1918–1920	Panama	(1) Support the constitutionally elected government against a revolution. (2) Maintain democracy. (3) Protect U.S. lives and the investments of U.S.-based MNCs.
1926–1933	Nicaragua	(1) Support the constitutionally elected government against a revolution. (2) Maintain democracy. (3) Protect U.S. lives and the investments of U.S.-based MNCs.

236

Year	Country	U.S. Priorities
1950–1953	Korea	(1) Repel an attack against South Korea by North Korea. (2) Restore peace in the area (multilateral intervention led by the U.S., but coordinated by the U.N.).
1958	Lebanon	(1) Protect Lebanon from an internal overthrow attempt allegedly instigated and supported by Nasser's Egypt.
1961	Cuba	(1) Overthrow Castro's government (conducted by a small force of Cuban exiles, based in the U.S. and trained and armed by the C.I.A.).
1962–1963	Congo	(1) Rid the Congo of the vestiges of Belgian colonial rule (multilateral intervention coordinated by the U.N.).
1964–1973	Vietnam	(1) Protect South Vietnam from aggression by the communist North. (2) Preserve the South Vietnamese peoples' right to self-determination.
1965	Dominican Republic	(1) Protect the lives of U.S. citizens. (2) Prevent a communist government from coming to power.
1975	Cambodia	(1) Rescue 39 Mayaguez crew members who had been captured by the Cambodian military while in international waters. (Successful)
1980	Iran	(1) Rescue U.S. hostages. (Unsuccessful)
1981–1991	Nicaragua	(1) Overthrow the communist Sandinista government (Although no U.S. combat troops were involved directly, funds and training were provided through the C.I.A. to the rebel "Contras" based in Honduras. The C.I.A. also assisted in the mining of Nicaraguan harbors in 1984.)
1983–1984	Lebanon	(1) Help the Lebanese army to restore order. (2) Protect the American embassy and the Beirut airport.
1983	Grenada	(1) Prevent the leaders of a pro-Soviet coup from coming to power. (2) Protect the lives of U.S. medical students allegedly endangered by the coup.
1986	Libya	(1) Retaliate against alleged state-sponsored terrorism (Tripoli was bombed, but no ground forces were used).
1989–1990	Panama	(1) Keep the Panama Canal open. (2) Restore democracy to Panama. (3) Protect the lives of U.S. citizens. (4) Arrest the leader of Panama on drug trafficking charges.
1990–1991	The Gulf War — Iraq	(1) Expel Iraq from Kuwait. (2) Return the Emir of Kuwait to power. Additional stated U.S. objectives included (3) Protect the lives of U.S. citizens. (4) Stabilize the region. (5) Prevent a "madman" from controlling a large share of the world's oil. (Multilateral intervention led by the U.S., but coordinated by the U.N.)
1990	Liberia	(1) Protect the lives of U.S. citizens from violence associated with an internal rebellion.

INDEX

Abrams, Elliot, on human rights, 198
Acheson, Dean, on morality versus
    national interest, 42–43
Action-forcing events
    Carter's response to, 179–185
    in foreign policy decision making, 5
    Reagan-Bush response to, 206–213
Adams, John Quincy, 94
    acquisition of Texas and, 91–92
Adelman, Kenneth, on prevention of
    weapon development, 78
Adoula, Cyrille, U.S. support for, 156
Afghanistan, Carter's response to
    Soviet invasion of, 184–185
Africa
    Carter's approach to human rights
    in, 180
    Kennedy's anticolonial policy on,
    155–156
    Reagan's policy on, 212
African slave trade, 96–97
Agency for International Development
    (AID)
    establishment of, 153
    Reagan and, 194
Alaska, purchase of, 95
Allende, Salvador, covert activity
    against, 166–167
Alliance for Progress
    criticism of, 154
    declaration of, 152
    goals of, 152–153
Angola, U.S. position on, 156
Aquinaldo, Emilio, 99
Aquino, Corazon, 202–203
Arbenz, Jacobo, 136–138
Argentina, 144
Aristide, Jean-Bertrand, 213
Armas, Carlos Castillo, 137–138

Bainfield, Edward
    on foreign aid, 130

    on foreign policy, 36, 131
Baker, James
    on foreign aid, 197
    Mideast Peace Talks and, 211
Baker Plan, 197
Baritz, Loren, on cultural distance and
    U.S. foreign policy, 74–75
Barre, Siad, 205
Batista, Fulgencio, 141
Begin, Menachem, 182
Biological weapons, 78
Boland Amendment, 206
Bolshevism, Latin American policy
    and, 114, 119
Bonker, Don, on U.S. foreign policy,
    18–19
Bordas, José, 112
Bosch, Juan, 160
Botha, Pieter, 212
Bretton Woods Agreement, 129,
    146–147
Burke, Edmund, on universal values, 8
Bush, George
    and action-forcing events, 209–212,
    213
        human rights approach of, 15–16
        moral position of, 16
    coup in Haiti and, 213
    covert action of, against Noriega,
    168–169
    environment and, 198
    foreign policy goals of, 214–215
    foreign policy strategy of, 191
    on Gulf War, 70–71
    and Kuwait, 209–211
    Liberian rebellion and, 213
    on Panama invasion, 70
    Progressive agenda and, 220
    on South Africa, 212

Calderon, Rafael Angel, on Costa
    Rican economic democracy, 46

239

expanded use of, 166–169
against Noriega, 168–169
Reagan and, 206
Cuba
Bay of Pigs invasion of, 154
and Eisenhower, 141–142
freeing of, 97–98
independence of, 105–106
missile crisis in, 155
Soviet military buildup in, 181

Debts
of Latin American countries,
106–108
Reagan-Bush approach to, 195–196
Delvalle, Eric Arturo, 204
Democracy
capitalism as challenge to, 61–62
promotion of, by Reagan-Bush
administration, 201–205
support of, in Latin American
policy, 119–120
Democratic administrations, foreign
policy agenda of, 21, 22–24,
120
Democrats, 221–222
Dependency theory, 58–59
Derian, Patricia, 175
Development Loan Fund (DLF), 139,
140
Dewey, George, 99
Dewey, Thomas, 133
Diaz, Adolfo, 114
Diplomacy
"big stick," 103–108
dollar, 60, 108–110
Doe, Samuel, 213
Dole, Robert, 232
Dollar diplomacy, 60, 108–110
Dominican Republic
Grant on annexation of, 95–96
instability in, Johnson's approach to,
160
support of elections/democracy in,
154
Wilson's approach to, 112
"Domino theory," 137
Donagan, Alan, on universal values, 7

Donnelly, Jack
on human rights in U.S. policy, 222
on human rights policies of Carter
and Reagan, 199
Draper, Theodore, on U.S.
intervention in Dominican
Republic, 160, 161
Dred Scott decision, 97
Drug lords, actions against, 77–78
Dulles, John Foster
on Development Loan Fund, 139
on Guatemala, 136–137
Duvalier, "Papa Doc," 154, 202

Eastern Europe, 230–231
Economic classes in Marxism, 53
Economic development
in foreign policy rhetoric, 219
promotion of, to stop communism,
125–147
Eisenhower and, 135–142
ends justifying means in, 142–144
goals of, 144–147
Truman and, 126–135
Third World, Reagan-Bush policy
on, 192–198
Economic expansionism, 95–96
Taft administration and, 103
Economic gain
aggregate imperialism based on, 57
Marxism on, 55–56
Economic imperialism, 54
Economic policies, Marxism on, 58
Economic relations, 177–178
Economic rights, 199–201
Efforts test
in foreign policy evaluation, 226–228
of motives, 72–73
Eisenhower, Dwight D., 135–136
on assistance to Third World,
138–140
Bay of Pigs invasion and, 154
counterrevolutionary tendencies of,
145
covert action and, 136
Cuba policy of, 141–142
on "Domino theory," 137
military alliances and, 135–136

Lebanon
  intervention in, 209
  military forces in, 141
Lefever, Ernest, on human rights,
    198–199
Lending agencies, 57–58
Lenin, Vladimir Ilyich, on economic
    imperialism and war, 54
Liberia, 213
Libya, 208
Lippmann, Walter, on stages of
    expansion, 89–90
Lipset, Seymour, on stabilizing effects
    of democracy, 130
Lipson, Charles, on Hickenlooper
    amendment, 157
Loan funds for Third World economic
    development, 139–140
Loans from International Bank for
    Reconstruction and
    Development, 129–130
Lumumba, Patrice, 156
Luxemburg, Rosa, on imperialism and
    need for markets, 56

Machiavelli, on objective of foreign
    policy, 31
Madison, James, on prevention of
    abuse of power by government
    officials, 30
Mandela, Nelson
  on Kennedy, 156
  release of, 212
Manifest Destiny, 92–93
Marcos, resignation of, 202–203
Market economies, Progressivism and,
    38–39
Markets
  economic expansionism and, 95–96
  need for, 56
Marshall Plan, 132
Marxism, 53–65
  capitalism and, 54
  class conflicts in, 53–54
  dependency theory and, 58–59
  economic classes in, 53
  economic imperialism and, 54, 56
  empirical argument of, 53–60

expansionist economic policies and,
    58
  human rights abuses and, 59–60
  mainstream response to, 60–64
  proper ends and means of, 64
  U.S. foreign policy and, 54–60
McCarthy, Joseph, 132
McKinley, William
  as Exceptionalist, 9, 37
  on fate of Philippines, 98
Means and ends, 74–82
  during Cold War, 142–144
  covert action and, 79–81
  drug lords and, 77–78
  intervention and, 75
  moral positions on, 81–82
  self-determination and, 78–79
  terrorism and, 76–77
  weapons development and, 78
Mercantilist doctrine, 31–32
Merritt, Wesley, 99
Mexico
  acquisition of Texas from, 91–92
  Coolidge's policy on, 114
  expropriation of U.S. oil properties
    by, 116
  Wilson's approach to, 111–112
Middle East
  Carter Doctrine on, 184
  Carter's approach to, 181–182
  Nixon's policy on, 164
  Reagan and, 209
Mideast Peace Talks, 211
Military power, Nationalist position
    on, 32–33, 34
Monroe, James, on anticolonialism in
    Americas, 93–94
Monroe Doctrine, 93–94
  Kennedy on, 152
  Truman Doctrine compared to, 127
Morales, Carlos, 107–108
Moral foreign policy, definition of, 3
Moral obligations beyond national
    boundaries, objections to, 8–9
Moral positions, typology of, 3–27
  applications of, 11–16
  cycles of political party control in,
    21–24